SCANLON EPIC LEADERSHIP

Where the Best Ideas Come Together

*Edited by Paul W. Davis
and Larry C. Spears*

Max —

Thanks for all you do,
and who you are.

Warm regards,

Larry

04. 01. 09

ISBN: 978-0981598406
Printed in the United States of America

Scanlon Foundation
www.ScanlonFoundation.org

Scanlon Leadership Network
www.scanlonleader.org

SCANLON EPIC LEADERSHIP: WHERE THE BEST IDEAS COME TOGETHER

TABLE OF CONTENTS

Books Created and Edited by Larry C. Spears

Scanlon E.P.I.C. Leadership: Where the Best Ideas Come Together (with Paul Davis), 2008

Practicing Servant-Leadership: Succeeding Through Trust, Bravery, and Forgiveness (with Michele Lawrence), 2004

The Servant-Leader Within: A Transformative Path (with Hamilton Beazley and Julie Beggs), 2003

Servant-Leadership: A Journey into the Nature of Legitimate Power and Greatness (25th Anniversary Edition), 2002

Focus on Leadership: Servant-Leadership for the 21st Century (with Michele Lawrence), 2001

The Power of Servant-Leadership, 1998

Insights on Leadership: Service, Stewardship, Spirit and Servant-Leadership, 1998

On Becoming a Servant-Leader (with Don M. Frick), 1996

Seeker and Servant (with Anne T. Fraker), 1996

Reflections on Leadership: How Robert K. Greenleaf's Theory of Servant-Leadership Influenced Today's Top Management Thinkers, 1995

As Contributing Author-Only

Robert K. Greenleaf: A Life of Servant Leadership, by Don M. Frick, 2004

Cutting Edge: Leadership 2000, edited by Barbara Kellerman and Larraine Matusak, 2000

Stone Soup for the World, edited by Marianne Larned, 1998

Leadership in a New Era, edited by John Renesch, 1994

What Others Say

Those of us who knew Joe Scanlon realize how important he was in humanizing the workplace and helping create today's workplace of ideas. How sad that so few people even know his name. This book should right that wrong by introducing a new generation to Joe Scanlon's inspired vision.

—**Warren Bennis**, author, *On Leadership*

Joseph Scanlon was an Irish lad of humble origin who was a prize fighter and a cost accountant; later he went to work in a steel mill, became a local-union president, then research director of the United Steelworkers of America, and finally a lecturer at M.I.T. He was an innovator. I think time will show that he has had a remarkable impact on our society.

—**Douglas McGregor**, author, *The Human Side of Enterprises*

The great strength of Scanlon is the potential unleashed by freeing an entire organization to do its best . . . Can those of us who are committed to the elegant breadth of the Scanlon idea begin to consider ourselves the custodians of social innovation? Why not? Who better than the companies who believe deeply in the Scanlon idea to be the launching pad for the next wave of effective activists? Who is better equipped to marshal the organizational experience, integrity, hope, and confidence needed to produce a broad renewal in our social condition? Those without vision perish.

—**Max DePree**, author, *Leadership is an Art*; retired
   Chairman, Herman Miller

Underlying Joseph Scanlon's efforts was a deep and fundamental belief in the worth of the human individual, in his capacity for growth and learning, in his ability to contribute significantly "with his head as well as his hands" to the success of the company which employs him. Scanlon, unlike many who make similar professions, really respected human beings.

—George P. Schultz, former United States Secretary of State

Many company executives spend a great deal of time looking for the next new management concept and very little time making the last one they learned work. Such is the case with popular management concepts including participatory management, quality circles, and others that in some companies, are no longer considered to be "hot enough" to emphasize in training related programs.

It's refreshing to find companies that are truly committed to programs for employee involvement, quality and service over the long haul. And it's not surprising to find that such companies are more likely to be successful.

A case in point is Atwood Industries located in Rockford, Ill. Atwood practices participatory management, employee involvement, and open communication. It also has quality circles, productivity plans, and a suggestion program—all wrapped into one program known as the Scanlon Plan. While the Scanlon Plan is not a recent management innovation, it is one that has worked well for Atwood, in large part because the company stuck with it. It wasn't started on a whim or the wave of a fad, but instead on the solid belief that people could work together in greater harmony and in doing so be more productive.

Most officers of the company agree that the Scanlon Plan is the major reason for the company's past and continuing success.

—Dr. Ken Blanchard, author, *The One Minute Manager*

Although profit sharing and employee stock ownership have long histories—and AT&T, General Foods, Xerox, and Honeywell experimented with employee decision making in the 1960's and 1970's labor organizer Joseph Scanlon first recognized the importance of pairing these two conditions in the 1950's.

—James O'Toole and **Edward Lawler**, authors, *The New American Workplace*

The Scanlon Plan is an innovative management process for total organization development. It consists of a set of assumptions about human motivation and behavior, general principles for the management of organizations based on those assumptions, and specific procedures for implementing these principles.

—**Carl Frost**, author, *Changing Forever*

If the fundamentals of participation and partnership are properly developed, the incentive to produce at the highest possible degree of efficiency is constant.

—**Joseph N. Scanlon**, originator of the Scanlon Plan

Thomas Jefferson and Joseph Scanlon knew that business could be a place for greatness. Let's make it so.

—**John P. Schuster**, author, *The Power of Open Book Management*

The philosophy of servant-leadership is increasingly viewed as a solid foundation for many businesses and organizations. Some servant-led companies have taken it a step further and utilize the framework of the Scanlon EPIC principles (Equity, Participation, Identity, and Competence) as a particular expression of servant-leadership. In so doing, they are helping to create the "better, more caring world," that Robert K. Greenleaf urged all of us to seek.

—**Larry C. Spears**, editor-author, *Insights on Leadership*; President & CEO, The Spears Center

A business that satisfies all partners will be able to attract a greater contribution from all partners. A management team that creates a culture where all the partners are actively looking for ways to serve one another may well discover the most powerful motivational force ever seen in business.

—**Robert Doyle**, author, *Gain Management*

People need to be needed, want to be productive, need to be responsible, have the right to know, need and want to own the problem. The Scanlon Plan can answer such needs.

—**Hugh DePree**, author, *Business as Unusual*; retired Chairman, Herman Miller

The purpose of the Frost/Scanlon principles is to transform the culture from an "us versus them" philosophy to one of partnerships committed to delivering results for all stakeholders.

—**Randy G. Pennington**, author, *Results Rule: Build a Culture that Blows the Competition Away*

You must take these values, these philosophies, these Scanlon principles off the shelf and introduce them into day-to-day relationships and weave them into the fabric of the organization . . . It's the only way to build a long-term foundation for survival. If you want a corporation to survive a hundred-plus years, and to be strong, and be capable of renewing itself, you have to have the human element more deeply woven into the way you do business. Otherwise, it's like sand in the hand, and you'll never make it through the rough times.

—**Robert H. Rosen**, author, *Leading People: Transforming Business from the Inside Out*

Organizations must deliberately work to keep their management principles and mechanisms aligned to protect their most important asset—integrity.

—**Terry VandeWater**, author, *Principle Based Participative Management*

If you really want to partner with your employees . . . one such model is the Scanlon Plan and it is one of the best kept organizational secrets for successful employee involvement, through equity and responsibility sharing.

—**Ray DuPont**, author, *The Art of Partnering*

The Scanlon Plan is one of the best kept secrets in American Business. Every company using it properly has had dramatic, measurable improvements in productivity and profitability.

—**Chris Hegarty**, author, *How to Manage Your Boss*

All too often the Scanlon Plan—like all profit-sharing plans—is thought of only as a device for increasing the motivational forces arising from the economic needs of the members of the organization. As Scanlon emphasized however, the plan requires the development of an interaction influence system in which the ideas for developing better products and processes and for reducing costs and waste can flow readily, be assessed, improved and expeditiously applied. Such an interaction-influence system is appreciatively more characteristic of System 4 than any other management systems.

—**Rensis Likert**, author, *The Human Organization*

The most sought after labor relations advisor in the U.S. today is Joe Scanlon, 56, onetime prizefighter, open-hearth tender, steel company cost accountant, union local president and now a lecturer in industrial relations at the Massachusetts Institute of Technology.

—**Time Magazine**, Monday, September 26, 1955

When Scanlon Plans are no longer news, we shall have licked the great problems of the industrial age, how to tame the machine for liberty and democracy.

—**Life Magazine**, 1952

Does all this sound too good to be true?
Does it presume mankind is better than it really is?
Does it demand a change of heart by many people?
Are we being presumptuous?
Yes to all four of these questions.

—**John Donnelly**, former CEO, Donnelly Corporation

PREFACE

Paul W. Davis and Larry C. Spears

EPIC Leadership: Where the Best Ideas Come Together is about the dream of steelworker, Joe Scanlon. Joe dreamed that "together we can achieve the impossible." He believed workplaces could be created where people want to come to work, where everyone contributes their ideas, where leaders serve their followers and where customers, investors and workers all benefit from our free enterprise system.

Joe often wondered whether his ideas were like a pebble placed in a pond: that is, would the ripples soon die out? Far from it! They have not died out after seventy years! They have contributed to the creation of a mighty river of change with tributaries that now reach far from the source. Scholars at the Massachusetts Institute of Technology (MIT) and Michigan State University (MSU) contributed to the flow of ideas. Business leaders like John Donnelly, Seth Atwood and D.J. DePree navigated their organizations on the river of change Joe helped to set in motion.

This book is about how the dream helped to lead to advancements in labor management cooperation, gainsharing, employee involvement, teamwork, servant-leadership, lean systems, six-sigma and open-book management. It is about how the dream which started in the 1930's continues to both attract and challenge business leaders today.

It is also about leadership, and how the ideas of men like Robert Greenleaf and Max DePree have deepened even further our understanding of Scanlon principles that are grounded in servant-leadership. It is about how the value of the leader can be seen in the strength of the followers. It is about how our beliefs and assumptions determine how we lead and the types of organizations we create.

It is about the reality of continual change and how the ability to adapt to change is the key to individual and organizational survival. It is about the four EPIC Principles for individual and organizational effectiveness developed by Dr. Carl Frost. It is about how the four EPIC Leadership Principles create high performance work cultures.

It is about how organizations like Adamson, Advanced Business Graphics, Atlantic Automotive, ARaymond, Atwood, American Tape, Beth Israel Hospital, Bradford, Bridgestone-Firestone, Briggs & Stratton, Canon, Dana, Fairchild Burns, Ferro, Harley-Davidson, Hitachi Magnetics, Huron Signs, ITT, Kysor-Cadillac, Lapointe, Landscape Forms, Limerick Veterinary Hospital, Lorin, Magna-Donnelly, Martin-Marietta, Meier, Michigan Bell, Motorola, National Manufacturing, Neelon Castings, Nicholas Plastics, Pacific Cast Technologies, Parker Pen, Pohlman, Quality Container, Raynor, S & L Plastics, Sara Lee, Sears, SGS Tool Company, Sligh, Spring Engineering, Thermatron, Thomson-Shore, TG Fluid Systems, Trans-Matic, United Building Centers, US Vision, Watermark Credit Union, Wescast, Westan, Westling, Wolverine Worldwide, Xaloy and countless other organizations dreamed the dream and experimented with EPIC ideas.

Finally, it is about a proven roadmap and a plan designed to help the reader achieve the impossible—to create more democratic, more focused, more responsive, more efficient and more human workplaces.

Robert Greenleaf wrote in his essay *The Servant as Leader*: "Not much happens without a dream. And for something great to happen, there must be a great dream. Behind every great achievement is a dreamer of great dreams. Much more than a dreamer is required to bring it to reality, but the dream must be there first."

Joe Scanlon believed in a great dream. He worked tirelessly to bring that dream of cooperation into reality in workplaces. Many others were inspired by his dream, adding to it and constantly refining and testing various ways to create better more cooperative workplaces. People like Dr. Carl Frost and

Fred Lesieur kept the dream alive, installing Scanlon Plans in organizations throughout North America, and conducting conferences and writing about their experiences. Dr. Frost took Joe Scanlon's ideas and refined and distilled them into the four EPIC Leadership Principles from which this book takes its title.

Joe Scanlon did not create all modern leadership practices. Nor did Joe arrive at his ideas alone. During his lifetime he was influenced by Dr. Douglas McGregor and the countless clients where he tested his ideas. Later Scanlon practitioners embraced the ideas of great thinkers like Robert Greenleaf, and Peter Drucker and incorporated them into Scanlon Plans. Today the Scanlon Network strives to be the place "where the best ideas come together."

All of us owe a debt to the humble steelworker and the EPIC ideas he helped to set in motion. In a 1952 editorial in *Life* Magazine they wrote this about Scanlon: "When Scanlon Plans are no longer news, we shall have licked the great problems of the industrial age, how to tame the machine for liberty and democracy."

It is our hope that this anthology of Scanlon ideas—the first book of its kind—will inspire readers to continue to dream great dreams and to tame machines and systems for liberty and democracy. Together we will achieve the impossible.

If you are intrigued or inspired, please contact:

> Scanlon Leadership Network
> 2875 Northwind Drive, Suite 121
> E. Lansing, MI 48823
> 517.332.8927 (phone)
> www.scanlonleader.org
> office@scanlonleader.org

Paul W. Davis, E. Lansing, Michigan
Larry C. Spears, Indianapolis, Indiana
March 2008

FOREWORD

WARREN BENNIS

Joe Scanlon is the management guru time forgot. It is tragic that someone with so prescient a vision of the shared fate of workers and their leaders is now so little known, but it is not altogether surprising. Unlike today's tireless self-promoters, Joe Scanlon was an unpretentious man. I knew him when he was a lecturer at MIT in the 1940 and '50s. Like Kurt Lewin, with whom he had little in common but greatness, Scanlon had been brought to the university by my mentor, Douglas McGregor. Often called the father of organizational development, McGregor was what chaos theory describes as a "strange attractor." He had an unerring eye for original thinkers and understood that the most remarkable things could happen when truly creative individuals had adjoining offices. McGregor loved the idea of bringing dissimilar geniuses together and watching the sparks fly.

Remember what MIT was like in those days. Paul Samuelson, who would win the Nobel Prize in economics, was the dominant presence in a place where mathematics was True North. It was a given that MIT faculty had prestigious advanced degrees. Unlike his fellow faculty, Joe Scanlon was a union man, a prize-fighter and former steelworker, who never went to college. Scanlon had acquired his wisdom in the streets, in steel plants, and in smoke-filled rooms where union representatives and management fought out the terms that would determine the fates of companies and the quality of workers' lives. At the university, I never saw Scanlon wear a tie. His uniform was a suit-jacket and a white shirt, open at the neck. When his lectures really began to smoke, the jacket would come off and he would roll up his sleeves.

Scanlon preached what was called the Scanlon Plan. It evolved over time, but its heart was an arrangement whereby labor and management collaborated on how to reduce costs, boost productivity and eliminate waste. The resultant savings were shared by company and workforce. It was a deceptively simple plan. The shared bonus that was its ostensible goal was the least of its rewards. In order to make the plan work, management had to share responsibility and information with workers. Employees had to become more productive, more resourceful, and more flexible. Perhaps most important, workers and managers had to sit down together and talk to each other. And because labor and management were working together toward a common goal, they inevitably began to see themselves, not as opponents, but as colleagues. Scanlon described his message this way: "What we are actually trying to say is simply this: That the average worker knows his own job better than anyone else, and that there are a great many things that he could do if he has a complete understanding of the necessary. Given this opportunity of expressing his intelligence and ingenuity, he becomes a more useful and more valuable citizen in any given community or in any industrial operation."

Scanlon had developed his plan during the Depression, at a time, almost unimaginable now in the United States, when loss of a job could mean a family's starving to death. In those terrible days, Scanlon had helped laid-off steelworkers feed themselves and their families by finding land to turn into gardens. During that era, labor and management were often at each others' throats, with government almost always backing management. Both sides sometimes resorted to violence. As a worker and the son of a worker, Scanlon was a passionate supporter of labor, but he did not hate management. His vision required mutual respect, a recognition that we are all in any community or corporate enterprise together and that what is good for one side will ultimately help the other. For me, as a young MIT faculty member from a working-class family, Scanlon was a romantic figure. I admired the way the stocky, straight-talking Irish American had earned a place in an elite university while remaining true to his blue-collar legacy. Widely admired by his faculty colleagues and beloved by students, Scanlon refused to kowtow to either. His very presence was a reminder that something vital and important lay outside of the halls of academe. Lest his graduate students forget, each was required to spend a summer working as a foreman in a factory.

Like Doug McGregor, Scanlon died far too young, in 1956 at the age of 56. But his vision of a collegial workplace—even a collegial factory—had legs. First to be influenced were those who worked beside him at MIT. Freddy Lesieur was a machinist and a union man when he first met Scanlon. Lesieur followed him to MIT and continued to advance their shared ideas after Scanlon's death. Dr. Carl Frost was another who worked with Joe at MIT and then brought the ideas to Michigan State University. You can see the impact of Scanlon's ideas about the interdependence of leaders and followers in the theory of servant-leadership promulgated by Robert Greenleaf, another protégé of Doug McGregor. And Scanlon's egalitarian beliefs surely had a role in shaping McGregor's Theory Y view of management. Like Scanlon, McGregor believed that those organizations most likely to thrive were those that loosed the human potential of all their members. Implicit in that view was recognition that an individual's life and work must be more fully integrated. McGregor wrote that human potential would be unleashed in organizations "only as we succeed in creating conditions that generate a meaningful life . . . Scanlon's lasting contribution is his recognition . . . that one cannot successfully tackle this central task of management with gimmicks or procedures or programs. The real task of management is to create conditions that result in genuine collaboration throughout the organization. To create such conditions is to create a way of life."

Although Scanlon's name is rarely heard today, his ideas are more widespread than ever. Donnelly, Herman Miller, Parker Pen, Atwood, Motorola and a few other companies successfully implemented the formal Scanlon plan. But its underlying assumptions have become more and more common, despite the dramatic decline of the labor movement that Scanlon championed throughout his lifetime. When much of America's economy depended on manufacturing, management could choose to align itself more closely with its workforce or ignore Scanlon's wise advice. In today's idea-driven economy, the talent *is* the company: the workforce is understood to be its greatest asset. In firms such as Google, workers demand to be treated with respect or they simply go elsewhere. Scanlon's implicit recognition that workers are, above all, human beings with gifts and dreams and lives is no longer seen as revolutionary. But now as then, that recognition is the first step in unleashing the extraordinary power of creative collaboration required to succeed in today's fast-moving global economy.

Those of us who knew Joe Scanlon realize how important he was in humanizing the workplace and helping create today's workplace of ideas. How sad that so few people even know his name. This book should right that wrong by introducing a new generation to Joe Scanlon's inspired vision.

INTRODUCTION

"The Scanlon Plan puts it all together—
worthwhile employment, worthwhile goods and
services, and worthwhile investments.
—Dr. Carl Frost

Epic: Webster's Dictionary (adj.) Marking an important date in history; of very great size. Synonyms: historic, momentous, epochal, fateful, enormous, immense, and monumental.

EPIC: The essence of Scanlon Leadership which stands for Equity, Participation, Identity and Competence, and the source for the title of this book.

The Scanlon Plan and Principles attempt to create worthwhile organizations within a free enterprise economy. By ensuring accountability to key stakeholders (Equity), by allowing those most competent to influence decisions (Participation), by educating all employees to the reality of their organization (Identity), and by constant commitment to personal, professional and organizational development (Competence), Scanlon organizations create competitive advantage for investors, customers, and employees.

The great Scanlon leader D.J. DePree wrote, "A company is rightly judged by its products and services but it must also face scrutiny as to its humanity."

Scanlon organizations have become the best places to work in their industries, valued members of their communities, and trailblazers in environmental stewardship.

In the process Scanlon also develops individuals. People who are exposed to the Scanlon EPIC Principles are more in tune to reality, less dependent, more able to work with others, more satisfied with their work and are more competent at work and at home.

While the ideas in this anthology have their origins in the life and work of Joe Scanlon, they evolved after his death in the 1950's to include ideas from many others. We have continued to call the ideas "Scanlon" whether they originated from Joe Scanlon or from those who followed after him.

This anthology contains in one place the writings of the original great Scanlon thinkers/practitioners, including Joe Scanlon, Douglas McGregor, Fred Lesieur, and Carl Frost. It also contains contributions from many of the succeeding generation of Scanlon thought-leaders like Max DePree, Dick Ruch, Dwane Baumgardner, Peter Scontrino, Terry Vande-Water and Richard Frost.

This book also contains separate chapters on Servant-Leadership, Open-book Management, Lean Systems, and Six-Sigma. Each of these concepts represents a particular tradition which may be helpful to the reader in better understanding how these ideas have either evolved from the Scanlon tradition or are otherwise linked to it. Where Scanlon thought had an influence on these traditions, or where they have had an influence on current Scanlon practice it is noted.

Finally this anthology attempts to bring up to date what the Scanlon idea is today in short cases, testimonials, culture studies, and even an analysis of Scanlon failures.

In choosing which chapters to include, the editors felt it was important to include a handful of the original historical writings, instead of excerpts or summaries. Readers are able to form their own opinions of the ideas without any editorial filtering. You may wish to keep in mind that a few of the older articles were written as long as sixty years ago. Joe Scanlon's chapter is the oldest, and refers to the period up to and including World War II. Fred Lesieur and Douglas McGregor's articles are from the post-WWII period up until the 1960's. Carl Frost's chapter was written in the 1970's. Most of the remaining chapters have either been written expressly for inclusion in this volume, or in the last few years. *Scanlon EPIC Leader-*

ship is therefore a superb mix of both the historic, foundational writings and more contemporary thought and practices.

As Scanlon ideas have evolved over the past seventy years, a unique language has been created that is comfortable to Scanlon practitioners, but which may be confusing to those who are new to the ideas. We think it may be helpful to you, our reader, if we provide the following brief "Primer" on Scanlon thought and history—

- A "Scanlon Plan" is a written document that explains how Scanlon Principles are practiced in an organization. Each plan is unique to the organization that created it.

- The Scanlon Principles today are called the EPIC Principles (from which this anthology takes it title). Historically, the Principles were first written as I.P.E.C. to reflect the importance of the "Identity" Principle. Identity, Participation and Equity were the first three Principles to be developed by Carl Frost based on his association with Joe Scanlon. The last Principle—Competency did not appear in writings until the 1970's. At first it was called Managerial Competency, but over time it evolved into Competency for all levels and functions.

- There are no universal definitions of the four Scanlon Principles. While the broad concepts imbedded in each Principle are clear to most Scanlon practitioners, there are many variations in how they are defined and interpreted. The chapter by Terry VandeWater will help the reader better understand the Principles and how they are defined.

- Scanlon Plans are generally created using an organizational change process called the "Scanlon Roadmap." The Roadmap begins with a "mandate" for change developed by the top leadership inside of an organization. The chapter by Dr. Carl Frost explains what a mandate means to a Scanlon practitioner. The Roadmap includes a series of steps that include secret ballot votes, and the creation of an Ad-hoc or design team that creates the actual plan. Traditionally the votes have required a supermajority. The reader will find references to votes from 66% to 90% in the various chapters. Each organization following the roadmap determines the number of votes they will require and what level of approval is required to proceed. In Scanlon tradition the "vote" usually refers to the company wide vote taken to create a design team, or the vote to give the Scanlon Plan a trial period even though there are multiple votes.

- In the early Scanlon Plans references were often made to Production Committees and Screening Committees. Today, Production Committees would most likely be described as work teams or departments. Screening Committees are representative groups that "screen" or review ideas from the various teams or departments. Today they would be described as continuous improvement teams, or cross-functional teams.

- Reference is made to the Scanlon conference in various chapters. The Scanlon conference, we believe, is one of the oldest continuing gatherings of business leaders in North America. It began at the Massachusetts Institute of Technology (MIT) in the 1940's. Michigan State University (MSU) also hosted the conference for a number of years. Since the 1960's the Scanlon Leadership Network has hosted the Scanlon conference. The Scanlon conference includes delegates from various Scanlon organizations as well as guests. Conference delegates include front-line employees learning along with their top leaders. Together they listen to keynote speakers and attend workshops. They return from the conference with the expectation they will take what they have learned back into their organizations. The conference serves as a major renewal and organizational development tool in the Scanlon community.

- The Scanlon "Network" or "Association" or "members" mentioned in several chapters refers to the nonprofit network of Scanlon organizations formed in the 1960's to conduct Scanlon related research, to serve as a Scanlon information clearinghouse, to develop Scanlon related products and services and to gather Scanlon best practices. The Network serves as the custodian of Scanlon related thought and practice. Network members are organizations not individuals.

- The Scanlon Foundation was created by the Scanlon Network in 2002 to take Scanlon ideas to a larger audience, and to meet the charitable needs of the Scanlon movement. The Foundation has made possible the creation of this anthology. Individuals who wish to keep the dream of "Joe the steelworker" alive are welcome to join the Foundation. Donations to the Foundation are tax deductible.

- When a Scanlon practitioner inquires, "What day is it?" He has not lost his calendar. It is a type of Scanlon-speak shorthand, which means: Do you understand reality? Do you know who your customers are? Do you know who your competitors are? Do you know if you are making or losing money?

- When a Scanlon practitioner refers to the "Equity Triangle" or simply "the triangle" they are referring to the major stakeholders in the organization who are often pictured on an equilateral triangle. Traditionally the triangle has included employees, customers and investors. Some Scanlon organizations like Watermark (a nonprofit) have modified the stakeholders changing investors to "organization" and customers to "members." Donnelly modified the triangle into a pentagon to include suppliers and community as key stakeholders. What is important is not the labels, or how many stakeholders who are identified, but the fact that Scanlon organizations strive to meet the needs of multiple stakeholders—not just stockholders.

- When a Scanlon Practitioner refers to "gainsharing," "goalsharing," "the bonus," or "the ratio" they are referring to a group incentive system common in most Scanlon organizations. Each organization creates their own system often with the assistance of the Network or an approved Scanlon consultant.

Scanlon practitioners' assumptions about human motivation are what Douglas McGregor later labeled "Theory Y." We believe that people are self-motivated, and there is great creativity widely distributed in the human family. We believe given the right work environment people can routinely achieve the impossible. We strive to build systems and structures to create the right environment. Scanlon practitioners pioneered many methods and tools like employee involvement, teams, gainsharing, open-book management, labor management cooperation, lean systems, etc. based on Theory Y beliefs.

Some organizations have adopted Scanlon tools without a commitment to the underlying Scanlon beliefs. The great Scanlon leader, Max DePree wrote, *"Managers who have no beliefs but only understand methodology and quantification are modern day eunuchs."* It takes a special type of leader to lead in the Scanlon way. Max DePree has also taught many of us that, *"the first responsibility of a leader is to define reality. The last is to say thank you. In between a leader must become a servant."*

Scanlon leaders are servant-leaders. Shortly after I came to the Scanlon Leadership Network in 1993 I met my co-editor and contributing author to this book, Larry C. Spears, and we struck up a friendship which has deepened over the years. Larry, President & CEO of The Spears Center for Servant-Leadership, is the editor and contributing author to numerous books on servant-leadership. Max DePree was an early keynote speaker at the 1993 servant-leadership conference. Larry Spears and Jack Lowe were keynote speakers at the 2006 Scanlon Conference. The Scanlon community and the servant-leadership community share much in common while maintaining their own unique identities.

Servant-leadership is a philosophy of life and a way of being which is not defined by any single organizational expression of it. That is to say, some servant-led organizations have adopted the Scanlon Plan, while other organizations follow different models. Readers interested in learning more about servant-leadership are invited to explore The Spears Center's publications (www.spearscenter.org).

Larry's involvement in this book is both an expression of our personal friendship as well as his belief in the possibilities of the Scanlon Leadership Network and the work that we do. Scanlon traditions are mostly oral. While volumes have been written about Scanlon and Scanlon companies, rarely have Scanlon practitioners told their own story. Larry's dedication, encouragement, and editorial competency have made this book possible. On behalf of Scanlon practitioners everywhere— past, present and future—we offer Larry our deep and sincere appreciation.

This anthology is about monumental worthwhile ideas, and how those ideas have evolved in organizations for over seventy years. We hope that this anthology may serve as a definitive guide for a new generation of practitioners, scholars and servant-leaders embarked upon their own EPIC journeys.

Paul W. Davis
March 2008

Part I

Equity

"The Proper man understands equity
the small man profits"
—Confucious

"The quality of Equity must be assured among all the
parties—customers, investors, and employees. When
quantitative records of production are made at the expense
of safety, quality, or customer service, there is no reason to
celebrate with a bonus. Equity is often in the eye of the
beholder, so it is essential to assess continually the perception
of the organization's members—customers, investors, and
employees. Are they convinced of equitable return
on their investment in the company?"
—Dr. Carl Frost

CHAPTER 1

JOSEPH N. SCANLON: THE MAN AND THE PLAN

Daniel A. Wren

Joseph N. Scanlon

A reporter described Joseph Scanlon as a "cocky, gay, tough-hombre Irishman . . . [and] an ex-featherweight boxer and Navy oiler whose hands betray the faulty mending of bad bone breaks" (Chamberlain, 1944: 215). The son of Irish immigrants, Scanlon was born in Cleveland, Ohio March 21, 1899. He enlisted and served in the U.S. Navy from July 5, 1918 to September 30, 1921 and was honorably discharged (National Archives and Records Administration). Afterward, "Joe Scanlon chose a professional boxing career over a college education and had a few years experience in the ring before he came to work for [Empire Steel] in Mansfield [Ohio] in 1924" (Cross, 1939). At Empire Steel, his first job was as a cost accountant, possibly a result of attending night school.

His first marriage came in 1924 and he and his wife had one daughter, Mary Lou, who was born in 1926 (Meehan, 2005). While at Empire Steel, he continued boxing, a carry-over from his Navy service, "sometimes getting $1,000 a fight [but management] told him he could not hope to rise as an accountant if he came to work with black eyes" (Chamberlain, 1946: 97). Scanlon chose to give up accounting and selected the workers' world as an open hearth tender for Empire Steel.

3

Empire Steel

Empire Steel was incorporated in 1927 as a consolidation of six smaller steel companies, had 5,000 employees, and the capacity to produce 400,000 tons of rolled steel products. The Depression hit the firm hard and it went into receivership in 1931 and was reorganized in 1933 as the Empire Sheet and Tin Plate Company with 1,900 employees and the capacity to produce 300,000 tons of rolled steel. Technological changes put Empire in an increasingly competitive disadvantage as other firms adopted more advanced methods of the continuous rolling of steel.

The steelworkers at the reorganized Empire Sheet and Tin Plate Company were represented by the American Federation of Labor's Amalgamated Association of Iron, Steel, and Tin Workers (hereafter Amalgamated Association), Delano Lodge of Mansfield, Ohio

Leadership Changes at Empire

The first president of the steelworkers' union at Empire was Joseph Snyder, described as a "militant president under whose leadership the union was mainly interested in solving petty grievances" (Cross, 1939). Snyder served one year and in 1937 Scanlon was elected President of Lodge 169, Steel Workers Organizing Committee (SWOC). His daughter wrote "It was a rough and tough time. He received threatening phone calls and was called a Communist (someone painted RED on our home)" (Meehan, 2005). Scanlon and his fellow lodge members formed a relief committee, developed a cooperative to buy food directly from wholesalers, enlisted gratuitous medical services from community physicians, and cut and delivered wood to needy families. The union lodge was the linchpin for members to survive economic deprivation and to demonstrate to non-union members the value of belonging. His daughter recalled "during the Depression my father and grandfather cut grass and helped maintain a cemetery. My parents really struggled but we survived and sometimes I feel we were more closely knit at that time than any other" (Meehan, 2005).

Another leadership change was the arrival in 1937 of James M. Hill, previously a Republic Steel executive, as the new President of Empire Sheet and Tin Plate Company (Cross, 1939). The steel industry had a brief recovery in early 1937 but by December, 1937 production had dropped drastically and it was estimated that fifty percent of the steel industry workers were unemployed (Harbison, 1942: 527). Empire reduced its workforce to 900 and many of those were working a reduced work week. Empire showed a slim net profit of $1,486 on sales of $8,264,195 in 1937; in 1938, however, it incurred a net loss of $423,979 on sales of $2,698,898 (*Moody's Manual of Investments*, 1938: 2092; 1939: 827).

Faced with this continuing decline, Hill asked all Empire executives to take a 25 per cent salary cut, which they did, and Hill also asked the workers to also take a pay cut. The workers suspected this was another management game to get more for less and appealed to the SWOC headquarters to substantiate the firm's financial condition. When it was learned that the firm was indeed headed for bankruptcy, the union members voted a 25 per cent cut in pay.[1] Union leaders and management agreed this was a tourniquet and not a long-term solution (Cross, 1939).

The Trip to Pittsburgh

In June 1938, Hill, A.L. Allen, Director of Personnel, Scanlon, and William Bell, Vice President of Lodge 169, visited Clinton Golden in SWOC Headquarters in Pittsburgh. The question the group posed to Golden was "What are we going to do? We don't want to lose our jobs . . . we like our community, we get along remarkably well with the management . . . How are we to survive?" (Golden, quoted in Schultz, 1951: 53).

---

[1]This 25% wage reduction was restored as the firm's profitability improved: 5% in October 1938; 2.5% in July 1939; 2.5% in August 1939; 10% in November 1939; and 5% January 1, 1940 (Cross, 1939).

Golden recalled his advice was ". . . go back to your company . . . talk it over . . . develop some method for reaching down into the mind of each employee and see what he has got to propose that may possibly result in a reduction of cost or improvement of the quality of the product . . . See if you can [work] together to save your company" (Golden, quoted in Schultz, 1951: 54).

The outcome was the creation of a Joint Research Committee to meet monthly to hear worker suggestions on cutting waste and improving productivity and profitability. President Hill was "surprised" that the union was interested in controllable production costs but agreed to try this idea (Cross, 1939). One of the earliest problems identified was of "alligator hide" on finished steel sheets, resulting in a scrap rate of 60%. A consulting metallurgist was called in, but was unable to solve the problem. The workers, however, stated that this rough finish was caused by the steel sheets being too long in the "pickling furnace." In turn, the extra time in the pickling furnace occurred because "the pickler was working short-handed and was unable to get them back fast enough to keep the furnace going" (Cross, 1939).[2] Management added three workers for the pickling operation and the alligator hide problem was solved.

There is no evidence the workers shared in these cost savings, a feature that would be developed later by Joseph Scanlon, but worker participation and cooperation by management enabled the firm to survive, restore the previous wage cuts, and eventually increase the number of workers' jobs. In 1939, Empire Steel earned a profit of $39,141 on sales of $4,990,256; and 1940 profits were $41,951 on sales of $6,025,699 (Moody's, 1941: 452). Orders for Empire's steel products doubled in 1941, enabling profits of $486,702 and an increase in the workforce to 1,200 (Moody's, 1942: 935).

The results of union-management cooperation at Empire Steel during this period indicate success in saving jobs and staving off bankruptcy. As America came to the aid of its allies in

---

[2]A "pickler" operated equipment that chemically cleansed foreign matter from metal to prepare it for further processing, such as electroplating or galvanizing.

1940 and 1941 and entered World War II in late 1941, Empire Sheet and Tin Plate continued to prosper.[3]

The Steel Workers and World War II

Clinton Golden called Scanlon the "sparkplug" of the successes at Empire Sheet and Tin Plate, was familiar with his cost accounting background, and realized his capabilities as a union leader. When John L. Lewis resigned the CIO presidency in 1940 and was succeeded by Philip Murray, Golden convinced Murray that Scanlon was needed at Pittsburgh headquarters. Scanlon joined the staff in 1940 as head of a newly established "Industrial Engineering Department."

The Adamson Company

The Adamson Company, founded and owned by Cecil Adamson, was unionized as part of the U.S. Steel-SWOC agreement of 1937 and had a history of sound labor-management relations with its 100 member workforce. The Adamson Company grossed approximately one million dollars per year annually by manufacturing and selling 100,000 welded steel storage tanks for oil companies and gasoline stations (Chamberlain, 1946). Adamson had tried profit sharing plans but "had not reckoned with wage stabilization," that is, the NWLB limits on wage increases unless the increase was somehow connected to increased productivity (Scanlon, 1947: 11). Adamson sought the advice of USW headquarters and he and Scanlon began to work on a formula that would pass the test. Scanlon's cost accounting experience helped and the proposal to the NWLB was a 50-50 split between management and labor of profits before taxes based on the "ratio of labor costs to sales value of production" (Scanlon, 1947: 11). An increase in sales value of production or a reduction of labor cost would lead to savings

[3]The post-war years were less prosperous and Empire Sheet and Tin Plate Company was acquired by the Studebaker Corporation December 31, 1947.

and a joint labor-management production committee began to seek means of accomplishing improvements in this ratio. By the end of 1945, production efficiency increased 54 per cent and the workers averaged bonuses of 41 per cent of monthly earnings. For 1946, profits doubled the 1945 level and worker bonuses were 50 per cent more than in 1945.

The Adamson Company became the poster-company for Joseph Scanlon to build upon in his future work. Regardless of Adamson's success, Scanlon provided a caveat: "Unless both union and management are prepared to change their accepted way of thinking about each other and are willing to spend all of the time, effort, and care necessary . . . they would be well advised to steer clear of the idea of profit sharing" (Scanlon, 1947: 12). War-time circumstances encouraged labor-management cooperation in unionized as well as non-unionized firms; national wage stabilization policy and the decisions of the NWLB to conform to that policy, however, restrained Scanlon's goal of tying rewards to productivity gains until the opportunity was presented at the Adamson Company for a gain sharing plan. After the war and in a new position, Scanlon was able to advance and refine what became known as the Scanlon Plan.

Moving On

Thomas Brooks, Clinton Golden's biographer, found in a May 5, 1946 entry in Golden's diary that read "It seems most of the effort Joe Scanlon and I particularly have put forth to both advocate and build cooperative relationships has been undone by our associates" (Golden, in Brooks, 1978: 226). Philip Murray's comment at a union wage policy committee that he "was not among those who believed that any substantial part of management want to get along peacefully with the Union" was interpreted by Golden as an end to union-management cooperation (Brooks, 1978: 239).

When interviewed by John Hoerr, a long-time reporter on the USW for *Business Week*, Harold Ruttenberg said he did not like the direction Murray was taking the union. Ruttenberg recalled the progress of union-management collaboration during the steel worker organizing days: "It became very apparent to me, and to Golden, that you have to have union-management cooperation . . . we've got to continue this program, and if we don't, we are going to bankrupt our companies . . . unless you followed a policy of trying to feed the cow, you're going to milk it to death. You can't just milk it. You've got to feed it" (Hoerr, 1988: 282).

Scanlon's family life would change in Pittsburgh. His daughter recalled: "He came home on weekends for awhile and then my mother and I spent a year with him in Pittsburgh" (Meehan, 2005). The marriage failed, a divorce ensued, and Scanlon's wife and daughter returned to Mansfield, Ohio. While working with a steel local in Washington, Pennsylvania, Scanlon met Virginia White, daughter of the president of a local bank. Later, they would marry in Boston and "sailed on the Queen Mary the next day for six weeks in England as the guest of Sir Arthur Deacon of the Labor Party. Joe had been asked to evaluate and respond to England's entrenched productivity doldrums and loss of morale. Joe came back tremendously discouraged" (Frost, 2005).

Meyer Bernstein, a close friend of Joe Scanlon, told Hoerr that Scanlon felt he could make no headway after Golden left: "He [Scanlon] had ideas, but he couldn't get any support for them" (Hoerr, 1988: 284). Scanlon had been involved with and had seen union-management cooperation succeed at Empire Sheet and Tin Plate and at other companies while with the SWOC and the USW. World War II did not present the opportunities to develop fully what was to become known as the Scanlon Plan but it did promote Scanlon's idea that mutual collaboration could work and the gain sharing plan at Adamson Company reinforced this belief. His resignation from the USW came in October, 1946 and he accepted an invitation to join the Industrial Relations Section in the Department of Economics and Social Science at the Massachusetts Institute of Technology (MIT).

Scanlon at MIT

Joseph Scanlon was no stranger to the Industrial Relations faculty at MIT. In January 1945, the faculty organized a three week series of seminars on topics relating to union-management relations, labor-management cooperation, personnel administration, women in industry, and related subjects (*Technology Review*, 1945). Ten outside speakers participated and Scanlon was the only one from a labor union. MIT Professor Douglas McGregor knew of Scanlon's work at the Adamson Company and invited him to the seminars and, subsequently, was instrumental in bringing Scanlon to MIT as a Lecturer.

In announcing Scanlon's appointment, James R. Killian, Jr., then a MIT Vice President, noted: "educational institutions must help to educate labor leaders . . . In appointing Mr. Scanlon to its staff, the Institute seeks to broaden it educational facilities in the important field of industrial relations with the object of bringing about a better understanding of union-management relations" (*Technology Review*, 1946: 46). Killian commented on Scanlon's prior experiences in the union movement and his participation in industrial relations seminars and conferences at Harvard, Princeton, the University of Pennsylvania, the University of Chicago, and Holy Cross College.

At MIT, Scanlon would join a galaxy of scholars. Rupert Maclaurin, son of MIT's sixth president, formed an Industrial Relations Section in the Department of Economics and Social Science in 1937, creating one of the earliest institutions for the study of industrial relations (Killian, 1985). Under Maclaurin's leadership, the Industrial Relations Section employed seminal scholars such as Paul Pigors, Charles A. Myers, and Douglas McGregor; for economists, there were Paul Samuelson, Walter W. Rostow, George P. Schultz, Robert M. Solow, Charles P. Kindleberger, and other prominent scholars.

The Lapointe Machine Tool Company was the first application of Scanlon's ideas after joining the MIT faculty. Lapointe made broaching machines, that is, machine tools that shaped non-round holes in metal, and had a checkered history of relations with its United Steelworkers Union. Frederick Lesieur was President of the local union and convinced Vice President Edward Dowd to contact Scanlon as a consultant to determine if Lapointe could achieve the successes of the Adamson Company (Davenport, 1950). Scanlon was agreeable and began with his standard approach: first, determine "normal" labor costs based on past experiences; second, establish joint labor-management production committees to invite and review employee suggestions for cost savings which would be sent to a joint screening committee for final approval; finally, establish a cost-sharing program to be divided among all employees.

In the first three months (December, 1947 and January–February, 1948), efficiency increased 33, 28, and 21 per cent and corresponding bonuses were paid to all employees, except upper management executives whose bonuses were tied to sales. Bonuses were paid in only one of the following six months and the employees became discouraged. Scanlon traced the problem to a backlog of orders which the added efficiency had cleared out, but the sales personnel had not brought in new orders, thus losing their bonuses. Scanlon recognized that sales and production had to work better together and allowances had to be made for up and down months for inventory changes. In joint meetings, a new plan emerged: management had to be more diligent in getting orders; inventory changes, positive and negative, had to be included in the formula; and a reserve needed to be established to level out the high and low months for bonuses, with any surplus becoming an end of year bonus (Lesieur, 1958). With these changes, bonuses resumed and averaged 15 per cent per month from January, 1949 to September, 1952 (Schultz & Crisara, 1952).

The lesson learned at Lapointe was each firm had different circumstances and no one plan was appropriate for all; the only essential, for Scanlon, was labor-management cooperation in seeking cost savings and sharing these gains with the employees. The Market Forge Company was a job-lot shop for fabricating various steel products; each order was custom made so inventory figures were less important. Market Forge was one of Scanlon's less successful cases (*Time*, 1955). Stromberg-

Carlson manufactured radio, television, telephone, and sound recording equipment and had 6,000 employees, the largest number encountered thus far for Scanlon's ideas. Stromberg-Carlson had three product divisions, each a profit center, which made plant-wide bonuses more difficult to determine because the employees in one group could have a positive or negative influence on employees in other divisions. The employees voted to keep the plan in preference to the previous piecework arrangement and, by 1953, Stromberg-Carlson's screening committee had considered 2,100 suggestions, adopted 1,270 of them, and distributed $1,227,034 in bonuses and the plan was deemed successful (Gehman, 1953).

Murray Manufacturing, making safety switches and employing 360, was another success along with Welch Grape Juice, Towle Silver Company and others which reflected the diversity of firms that adopted Scanlon's ideas (Gehman, 1953). His ideas were also successful in union and nonunion firms, large or small, whether the joint committees were elected or appointed, whether profitable or on the brink of disaster, and in diverse manufacturing industries such as "shoes, silverware, pens and pencils . . . door handles . . . railroad ties, tanks for processing chemicals . . . [and] packaging equipment" (Schultz, 1958: 102–103). Exceptions could be found in continuous processing firms, such petroleum refining, where productivity was more likely to be connected to technology.

Time magazine called Scanlon the "most sought-after labor-relations consultant in the U.S. today" with successful installations of his ideas in 60 plants in a variety of firms (1955: 88–89). Parker Pen of Janesville, Wisconsin was cited as an example of a profitable firm with all modern facilities that disproved allegations that Scanlon's ideas worked only in small or failing firms. Parker Pen had eight joint production committees, one for each department, and a 17 member joint screening committee. The employees received 75 per cent, management 25 per cent of the efficiency bonus which averaged 27 per cent for 1953 and 1954. The ingredients of Parker's success were "a strong union, able to guarantee the support of its members . . . [and] a management willing to open its books and innermost production secrets to union members" (*Time*, 1955: 90).

The Scanlon Conferences

MIT decided to host a conference on Scanlon's ideas in 1947, but those who came had difficulty finding the site. Better directions were needed and "Labor-Management Production Committee's Saving-Sharing Plan Conference" proved unwieldy as signage. The signs were changed to read "Scanlon Conference" and this provided the necessary guidance. Scanlon objected and told a colleague "his work was like dropping a pebble in a pond and like the ripples it would just disappear" (Frost, 2005). Instead, the Scanlon Conference became an annual event and Scanlon served as chair until his health began to fail and the 1955 and 1956 conferences were cancelled.

Human Relations and the Scanlon Plan

Douglas McGregor and Joseph Scanlon were quite unlike in many ways until they found a common ground through their work at MIT. McGregor attended Oberlin College intending to be a minister, but changed his interest to psychology and received his Ph.D. from Harvard University. Scanlon's formal education was less formal and he spent his younger years in the Navy, as a prizefighter, cost accountant, and open-hearth steelworker before becoming involved in the union movement. Their common ground from divergent backgrounds involved employee participation in workplace decisions. As members of the Committee on the Causes of Industrial Peace under Collective Bargaining, they co-authored the case study of the Dewey and Almy Chemical Company and the International Chemical Workers Union. Dewey and Almy had progressed from the policies of its paternalistic founders and made significant progress in its relationship with the chemical workers union. To progress further, however, "it [the company] must soon move into the third—cooperative—stage if it is to remain healthy . . . [and] recognize the possibilities in union participation on problems of production efficiency and cost reduction" (McGregor & Scanlon, 1948: 65–66).

McGregor devoted a full chapter to the Scanlon Plan as an example of "management by integration and self-control . . . a way of industrial life—a philosophy of management— which rests on assumptions entirely consistent with Theory Y" (McGregor, 1960: 110). The Scanlon Plan's bases of cost reduction sharing and participation could work well in union- ized and nonunionized firms, according to McGregor, because it "helped managers discover the true nature of the organization's human resources" (1960: 118). A MIT doc- toral student who studied under Scanlon from 1947–1950 also stressed participation as a way "of utilizing the experi- ence of all members of the organization in developing better solutions to production problems faced by the organization" (Krulee, 1955: 104). Whyte and his colleagues praised the shared rewards in contrast to individual pay-outs and the sug- gestion system that was planned "discovery, development, and implementation of suggestions" as being more conducive to improved labor-management relations than the typical sugges- tion box on the wall (Whyte, et al., 1955: 173, 176). Others agreed: "The Scanlon Plan is one of the most promising approaches yet suggested to securing widespread employee participation and obtaining industrial peace and higher pro- ductivity as well" (Strauss & Sayles, 1960: 670). Despite its promise, the Scanlon Plan required changed attitudes for both labor and management which were not easily attainable (Strauss & Sayles, 1957).

These representatives of human relations thinking empha- sized the group, not individuals, and participative decision mak- ing. Human relations assumptions and conclusions would be challenged, but for this time in history Joe Scanlon's ideas fit well into and likely had a positive influence on human rela- tions in the workplace.

The Death of the Man but not the Plan

A close friend and colleague described Joe Scanlon as an "inveterate smoker" whose later years became "increasingly difficult because of [his] deteriorating emphysema condition which now required oxygen availability" (Frost, 2005). In these latter days Joe asked Fred Lesieur to leave Lapointe Machine Tool and join him at MIT in 1950.

Scanlon also encountered difficult times in his personal life. He and Virginia White Scanlon had a son, James Joseph Scanlon, but "unfortunately and tragically Jimmie Joe suffered severe injuries during the birth process" and was mentally retarded (Frost, 2005; Meehan, 2005). "This fact cast a prioritized agenda over every facet of Joe's personal and professional life. Joe tried desperately to cope" (Frost, 2005). It was a losing battle and Joseph N. Scanlon died of emphysema February 10, 1956, age 56, at the New England Medical Center (*Technology Review*, 1956). Memorial services were held at the Unitarian Church in Lexington, Massachusetts. His long-time friend and colleague of 20 years, Clinton Golden, was unable to attend these services but gave a eulogy at ceremonies honoring Scanlon at the Lapointe Machine Tool Company in Hudson, Massachusetts:

> Joe Scanlon was an American worker with a deeply rooted faith in Democracy and democratic processes. He believed that Democracy, while not perfect, is perfectible . . .
>
> He believed every worker, no matter how humble and seemingly unimportant his task, is capable of making a contribution not only to the success of the enterprise that employs him but to the happiness and well-being of his fellows . . .
>
> [He] was an unassuming, lovable, and unselfish human being, richly endowed by his Creator with the ability to *serve* rather than to *command* . . .
>
> He loved his country, he was proud of the heroic past, dissatisfied with the present, confident of the future . . .
>
> I have never grasped the hand of a better, truer, more unselfish friend than Joe Scanlon (Golden, in Brooks, 1978: 348).

After Scanlon's death, Fred Lesieur resumed the annual Scanlon Conferences at MIT in 1957 and these continued until the 1980s (Davis, 2005)

Carl Frost, who worked with Scanlon and McGregor at MIT and later moved to the Department of Psychology at Michigan State University, would take a different path regarding Scanlon's work. He published widely, formulated the "Frost/Scanlon Principles" (Frost, 1996), and developed the "Scanlon Roadmap" for organizational change and development.

Frost centered his work at Michigan State University and formed the Scanlon Plan Associates which continues today as the Scanlon Leadership Network with a web site and frequent conferences on leadership and organizational and personal development.

Conclusions

Joe Scanlon's experiences provided a unique perspective that created the most widely studied labor-management relations plan that bears his name. Through archival sources we have seen how his cost accounting background led to the original formula for sharing efficiency gains; how his life as a steelworker, union member and local union leader took him from the ranks to a national leadership position; and how his colleagues at MIT provided the means to nourish and expand his ideas. The Scanlon Plan has outlived many fads and evolved through human relations thinking to organizational change and development to an ever increasing body of gain sharing literature. It remains a viable means to promote and reward labor-management cooperation and improve efficiency and competitiveness. The Scanlon Plan is a future means of improving labor-management relations and work practices as well as part of its past.

References

Brooks, Thomas R. 1978. *Clint: A Biography of a Labor Intellectual, Clinton S. Golden*. New York: Atheneum.

Chamberlain, John. 1944. "The Steelworkers." *Fortune*, Vol. 29, No. 2 (February), pp. 165–166+.

Chamberlain, John. 1946. "Every Man a Capitalist." *Life*, Vol. 21, No. 26 (December 23), 93–103.

Cross, Ira B. 1939. "Empire Sheet and Tin Plate Company." Unpublished manuscript, no pagination, Ohio Historical Society, VFM 3208. Columbus, OH.

Davenport, Russell W. 1950. "Enterprise for Everyman." *Fortune*, Vol. 41, No. 1 (January), pp. 55–59+.

Davis, Paul. 2005 (June 2), to author. pdavis@scanlonleader.org

Frost, Carl F. 1996. *Changing Forever: The Well-Kept Secret of America's Leading Companies.* E. Lansing, MI: Michigan State University Press.

Frost, Carl F. 2005. To author (June 11).

Gehman, Richard. 1953. "Workers' Ideas Pay Everybody." *Nation's Business*, Vol. 41, No. 8 (August), pp. 65–70.

Harbison, Frederick H. 1942. "Steel," in Harry A. Millis (ed.), *How Collective Bargaining Works: A Survey of Experience in Leading American Industries*, pp. 508–570. New York: Twentieth Century Fund.

Hoerr, John P. 1988. *And the Wolf Finally Came: The Decline of the American Steel Industry*. Pittsburgh, PA: University of Pittsburgh Press.

Killian, James R. Jr. 1985. *The Education of a College President: A Memoir*. Cambridge, MA: The MIT Press.

Krulee, Gilbert K. 1955. "The Scanlon Plan: Cooperation through Participation." *Journal of Business of the University of Chicago*, Vol. 28, No. 2 (April), pp. 100–113.

Lesieur, Frederick G. 1958. "What the Plan Is and What It Isn't." In Frederick G. Lesieur (ed.). *The Scanlon Plan . . . A Frontier in Labor-Management Cooperation*, pp. 34–49. Cambridge, MA: The Technology Press of Massachusetts Institute of Technology.

McGregor, Douglas, and Joseph N. Scanlon. 1948. *The Dewey and Almy Chemical Company and The International Chemical Workers Union: A Case Study*. Case Study No. 3. Washington D.C.: National Planning Association.

McGregor, Douglas. 1960. *The Human Side of Enterprise*. New York: McGraw-Hill.

Meehan, Mary Lou. 2005. To author (June 5).

Scanlon, Joseph N. 1947. "Adamson and His Profit Sharing Plan." Production Series #172, pp. 10–12; "Discussion," pp. 29–34. New York: American Management Association.

Schultz, George P. 1951. "Workers Participation on Production Problems: A Discussion of Experience with the Scanlon Plan." *Personnel*, Vol. 28, No. 3 (November), pp. 201–211.

Schultz, George P. 1958. "Variations in Environment and the Scanlon Plan." In Frederick G. Lesieur. *The Scanlon Plan . . . A Frontier in Labor-Management Cooperation*, pp. 100–108. Cambridge, MA: The Technology Press of Massachusetts Institute of Technology.

Strauss, George. 2006. "Worker Participation—Some Under-Considered Issues." *Industrial Relations*, Vol. 45, No. 4 (October), pp. 778–803.

Technology Review (The). Courtesy of the MIT Museum. 1945. Vol. 47, Issue 3 (January), pp. 138–139; 1946. Vol. 49, Issue 1 (November), p. 46; 1956. Vol. 59, Issue 6 (April), p. 296.

Time. 1955. "The Scanlon Plan." Vol. 41, No. 5 (September 26), pp. 88–90.

Whyte, William F., Melville Dalton, Donald Roy, Leonard Sayles, Orvis Collins, Frank Miller, George Strauss, Friedrich Fuerstenberg, and Alex Bavelas. 1955. *Money and Motivation: An Analysis of Incentives in Industry*. New York: Harper and Brothers.

CHAPTER 2

THE SIGNIFICANCE OF SCANLON'S CONTRIBUTION

Douglas McGregor

I have been thinking about three remarkable men whom I have had the privilege to know during my lifetime. One of them was a Jew who came out of the ghettos of Europe. He was born before the turn of the century, became a professor of psychology at the University of Berlin, left there along with Albert Einstein back in the early Thirties when the handwriting on the wall became clear. He lived and worked in this country until his death about ten years ago. He was a remarkable innovator—a man who has had as much influence as any man in his profession on the field of psychology during the last generation. His name was Kurt Lewin, and he was the father of what we now refer to as group dynamics—the study of what goes on in the face-to-face group and of the kinds of things that effect productivity and effectiveness and group morale.

The second man was an Ohio farm boy, also born in the last century, who at eighty today is a multimillionaire, a very famous man, also an innovator. He has had a profound influence on our society. His name is Charles Kettering, and he was research director of General Motors for many years. I know him because he was on the Board of Trustees of Antioch College where I was for a number of years, and I spent many hours sitting in my office discussing life with Ket.

The third man was an Irish lad of humble origin who was a prize fighter and a cost accountant; later he went to work in

19

a steel mill, became a local-union president, then research director of the United Steelworkers of America, and finally a lecturer here at M.I.T. He was another innovator. I think time will show that he too has had a remarkable impact on our society. His name was Joseph Scanlon.

The differences between these three men are at first glance so great as to make you wonder why I even mention them in the same breath. But as I said, I have been struck with certain similarities among them which to me are impressive.

First of all, their point of view was always toward the future and never toward the past. Joe was fond of kidding people, sometimes quite seriously, about "facing the past and backing into the future." He had no use for the things that had been done, or for the milk that had been spilled; he wanted to look ahead and see what could come next. This was equally true of Kurt Lewin and is still true of Ket.

Even at eighty, he is impatient with the way things are now being done, looking eagerly to what can happen next. These three men, although they undertook things which were highly risky in terms of the chances of failure, never seemed to feel that risk was any more than an exciting challenge. The danger of failing never slowed them up, deterred them, or worried them. They were always emphasizing the chance of success. Kettering is fond of saying that he does not like the term "trial and error" because it carries the wrong implication. "You make trials, and you make mistakes, and you have errors, but you're aiming at success. What counts is the success that comes at the end of the road."

All three men had an experimental point of view. However, it was a rather unique one. It was not the experimental point of view of the physicist in the laboratory nearly so much as it was a practical concern with life itself. I have heard Ket say that with respect to the inventions in the automotive field that he has been concerned with, there were no formulas, no scientific laws that could give him the answers he was seeking. He had to turn to the engine. He said: "When you want to find out how to design a high-compression head, you can't find out with a slide rule how to cut the spaces in the head; you have to ask the engine—make a head, fit it on, and see how it runs."

Kurt Lewin was fond of what he called "action research." Though he fostered much research in the laboratory, he liked to get out into the field and deal experimentally with real-life situations. And Joe Scanlon operated exclusively with a kind of experimental approach to the real life of industry.

None of these three men was ever intimidated by "what is known." There are many things in books that are not so. Those who are wise enough to realize this do not depend too heavily on the books for their answers. Again I think of many stories I have heard Ket tell about his experiences, for example, with the diesel engine. He was told by physical scientists at eminent institutions that the ideas he was working with were impossible—that he could not design an engine to do the things he was asking an engine to do. Ket tells with some amusement about talking to famous physicists about the principles that he finally used in the design of the diesel engine, about hearing them say they wouldn't work, at a time when Ket was able to reply: "There goes one down the track."

Kurt Lewin was the same way in his work with groups. If he had depended exclusively on what was in the books, he probably would have been deterred even before he started in the important work which he carried on. In the books he could find a lot about how a group was simply a collection of individuals, that all he needed to do was study them individually and then put them together, and that the sum of their individual efforts would give him his answers. Kurt knew from his observations of life that a group was more than a sum of individuals; his experiments helped to prove this and to show why. He contributed to human knowledge because he was able to put the books in perspective, read them, but not be intimidated by them.

In the same way, Joe, with his approach (for example, to the problems of incentives) was not a bit intimidated by the fact that we have thousands of volumes on incentives and on industrial-engineering practices related to them. He was prepared to go beyond these because his knowledge of life was such that he knew the books did not have all the answers.

I remember one experience with Kettering along this line which illustrates how he felt about this whole matter. I went to him for financial help for Antioch, and after some discussion he agreed to give us a library. The very fact that Ket would give a library was in itself an interesting thing. When I was talking with him later, when the library was being designed, I said: "Ket, what do you want inscribed over the door?" He looked at me for a moment, and then he grinned as he said: "You won't do it, but I'll tell you what I'd like over the door—Enter Here at Your Own Risk."

His research over the years included much that was going on at the Antioch campus under Ket's auspices. He had people studying about why plants are green—the subject of photosynthesis—which Ket believes in the long run is going to lead us to an understanding of sources of energy that will make atomic energy look like peanuts. This research is still in its early phases, but it is being actively pursued in the Kettering Laboratory at Antioch, among other places. Ket's way of handling his staff on this project reflected this same idea. Whenever they hit on a new notion of something to do experimentally, he would say: "Let's try it first, and then go see if other people have done it." The normal process is the reverse of this. His fear was that in going too soon to see what was in the books his staff might put on blinders and never see the possibilities. This was also a characteristic of Joe that I very much admired.

There are two other qualities about these three people that have stuck in my mind and they are far more important than any I have mentioned so far. One was an abiding faith in their fellow men. They did not see themselves as elite and the rest of the world as a mass of ignorant people. Each of these three great men was simply a human being in his dealings with other people. (I speak of Ket in the past tense, but at eighty he is still as alive and active as a man can be. The other two having passed on, it is difficult to use the right tense in referring to all three.)

I remember an experience Kettering had when a ship was being built and one of his first diesel engines was being installed in it. As he was wandering around the shipyard just a few weeks before the launching, he noticed one of the workmen standing at the stern of this vessel looking at it. Ket walked up to him, got into a conversation with him, hauled up a nail keg, and sat down for a while. He had noticed the man staring intently at the stern of the ship and finally asked: "What are you looking at?" The fellow said: "That propeller." Ket said: "What about it?" He said: "It's too big." Ket said: "How much too big?" "Oh," he said, "at least five inches; maybe five and a half."

I think most people would have dismissed such a comment at this point. This was an ordinary workman; he was not a member of management; he was not an architect—just an ordinary guy. But Ket did not drop the subject. He called up the architects and asked them to check the plans and find out the diameter of the propeller on this ship. They did and after a little while came back with an answer. Then he said: "Will you send somebody out to measure it?" And of course they did. Somewhat later he got a phone call, very shamefacedly, from the architectural firm. They said they did not know who had made the mistake, but the diameter of that propeller was five and a quarter inches too great! Under the conditions of design of this ship, this was a serious error. This kind of belief in the intelligence of his fellow men was as characteristic of Joe Scanlon and Kurt Lewin as it is of Kettering.

Finally, all of these things I have mentioned indicate to me in these three people, as in others like them, a way of life, a personal philosophy and a view of what people are like and how one deals with them. This "philosophy" leads to an attitude toward risk and mistake making, to optimism about what can be done, a refusal to think that anything is impossible, no matter how difficult it looks. It seems to me that even though the differences are sharp, the similarities among these three innovative men are worth some reflection.

Several people have raised a question with me when the Scanlon Plan has been under discussion. They have asked: "Why is it, if the Scanlon Plan is so good, that it isn't more widely adopted?" I should like to comment just a moment on this. If you as management are considering the development of a new product or process in industry, you expect without question to devote a lot of time, money, and energy to turning your initial idea into a working process or a finished product that can go on the market. The initial idea is very remote from the final product that appears on the market.

However, when we turn to look at the problems of managing people or to matters having to do with the organization of human effort, we find management attempting (quite unconsciously, I think) to shortcut this process completely and to assume that you can go from the original idea directly to the sale or use of the product without any intervening development process. For me, the growth of the Scanlon Plan since the middle Thirties represents a kind of development research that is still far from complete. This research has gone on in many companies rather than in one. There have been mistakes, there has been a lot of money, time, and energy put into it, and there will have to be a lot more before we realize the full potential of this complex and intricate set of ideas involved in Joe Scanlon's philosophy.

I have heard, over the days of the conference here, a number of questions implying that you wanted to have all the uncertainty taken out. Some of you seem to be saying: "If it's a good idea, tell me the gimmick; tell me how I can do it without any fear of failure; tell me how I can remove all the possible mistakes so that, when I go home and attempt to apply it, there'll be no risk involved." Now nobody said this in so many words, but this was the implication I got from some of the things that you said to each other. I should like to urge you to consider my analogy and realize that we are still at the pilot plant stage. These things we are talking about—this way of life, if you like—which are represented by Scanlon and his ideas, are still being developed. There is still risk for the innovators. The implication of this is that you are being asked to go out on the end of a springboard to jump off in pitch darkness, not knowing whether there is water or rocks underneath you. I don't think this is the case either.

Over the years, the thing that has fascinated me most about Joe Scanlon and the pilot plants which some of you have been operating is the similarity between the insights that you are developing and some of the ideas that have been coming out of research in the social sciences focused on people. The way these insights have coincided with our increasing scientific knowledge in this field has been to me an exciting and fascinating thing to follow. I should like to mention before I close just a few that have struck me particularly because of the parallel between the Scanlon Plan and what is going on—entirely independent of Scanlon's operations—within the social-science field and within the field of management, broadly.

First consider with me the knowledge and the insights that we have acquired within the last fifteen or twenty years about delegation and decentralization within industrial organizations. We have learned that, if we push decision-making down in an organization as far as we possibly can, we tend to get better decisions, people tend to grow and to develop more rapidly, and they are motivated more effectively. Most companies today of any size at all are persuaded that the principles of decentralization and delegation—applied with wisdom—are fundamental to the successful operation of their organizations. We recognize that no small group of management or no single manager can have all the answers; even if he does have them, he will lose a great deal if he attempts to make all the decisions. He will never have an organization that grows and becomes healthy in its own right.

For me this idea, although unrelated to the Scanlon Plan, is remarkably similar in some of its implications. What Joe Scanlon was driving for was broad decentralization and genuine delegation, clear to the bottom of the organization. Some of you have given evidence of what happens when this idea is applied in that way.

There have been many developments in the social sciences in the last fifteen to twenty years having to do with motivation. We are coming around to very different notions about why people behave the way they do, and about what motivates them. I am not going into this matter here, but I should like to mention that there has been much more evidence than we ever had before concerning the importance of the social motives of human beings. Man is still tremendously motivated to work with his fellows, gain their recognition, their acceptance; the motivations existent in a social group are powerful in influencing behavior.

Those of you who knew Joe have heard him say many times that social motivations, with their constructive and positive implications, have a great deal to offer management and workers alike. They are far more effective than what Joe called the "vicious" motivations stimulated by our attempt to use the carrot and stick with the typical individual incentive approach to motivation.

We have learned a great deal in recent years about the organization of work, and we have come to realize that the typical industrial-engineering approach—the "scientific-management" approach—of the last half century, which takes all the human elements out of work and turns man essentially into a glorified machine tool, is a waste of the most important resource of the organization. You see today in the concept of job enlargement and similar ideas (again entirely divorced from the Scanlon Plan) the same concern with using the knowledge, the skill, the ingenuity, and the ability of the individual with respect to his own job, and the same concern with building responsibility back into jobs that we have defined far too narrowly.

We have had at M.I.T. for a number of years an activity that some people might regard as industrial-engineering. The faculty members who head it refer to it as "the management of improvement." They have made a sharp break with traditional industrial-engineering approaches. They are concerned with participative methods that can be used to improve performance on the job. Here is something right here at M.I.T. which has been completely independent of the Scanlon Plan but which has gone parallel with it to a remarkable degree.

Finally, there is one other independent development which parallels Joe's work. It is the notion that, by and large, people are capable of being mature adults in their relationships with each other—that they are capable of *self*-direction, of *self*-discipline, of *self*-control. Our whole managerial philosophy for the past several centuries has been built on the notion that people are like children, incapable of directing their own activities within the organization, incapable of controlling and disciplining themselves. If we take this point of view, the task of management must be that of directing them, manipulating them, and controlling them in doing the job that has to be done.

I think we are beginning to get evidence from a variety of sources that this is not true, and I suspect that our conception of management as a manipulative, directive process is one day going to be supplanted by a very different notion that people are, after all, adults and capable of self-direction. When we begin to treat them that way, we shall have some different consequences in organizational behavior.

Much of the behavior we see in typical industrial organizations today is not a consequence of human nature; it is a consequence of the way we organize, of the way we manage people. Resistance to output, antagonism to management, and all kinds of subtle ways of defeating the purposes of the organization are not inherent expressions of human nature; they are results—consequences of the fact that we have built organizations and methods of control that bring about exactly these behaviors.

We have evidence in the companies that are experimenting with the Scanlon Plan concerning the different behavior you begin to get when you set up a different kind of organization with a different management philosophy, based on the idea that people are, after all, capable of behaving like adults. We have heard illustration after illustration which on the surface sound pretty odd. Says one man: "We don't have fights any more about moving a man from this operation to that one. He doesn't quarrel about the limits of his job; we don't have to go back to the contract to see whether he can be moved around." We have heard examples of people helping each other on their jobs. When one fellow runs out of work he goes over and helps another man on with his job. We have been told that the issue of management prerogatives has ceased to be an issue.

To my way of thinking what really is being said is that when we set up a different way of life in the industrial organization, we can expect people to behave differently. And this is exactly what some of you have discovered. It looks strange to those on the outside whose experience has been different. Perhaps it explains why some of us are worried about the legal limits we would have to put on the Scanlon agreement to make sure that this or that or the other thing does not happen. We are habituated to seeing people respond in certain ways to the typical managerial philosophy that we have been using for so long.

I should mention before I close one important caution to any of you who perhaps are thinking of shifting in the direction of this different way of life, this way of treating people as if they were capable adults. It is simply this: we can't learn to run until we learn to walk. It takes time and lots of mistakes before we can grow from the pattern that we may be accustomed to, of treating people like children and having them respond like children, to the pattern of having them react like adults. It's easy enough, of course, to use this as an excuse to continue past practices. But even if you adopt a way of life that is built on a genuine belief that people can grow, can learn together, and can solve their mutual problems together, you must still expect the process to take some time. And the spotty picture that we have seen among the companies represented here—different degrees of success and failure, different experiences, different kinds of mistakes that have been lived through—simply reflects this natural but difficult process of growth and development which goes on when one attempts to practice a new managerial philosophy.

I should like to close by reminding you once more of my initial comment about the three men: Kurt Lewin, Charles Kettering, and Joe Scanlon. In my honest opinion these were three great men. They had many qualities of greatness among them, but the most important one, the one that will make them stand out through the years, was their abiding conviction that they and their fellow men together could achieve the impossible.

CHAPTER 3

THE SCANLON PLAN THROUGH A PSYCHOLOGIST'S EYES

Douglas McGregor

The Scanlon Plan is a philosophy of organization. It is not a program in the usual sense; it is a way of life—for the management, for the union, and for every individual employee. Because it is a way of life, it affects virtually every aspect of the operation of the organization. In this fact lies its real significance. Underlying Joseph Scanlon's efforts was a deep and fundamental belief in the worth of the human individual, in his capacity for growth and learning, in his ability to contribute significantly "with his head as well as his hands" to the success of the company which employs him. Scanlon, unlike many who make similar professions, really respected human beings.

The Scanlon Plan is what he evolved out of his experience to implement his fundamental belief in people. Although he was anything but a theoretician, and although he was only casually familiar with the research findings of the social sciences, the Plan he conceived fulfills to a remarkable degree the requirements for effective organized human effort that have been highlighted by such research. In addition, the actual experience of Scanlon Plan companies provides significant verification of the predictions the social scientist makes on theoretical grounds. The Plan implements Scanlon's underlying belief by establishing three broad conditions within which it becomes possible and natural for all members of the firm to collaborate in contributing to its economic effectiveness. These conditions are:

1. A formally established "area of collaboration" and machinery (production and screening committees) for coordinating such collaborative efforts throughout the whole organization. This is accomplished without undermining collective bargaining or weakening the local union.
2. A meaningful, realistic, common objective (the "ratio") in terms of which such collaborative efforts can be objectively measured.
3. A psychologically adequate system of rewards (non-economic as well as economic) for a wide range of contributions to the effectiveness of the enterprise. (Traditional incentive wages, profit sharing, and suggestions system awards are quite inadequate in terms of modern psychological theory.)

As a consequence of establishing these three conditions, the employees and the managements of Scanlon Plan companies literally discover a new way of life. The process is not easy; some of the learning is rough indeed. There is little of a sentimental sweetness-and-light atmosphere, but there develops a mutual respect which cuts across even the most violent disagreements. The new relationship permeates in surprising but meaningful ways into every corner of the organization. It is some of these consequences and their relation to social-science theory and findings that I would like to examine.

Scientific Management and Human Capabilities

Many research studies have pointed out that, however persuasive the *logic* of "scientific management" may be, the consequences of its application are often contrary to expectation.[1] Informal but effective collusion to defeat managerial purposes takes many forms, and it is widespread. Less recog-

---

[1] Chris Argyris, *Personality and Organization*, New York: Harper, 1957. Chapters IV and V summarize the data succinctly.

nized, but perhaps more important than these consequences, is the failure of this approach to make effective use of the potentialities of people.

Treating the worker as though he were in Drucker's words, a "glorified machine tool"[2] is a shameful waste of the very characteristics which distinguish people from machines. Despite protests to the contrary, the approach of scientific management has been to treat the worker as a "hand" rather than a human being. The consequences of so doing have been attributed to the "natural" cussedness of workers and explained as the price of technological efficiency. Pleasant working surroundings and fringe benefits have been used to alleviate the negative aspects of assembly-line jobs. Fancy communications programs and Madison Avenue sales gimmicks have been used to persuade the worker of the vital importance of his tiny contribution to the enterprise. These are understandable but largely ineffective palliatives. However, work simplification and all the other paraphernalia of the industrial engineer—consistent with a view of the worker as a glorified machine tool—remain the commonly accepted way to utilize human effort in industry.

Scanlon knew better. He knew that what Drucker calls "industrial citizenship"[3] is perfectly possible even in the mass-production setting, provided management will recognize that workers have brains and ingenuity as well as muscles. The Scanlon Plan creates the necessary conditions for this discovery. Once these conditions are established, people collaborate because it is to their interest to do so. They don't need to be made to "feel" important; they *are* important and they know it. The most far-reaching consequence of this creation of genuine industrial citizenship is the virtual elimination of what Argyris calls the sense of "psychological failure" created by the traditional approach of scientific management. Among other things, the notion of the "nonproductive" worker, and, the "burden" concept of staff and administrative employees

[2]Peter Drucker, *The Practice of Management*, New York: Harper, 1954, pp. 280 ff.
[3]Peter Drucker, *The New Society*, New York: Harper, 1949, pp. 151 ff.

go out the window. Productivity, under the Scanlon Plan, is not confined to direct production workers, nor is the line organization the only part of the enterprise that is seen as carrying its own weight. Productivity is measured by reduction of the labor bill, and *everyone* can contribute to this objective. Improvement of the ratio, by every means, is everybody's business. The individual's contribution is not limited to doing "a fair day's work." The janitor and the stenographer, as well as the engineer and the manager, can, and often do, exercise human ingenuity in developing improvements entirely outside the limits of their own job descriptions. The area for collaboration covers anything that will contribute to the effectiveness of the enterprise.

The challenging opportunities that are inherent in every industrial organization for people to assume responsibility, achieve status, acquire new skills, learn, develop, and exercise creativity become apparent once this area of collaboration is carved out. The idea that workers are paid to do what they are told and management is paid to tell them not only prevents effective collaboration but automatically creates the feeling of psychological failure. It leads either to indifferent passivity or to active hostility. Genuine participation in problem solving removes the causes of these common reactions.

The Task of Management

It should not be supposed that management loses its responsibility to manage under a Scanlon Plan. Much to the contrary. One of the happier consequences is that the foreman ceases to occupy the impossible role that has been his in recent years and becomes a manager in the real sense of the term. He is no longer caught in the problem of divided loyalties and conflicting pressures. He is no longer the pawn of a variety of staff groups who "control" him to death under the label of serving him. He ceases to be a paper shuffler, an ineffective disciplinarian, a "master and victim of doubletalk,"[4] and becomes a manager willy-nilly. Sometimes the pressures that bring about this transformation are painful in the extreme. However, most supervisors come to relish their new role.

Further up the line there is considerably less tilting with the windmill of prerogatives and more genuine concern with managing the enterprise. One of the interesting phenomena among management people in Scanlon Plan companies is their inability to comprehend the questions that are frequently asked of them concerning their freedom to manage. Authority in the sense of the right to be arbitrary, to force subordinates to do their bidding, ceases to be a meaningful idea because the collaborative relationship almost eliminates the necessity for this kind of order giving.

The management task in Scanlon Plan companies becomes one of genuine leadership. The manager who is primarily a power seeker and a protector of management's right to be arbitrary finds little satisfaction in such a situation. The pattern of managerial behavior which tends to emerge is remarkably close to that of the "democratic" leader in the classic Lewin and Lippitt research.[5] However, this term "democratic" does not mean abdication; it does not imply that "everyone decides everything." Its essence is that it makes effective use of human resources through participation; it provides general rather than close supervision; it is "employee-centered"[6] it encourages responsible behavior and tough-minded self-control rather than reliance on external authority.

As mentioned above, disagreements flourish in Scanlon Plan companies. Management has the responsibility and exercises the authority in their resolution. The difference is that people usually disagree about the best way to do the job or to

---

[4]Fritz Roethlisherger, "The Foreman: Master and Victim of Doubletalk," *Harvard Business Review*, Vol. 23. No. 3, Spring, 1945, pp. 283–298.

[5]Kurt Lewin, Ronald Lippitt, and Ralph K. White, "Patterns of Aggressive Behavior in Experimentally Created Social Climates," *Journal of Social Psychology*, Vol.X, 1939, pp. 271–299.

[6]Rensis Likert, "Motivational Dimensions of Administration," *America's Manpower Crisis*, Chicago: Public Administration Service, 1956.

reduce costs or to improve the profit margin rather than about whose rights are what or what legalistic interpretation should be put on a work rule. This is a big difference.

The Scanlon Plan typifies Drucker's "management by objectives and self-control." General (as opposed to close) supervision and wide delegation evolve naturally as management discovers that it is no longer necessary to force people to do what needs to be done. It becomes possible to deal with people as mature adults rather than as children and thus to avoid much of the conflict between organizational requirements and the needs of the human personality which Argyris has so well delineated.[7]

Cooperation and Competition

The psychological significance of all of this is that the Scanlon Plan "fits together" the purposes of organization with the natural human tendency to collaborate when collaboration is the sensible way to do things. Industrial organizations are complex *interdependent* human entities. Unless the many related functions are smoothly interlocked, unless people are constantly adjusting to each other in terms of common objectives, organizations cannot operate effectively. Emphasis on individual competition, on narrow job responsibilities, and antagonism toward the natural tendency of humans to form groups characterize much of present-day managerial practice. This emphasis is 180 degrees out of phase with the need for collaboration in a complex system of interdependence.

The Scanlon Plan sets a meaningful common objective and creates the necessary conditions to bring practice and organizational need into phase. Instead of lip service to "teamwork" within a system which stacks the cards against it, the Scanlon Plan makes teamwork the natural way of life. And then it becomes no longer necessary to preach about its value! Competitive motivations—also natural to humans—are not ignored either. However, instead of competing with fellow workers, or

[7]Chris Argyris, *op. cit.*

saying, "To hell with the other department (or the other shift); I'm paid to do my job, not to worry about them," the competition is with other companies in the industry. In a capitalist economy what could be more natural?

Resistance to Change

A fair amount of research has pointed up the fact that resistance to change is a reaction primarily to certain methods of instituting change rather than an inherent human characteristic.[8] Leo Moore and Herbert Goodwin of the M.I.T. School of Industrial Management have coined the term "improvement management" to describe a way of gaining some of the benefits of scientific management without producing resistance to change.[9] The Scanlon Plan minimizes such resistance because it involves people in the process of creating change rather than imposing it on them. Improvement management is the Scanlon way of life because everyone is interested in improving the ratio. Significant examples of worker-generated change in the organization of work are common in Scanlon Plan companies. Ironically, these are frequently changes that management tried unsuccessfully to introduce in pre-Scanlon days. Resistance becomes instead active instigation. In fact, the Scanlon Plan company experience with the change process is one of the most clear-cut examples of the way in which the research-based predictions of social science are fulfilled in practice.[10]

It is perhaps needless to point out that restriction of output, feather-bedding, collusion to fudge production records, and

[8]Alvin Zander, "Resistance to Change: Its Analysis and Prevention," *Advanced Management*, Vol. 15, No. 1, January, 1950, pp. 9–11.

[9]Leo Moore, "Too Much Management, Too Little Change," *Harvard Business Review*, Vol. 34, No. 1, January–February, 1956, pp. 41–48.

[10]See, for example: Lester Coch and John R. P. French, Jr., "Overcoming Resistance to Change," *Human Relations*, Vol. I, 1948, pp. 512–532; Kurt Lewin, "Group Decision and Social Change," *Readings in Social Psychology*, rev. ed., New York: Henry Holt, 1952, pp. 459–473; A. T. M. Wilson, "Some Contrasting Cocio-Technical Production Systems," *The Manager*, December, 1955.

all the other ingenious group methods of defeating the managerial purposes of traditional incentive plans disappear completely in Scanlon Plan companies. Again, this is exactly what the social scientist would predict on the basis of his research into the causes of this phenomena.[11]

Human Motivation

Examination of modern theories of motivation points up further Scanlon's insight into human behavior. The Scanlon Plan production and screening committees, as well as the whole management-employee relationship which develops, provide ideal means for satisfying ego and self-actualization needs which are typically frustrated under the conditions of present-day industrial employment.[12]

There is no undervaluation of economic motives either. However, one happy consequence of the Scanlon Plan is the minimization of conflict over the workers' share of the proceeds of enterprise. The ratio is determined from accounting data, and even in unionized companies there is no instance on record of an impasse over this issue![13]

The economic rewards of the Scanlon Plan are fully consistent with present-day psychological knowledge. First, they are related to factors in the work situation which are controllable by employees. This is in contrast to most profit-sharing plans. Under the latter workers are rewarded in a fashion which is only remotely connected to their direct contribution. (I know

[11] William Foote Whyte, *Money and Motivation*, New York: Harper, 1955.
[12] Abraham Maslow, *Motivation and Personality*, New York: Harper, 1954, especially Chapters 4, 5, 8; Douglas McGregor, "The Human Side of Enterprise," *Management Review*, November, 1957, pp. 22–28; E. Wight Bakke, *The Unemployed Worker*, New Haven: Yale University Press, 1940; Robert W. White, *Lives in Progress*, New York: Dryden Press, 1952.
[13] Scanlon was insistent—and wisely so—that the Plan offer management no escape from meeting the standards of wage levels and other conditions of employment established generally by collective bargaining. To use it in this fashion would be the surest way to undermine the union's acceptance of the philosophy of collaboration. The Scanlon Plan would quickly be seen as a device to negate the legitimate gains of the labor movement.

of one profit-sharing plan where the profits which were shared for several years resulted primarily from the speculation of the treasurer of the company in the raw-materials market!)

Second, the payoff is within a sensible time span. It is well established that rewards become less effective the more remote in time they are from the behavior which is being rewarded. An annual payoff (typical under profit sharing) is too remote to be of much use as a motivator. The monthly payoff under the Scanlon Plan is meaningfully related in time to the behavior which affects the ratio.

Third, the plant-wide nature of the bonus is realistic in terms of the common objectives of the members of the enterprise. It does not eliminate individual differences in wage rates related to job responsibilities, but it creates the proper perception of "sharing" in a common endeavor.

Fourth, the bonus is paid for *all* contributions to the effectiveness of the enterprise rather than for the narrow contribution of output per man-hour which is common under conventional incentive plans. There are no problems in relating pay to fancy (and largely unrealistic) "standards" for measuring individual performance, particularly for maintenance, clerical, and other service jobs. Moreover, there is no longer any incentive to defeat the time-study engineer or to hide jigs and fixtures which have been invented to "beat the standard" or to establish collusive relations with tool-crib clerks, timekeepers, inspectors, and others in order to "make out."[14]

Finally, the payoff reflects the success of the enterprise in understandable terms. There is no necessity for interpreting the elaborate formulas of the industrial engineers (which workers are quite able to do, by the way), or for fathoming the formalized and often misleading gobbledygook of the balance sheet.

Mention of the balance sheet leads to one other economic point I would emphasize: the education for all participants in the economics of enterprise. American management has spent many millions of dollars in attempts to provide economic edu-

[14]William Foote Whyte, *op. cit.*, particularly Chapter 7.

cation to workers. The results have not been measured, but one may be permitted a certain skepticism.[15]

The Scanlon Plan, however, provides such education in the most direct fashion: through day-by-day involvement in the problems of the enterprise. A casual conversation with Scanlon Plan company employees often reveals an understanding of our economic system which is uncommon even among college graduates. And this fundamental and important educative process costs not one cent! It requires no films or brochures or discussion groups or lecturers. It is obtained in the normal course of daily life by direct, firsthand experience. Scanlon Plan company employees are believers in capitalism, and they know *why* they are!

Staff-line Conflict

Friction between workers and lower levels of supervision on the one hand and staff departments such as industrial engineering, accounting, personnel, inspection, inventory control, purchasing, and research and development on the other hand is widespread in industry today and it is a good deal more costly than management usually recognizes. Research studies and reports of participant observers have provided substantial evidence of this phenomena.[16]

A major cause of these frictions is the fact that staff departments are placed in the position of imposing their standards, their plans and procedures, their "expertness" on the line; this is a fact quite generally despite textbook assertions that the staff functions are those of service, advice, and counsel. The staff engineer tells the worker to "follow the blueprint" even when (as

[15]William H. Whyte, *Is Anybody Listening*, New York: Simon & Schuster, 1952; Douglas Williams in *Management Education for Itself and Its Employees*, New York: A.M.A.,1954, Part 4.
[16]William Foote Whyte, *op. cit.*; Chris Argyris, "Human Problems with Budgets," *Harvard Business Review*, Vol. 31, No. I, January–February, 1953, pp. 97–110; Charles A. Myers and John U. Turnbull, "Line and Staff in Industrial Relations," *Harvard Business Review*, Vol. 34, No. 4, July–August, 1956, pp. 113–124; and F. J. Roethlisberger and William J. Dickson, *Management and the Worker*, Cambridge, Mass.: University Press, 1939, Part IV.

happens all too often) the worker's knowledge of his tools and materials tells him that this is foolish or impossible. A substantial amount of paper work by the supervisor is summarized or scrutinized by the accounting department and turned over to others higher in the organization to be used frequently in a disciplinary manner ("Your variances are out of line," or "You have overrun your budget," or "You made an unauthorized expenditure").

The simple psychological fact is that external controls of this kind engender hostility and lead to the exercise of a substantial degree of ingenuity directed solely toward defeating the purposes of those who have instigated the controls. This is the exact opposite of management's desire; it is the antithesis of collaboration. Unfortunately, management at the top is rarely aware of the extensiveness of this internecine warfare, and the staff groups tend to interpret it as evidence of the stupidity or inherent hostility of workers and supervisors. The typical staff reaction is to tighten and elaborate the controls, which of course simply makes matters worse.[17]

The Scanlon Plan, when these groups are included, creates entirely different relations between staff and line. The need for external controls diminishes to the vanishing point as collaboration toward the common objective of improving the ratio becomes the way of life. The staff groups can help the line in a great many ways if this is what they are set up to do. The line learns to use and to value this, help as soon as the staff is relieved of a function which makes them appear to be policemen and spies. Evidence for this fundamental change in relations is to be found readily in Scanlon Plan companies. One nice example was the occasion at the Lapointe Machine Tool Company when the engineers voluntarily postponed their vacations in order to prepare specifications for a new order so that there would be sufficient work to avoid a layoff in the factory.[18]

[17]See Argyris, "Human Problems with Budgets," *op. cit.*, for a penetrating analysis of this set of problems.

[18]Fred Lesieur tells how the machinists in this same company, during pre-Scanlon days, would receive with glee a set of engineering specifications containing a major error and build the equipment exactly "according to specs" with full knowledge that it would ultimately have to be scrapped!

If the Scanlon Plan accomplished nothing else but to bring about effective collaboration between staff and line it would be a major contribution to organizational effectiveness. But this consequence is simply one of a large number of by-products resulting from a changed way of life. It is, in addition, a convincing demonstration of the well-established psychological fact that self-control is far more effective than externally imposed authority.

Conclusion

There are other ramifications of the operation of the Scanlon Plan which fit consistently with the implications of modern social-science findings. However, those discussed above serve to document my initial assertion concerning this consistency. They demonstrate, also, the difference between the usual personnel "program" and a genuine organizational philosophy, an industrial way of life.

No doubt other patterns of relationship will be found which yield results comparable with or superior to the Scanlon Plan. It is probable that the Plan as Scanlon conceived it would be difficult to establish in some kinds of industrial situations even if both management and union desired it. However, I will venture the prediction that we will succeed in increasing our utilization of the human potential in organizational settings only as we succeed in creating conditions which generate a meaningful way of life.

Scanlon's lasting contribution is his recognition—now effectively demonstrated in action—that one cannot successfully tackle this central task of management with gimmicks or procedures or programs. The real task of management is to create conditions which result in genuine collaboration throughout the organization. To create such conditions is to establish a way of life. This is the central conclusion to which the findings of social science are pointing today. And this is the lesson that Joseph Scanlon taught us all.

WHAT THE PLAN ISN'T, AND WHAT IT IS

Frederick G. Lesieur

The best way of describing the Scanlon Plan is the method used by Joe Scanlon on many occasions over the years before his death. This means spending just as much time telling you what the Plan isn't as what it is. Many of the stories that I am going to relate will be experiences that I personally have had under the Scanlon Plan. I was a machinist at the Lapointe Machine Tool Company and was also very active in the local Steelworkers' Union at that plant. These examples are combined with experience I gained during six and a half years of association with Joe Scanlon in the application of the Plan.

The Scanlon Plan is difficult to explain because it is not a simple formula. It is a set of principles or ideals that can be attained in industry.

A word that is pretty shopworn in industry today is "teamwork," so I am going to spend some time discussing teamwork as I see it. At just about all of the meetings of the many different industrial and management associations there is always a speech given by some company official concerning "teamwork" at his plant. I would venture to say that if you had the opportunity to go back to many of these plants where this so-called teamwork is going on, you might come to the conclusion that it is almost impossible to have teamwork because of the very system under which the employees have to work.

Let me start with some examples of what Joe Scanlon used to call the "restraining influences" that are prevalent in most plants today and how they affect "teamwork." One of the more

41

disturbing elements is the approach taken by many companies—
that to increase productivity you've got to appeal to the selfish
individual. You have to set the individual up in business for himself and make a "free enterpriser" out of him. I was one of those
individuals, as an incentive worker, in the plant where I worked.
Most incentive or direct workers feel that everybody else who
isn't a direct worker just hasn't any place in the enterprise. They
feel that they are carrying the load of the whole plant on their
backs. They think that the so-called indirect (that's the group
that the company claims they can't measure) are only in their
way, and if these people weren't around things would be much
better.

To cite another example, most of us working in plants have
always felt that the engineering department never gave any consideration to the tools or the equipment we had to work with
when they were developing or designing new products. We
always felt that they were living up in their ivory tower and in
no way concerned with how their creations had to be made or
with the success of the company. At least, that's what we
thought. Of course, later on, when I had the opportunity to discover for myself how they felt about their jobs and their relations with us in the plant, it certainly opened my eyes. They
weren't too happy when many of us incentive workers were
making more money than they were. You can readily see that
this "understanding" between engineering and the plant promotes "teamwork"! If anyone of us made a mistake in our work
and called engineering concerning this mistake, we were very
likely to get the answer back: "Follow the print." And when you
would plead with them—"Well, it is too late to follow the print,
I've already made a mistake!" it was still "Follow the print." In
some instances it would take nearly a day or two to get some
flexibility of agreement as to how you should proceed from
there. That's "teamwork" again!

Now let's take the next group, the office people. Many factory workers feel that most of the women in the office knit and
the fellows there just smoke cigars. From the factory worker's
point of view, office workers make very little contribution to
production. Again, I feel this is brought about by the very fact

that everybody is confined to the narrow limits of "my job"—
what "I," the individual, rather than what "we" in the enterprise, do. There isn't any consideration given to the fact that,
as Joe Scanlon always put it, there was never any such thing
as an "indirect" or "nonproductive" worker—that everybody
working in an enterprise had a contribution to make, whether
making the product or servicing it. And if they didn't have a job
to do, they ought not to be around. It wasn't until we got under
the Scanlon Plan that we recognized the contribution that the
engineering, office, and service people could make to whatever we were building.

Another group that has been weakened over the years is the
foremen. In many plants, if you go up to a foreman in a particular department and say, "How is this particular worker
doing?" he can't give you a quick answer. He has to look up
some record to see if that worker is doing so many hours or
whatever it might be, and then he says that the worker is doing
a good job. Yet the irony of it is, you may have just left that particular worker, and he has told you that he was spending his
time wandering around the plant! In many cases, industry has
done more to take away the foreman's job in the last twenty-
five years than to aid him to do his job. The fashionable thing
to do today seems to be to train him. Now I'm not saying that
some training isn't necessary or can't be of benefit, but I think
that you ought to concentrate on training him to do his job, not
to be a public speaker or a psychiatrist.

But I don't know how you train him to cope with the incentive worker. Looking back to my days in the shop, I can recall
that after a very important baseball or football game, we would
spend part of the next morning in the plant talking to some fellow workers about what happened at the game. My foreman
would walk past me two or three times and then get up enough
nerve to come over and say: "Fred, will you please go to work?"
And my usual reply was: "What do you mean, go to work? I'm
beating the day's work you set up; I'm beating the standard. It's
my money that I'm fooling with. If I want to spend a half an
hour talking here, it's my business, not yours. If I wasn't beating the standard, well, then you would have a right to talk to

me in such a fashion, but seeing that I am beating what you say is a day's work, then it's my time that I am spending here, whatever I might be discussing." Again, what "teamwork"!

Or, just picture the inspector, who probably is on day-work, being hounded on a particular day by the incentive worker to come over and check his work. The more work the incentive worker does, the more pay he gets; but the more work the inspector does, the same pay he receives—again "teamwork"! Even though they might be "brothers" in the same union, it doesn't seem to make much difference. On many occasions if a machinist on a particular job had spent an hour or more on a job than he actually did, three men might have been able to assemble it in three days rather than spending three weeks because shifts didn't line up, etc. "Teamwork" again, you see! Why, even in many situations the first thing an incentive worker does when he reports to work, on his or her shift, is to find out who the inspector is for that shift. This is because workers generally discover that all human beings are not the same and some inspect differently, so there is no need of doing more work on a part if the inspector will pass the part otherwise. I've actually seen instances where the foreman of one department will mess up the foreman in another department just to make himself look good. "Teamwork" again, you see. It's the old story—"I" seems to be the only important thing; the "we" attitude just doesn't prevail.

Now, I could go on and enumerate literally hundreds of other such problems that tend to make it impossible for people to work together. The industrial engineer, for instance, who comes out to the plant with his stopwatch certainly can often do more to control production than to increase it. You may think of this fellow as the expert, but actually the expert is the fellow who is doing the job day-in and day-out. He knows best how it ought to be done. The enemy, to this fellow on incentive, is this industrial engineer with the stopwatch; yet they're both working for the same company. "Teamwork" again, you know.

In talking about what the Scanlon Plan is, we need to get away from this "I" concept, and instead, go to "we." If there is to be an incentive in any organization then it ought to be on that product going out the door—more of a better product going out at a lower cost. Certainly, management has its job to do. The union and employees have their jobs to do, and it's how well all of them can do it together which spells the difference between success and failure in the enterprise.

What "I" do means very little, but "we" do is very important. How can you get this "we" environment? Frankly, I think you have to throw out everything that you presently have, whatever it might be in your individual companies, that makes it impossible for people to work together. You have to believe firmly that there is a contribution that people can make who are doing jobs day-in and day-out, that they do have ideas of how the job might be best done. Take the union, for instance. In many firms the only time the union and company get together is when there is trouble. This can be in negotiations; it also can be in the processing of a grievance. These are generally not pleasant associations. However, there is a third area that is left untapped, and that is the area of how to do your job.

You have to use your imagination a bit and realize that there is an area in which a union and a company can get together not as enemies, but as a team, and that is the area of how the product, whatever it might be, is made. We have discovered that we don't know what efficiency is. If a worker knows and understands why he or she is doing something, this can be very important to the outcome of that particular job. Joe Scanlon used to call it "giving people the tools they need to work with."

I would like to emphasize that the Scanlon Plan is not a substitute for leadership; it is something that will thrive on good leadership. The better leadership on the part of management, the better it can work. It means the foreman doing his job, not that of a clerk, but his job as foreman—working with people, planning the work, seeing that the schedules are met, having jobs ready so that when workers complete their job there is another waiting. The foreman under the Scanlon Plan is not a traffic cop trying to chase people out of the rest rooms and walking up and down the floor to make sure they are at their machines. This relationship calls for an entirely new approach—it calls for the foreman to sit down with his people and give them the help that he can by leading them. Under a plan such as this, you cannot have success if the union and the employees want it and the management doesn't want it. And you can't have success if the management wants it and the union and employees don't want it. It takes the combined efforts of both.

This plan doesn't mean turning the plant over to the union. This statement may sound strange, but I don't know any union that wants the responsibilities of running a plant. Under the Scanlon Plan, all we are talking about is providing the opportunity for people to say in an adult society how they think the job might be best done. It's up to management to take it from there. It means workers thinking a little bit more about who gets the job after them and how they might make it easier for them. The Plan means that the older, more experienced worker gives his ideas on how the job ought to be done to the newer worker. It means that the younger worker may be more physically able to help or make his contribution to the older worker. It means management makes decisions on what is good for the company and not on what's good for some personality down in the plant.

This plan doesn't mean giving people a "sense of participation"; workers don't want that. This plan means giving them real participation. You will discover that we have no set formula, that the Plan has worked in these situations because of the desire of both management and labor to get together and mutually solve problems that will help them be more competitive in this industrial society of ours. It means working with your brain instead of your back.

Before getting into a detailed description of what the Scanlon Plan is, however, there is an important group of people in a company that I would like to discuss briefly. This is the accounting department. In my work, I've been amazed to find how many accounting groups in companies have become so inflexible that they make very little constructive contribution. Rather than accounting servicing the company, it is often true that the company is servicing the accounting group. Why, even in some of these situations it seems to make little difference to the accounting people whether the company was losing or making money. This may seem a little harsh, but what I am driving at is that sometimes when suggestions are made to the accounting people that a change in their system or procedure might help the company, you run into a great deal of resistance. The accountant's answer: "We've got a perfect accounting system here, and under no conditions do we want to alter it." The fact that making even minor changes in procedures might help the plant was not important. The thing that seemed most important to these accounting people was "don't disturb our setup."

I share Joe Scanlon's conviction that this particular group can make a contribution that is probably unparalleled in the firm. This is the group that has the records of what is taking place in the firm. But, too often, trying to translate that record into something meaningful, which can be understood by the men and women in the plant, seems to be considered almost impossible. Certainly the jargon used by the accounting people has become quite confusing to the poor foreman out in the plant. I've even heard some foremen jokingly say that they thought a "labor variance" was a new tool to work with, rather than what it really is—excessive costs on a particular product.

Accounting is a very mysterious thing to most union people. Workers just don't understand a "profit." They feel that it can come about or be reduced or eliminated by the manipulations of some accountant. In fact, union people feel in many instances that the company has two sets of books, one for the union and one for the company. If you look at some cases, this is easy to understand. In some of the companies and unions that I have talked with the company began negotiations with the union by discussing how difficult things were and how they were losing money. Workers often feel that the company must have had a huge sum of money to begin with because the company loses money each year they negotiate. Then in these same situations, when the company faces some severe problems and is finally willing to discuss the real facts with its people, company officials are sometimes hurt to find that the people in the shop simply don't believe the accounting figures.

I believe that this is one area where the Scanlon Plan can bring about a significant change of great value to the company, by making it possible for the accounting people to become a real service group to the whole company. On many occasions I can recall Joe Scanlon saying: "If you want people to do something about a problem, give these people the tools to work with." Just saying to a working group, "We are losing money," is not enough. In a sense it is like going to a doctor and saying, "I'm sick, guess what I've got," or going to a lawyer and saying, "I've got a case, guess what it is." The important thing is "Where are we losing money?" Or for that matter, in a particular department, "What cost allowance do we have for this job?" In many cases, the standards set up are meaningless, because in order to get the job the company may have had to cut its price by 10, 20, or 30 percent. Under conditions such as this you could meet the standard and go broke, so what we are looking for is the best contribution that everybody can make in doing his job. That means accounting people working with these departments to give them the facts and figures, so that the production people might be able to tackle the problem and do something about it.

Just imagine if you can, the tremendous gain from getting all of these different functions in any one company to realize their importance to each other and to develop a willingness to work together. This is real teamwork, as I know it.

We are now ready to get into the two facets of the Scanlon Plan: (1) the measurement or norm, and (2) the actual participation process.

It was Joe Scanlon's premise that if something is to be effective with work groups, it should be simple and easy to understand. I would venture to say the work we have done in the area of measurements has been quite sloppy. In fact, during the course of a year under the Plan we have depended a great deal on the law of averages to see that the equity of both parties was served under the Plan. If at all possible, we have shied away from profit sharing as such. Our experiences have shown us that profit sharing can be very dangerous. In many situations this comes about because you are tying people down with responsibilities where they have no control. It was always Joe Scanlon's feeling that you can only relate people to problems which they can do something about.

To illustrate this point, several companies have come here to M.I.T. to talk to us about their problems under profit sharing. They all state that when profits were good things went along fine; however, when profits were no longer present, they ran into very serious difficulties with their employees. I think it's quite simple to see why. Under profit sharing a bonus can come about when the company makes a good purchase on materials, or gets a lucky break in some other area that has no real relationship with the operation in the plant. Consequently, in many instances, workers don't know why they got a bonus, so it is reasonable to understand they also don't know why they aren't getting one. The irony of the situation is that some companies have told us, despite the fact that there were no profits for the past few years, they were still paying the "profit-sharing bonus." They indicated that the people felt that it was only deferred wages anyway.

Another difficulty with profit sharing is that payments are too few and far between. A worker has a difficult enough time remembering what happened last week, never mind three or six or twelve months ago. Joe Scanlon always felt that the measurement should be simple and easy to understand, so that when workers received a bonus they knew why they got it, and when they didn't receive a bonus they knew why they didn't get one.

In all of the situations that we have worked with under the Scanlon Plan, the bonus payment has been on a monthly basis. We have generally developed a measurement to fit each individual situation. This meant taking into consideration the peculiarities of the specific plant or company, so that I venture to say that there aren't any two Scanlon measurements exactly alike. Each situation has had to have its own workable measurement. Most of these have involved comparing sales value of production to payroll costs. Now, when I say payroll costs,

I'm not just talking about the bargaining unit, I'm talking about the whole plant. Our feeling has been that if you are going to have a plan that's good for the company, everybody ought to be in it, and I mean from the top of the company on down. We have always recommended that you make the team as broad as possible. In fact we like to see everybody from the president of the company to the floor sweeper all in the same plan. I feel that's one of the strengths of the Scanlon Plan.

There is a great deal of mistrust and worry in most situations where you find several plans of remuneration present. Now I'm not just talking about how they might conflict with each other, but about the jealousy that you have when one person is on a more lucrative plan than the other fellow. And if we are talking about real joint participation, then there should only be one plan. I think you can adequately take care of the different skills and wage or salary levels by paying the monthly bonus on a percentage basis. A worker doesn't mind his boss getting a bonus when he is also getting one, but as it so often happens when there is more than one plan in the situation, he gets terribly disturbed when he hears through the grapevine that the boss is getting a bonus and he isn't getting one.

Furthermore, if you are going to have an incentive plan, the incentive ought to be based on more of a better product going out of the shipping room at a lower cost. In your respective companies, you all live or die by that product. We have leaned very strongly towards the dollar measurement, because we have felt that this is the one the worker best understands. The dollar is what he has to support his family on, and it certainly is much more meaningful to him than some far-removed and maybe technically correct standard. We have found that in developing measurements, the more you refine them, the more complicated they get and the more useless they are. The measurements that we have developed have had to be real and live with the times.

We have heard people say, "Take all the variables out of the measurement and once it is set you can live with it without change." I think that is the worst approach you can take. How can you teach people about our free-enterprise system unless they really live under it? Measurements that we have developed have had to change with conditions. Generally we have selected a year's performance as a basis to develop our ratios. The most recent year is always the best, despite the fact that some companies I know of would like to use the depression as a basis. I think you've got to be realistic. Certainly the most recent year is where you are and is probably the one base period that can work best. Now, it might have to have some adjustments to fit new developments or changes, but nevertheless it is the most realistic base that can be used.

At this point, I am reminded of a Canadian firm which, after reading the *Fortune* article on the Lapointe experience, proceeded on their own to install the Scanlon Plan. About eight months later, Joe Scanlon got a call from the president of the company, who introduced himself and told him that they had applied the Scanlon Plan. Joe's remarks were as follows: "That's fine. How's it working?" The president of the company indicated that it was working fine; the people had really increased productivity and were doing a good job. Scanlon countered this answer by saying: "Well, that's good, what are you calling me for?" "Well," the president of the company said, "we've got a serious problem." Joe asked, "What is it?" "Well," he replied, "we're getting an increase in productivity, our relationships with our people were never better, but the company's going broke." After some further discussion on the phone, arrangements were made for a team from the company, composed of both management and its people to come down to M.I.T. to meet with Scanlon to discuss their problems. We discovered that after they had read the *Fortune* article, they had developed their measurement just as the article indicated Lapointe did. The only fact that they didn't take into consideration was that the base year they were using for the development of their measurement was one in which the company had incurred severe losses. I merely bring this out to try to get across the point that what works at Lapointe will not necessarily work someplace else. So again I repeat, measurements must be tailored to the individual situation. Certainly in this Canadian company, consideration should have been given to the company's profitability or loss during the base year used. I am sure that if this had been done and discussed with all of the people under the Plan, it would not have been difficult to set a proper ratio or norm.

It is most important, whatever measurement is used, to put all of the cards on the table and hide nothing. You have to stay away from the mumbo-jumbo type of incentive measurements that are now plaguing many plants today. I don't care at what efficiency you think a worker has been performing, if you have accepted it from him day in and day out, that has become a "day's work" to him. To get him to do something different requires a sincere and honest understanding of your joint problem. Whenever we have had to make adjustments in a norm, in the application of the Scanlon Plan, the parties involved have understood why. It was then up to them to decide whether they felt they could do something about it or not.

The development of these measurements reminds me of the first time I was time-studied as a worker. I was new at the job when a young fellow with a board having a stopwatch attached to it, came down to my machine one day and indicated to me that he was going to make it possible for me to make more money. He was going to engineer my job for me. Well, since I was a fellow who could never make enough money, this sounded quite appealing. The engineer worked with me for some time and indicated to me that we had a lot in common. He knew I was a union member and said that his dad had belonged to the Sewer Cleaner's Union (or some such union), so after all we were brothers under the skin. Well, after he got through methodizing or engineering my job, he said: "Here's the pitch, because of the laborious type of job that you have, one-tenth out of every hour you can loaf." Well, that sounded pretty good to me, because in those days I was usually quite happy when I was loafing. And he followed it up by saying he knew I had personal needs to take care of, a drink of water, etc., so one-tenth out of every hour I could do that. "Now," he said, "if you will work diligently the other eight-tenths of the hour you can make yourself a 20 percent bonus." So help me, when he left my machine, I think I was already spending the money! However, the next day when I came to put his theory into practice, I discovered that what I had been doing day in and day out wasn't a day's work according to his computations. Before I could get into this 20 per cent area that he had discussed with me, I had to work about 40 percent harder!

Well, it's easy to understand that you only get fooled like that once, when you learn to play the game. The time-study engineer then becomes your enemy, and when you start playing the game with him, generally the company comes up on the short end. Because after all, this engineer is dealing with the real expert, the man who is doing the job day in and day out and knows its peculiarities and possibilities. Lo and behold, in many instances, he may come back five or six months later and instead of making 20 percent bonus, I am making 70 percent. Then he becomes quite disturbed because I have bastardized his engineering job. I am making too much money. So now an attempt will be made, of course, to re-engineer my job and change the rate. I believe this is quite similar to the Government imposing an excess-profit tax on the company. Let me tell you, workers don't like it any more than do companies.

I bring this point out because we are in the area of measurements. The consultants who come into a firm and say, "Look, there's 20 or 30 per cent cream that you ought to be getting that belongs to the company," is just so much hogwash. If there is that much cream in any of the plants that I'm talking about, then they ought to go out and get it from the workers, if they can. I think you have to be very realistic in applying a measurement. Certainly we have recognized the needs of a company in our work. We have found that a plan is only as good as the ability of both the company and the union to go down the same road together. The Plan just can't work if there are big bonuses to the employees and losses to the company. Conversely, it can't survive if there are huge profits to the company and no bonus to the people for their efforts. So that's why I've said that these measurements have to be realistic. They should be changed when conditions indicate that they should change. In fact, in the Memorandum of Understanding, used in the Scanlon Plan, we say anything that disturbs the equity of either side in the benefits of the plan requires a review of the presently applied ratio to ascertain if any change is necessary.

However, to avoid frequent minor changes, we have strongly recommended in all our work during the last six years, that the union and the company split the benefits of the Plan. Some of the earlier installations, such as Lapointe, were on full participation, in which a 1 per cent increase in productivity meant that a 1 per cent bonus was paid. But now we strongly recommend a split in the benefits, and the one most often used is 75-25, 75 percent going to the participants under the Plan and 25 per cent going to the company. This means that as the people increase productivity by 4 per cent the company retrieves 1 per cent. Therefore, it is attaining its objective of getting lower labor costs, along with the people getting a fair return for their efforts. By having a split in the benefits, the company does not have to adjust that ratio meticulously for every minor change that comes about.

Earlier I said that most of our measurements have involved the total payroll measured against the sales value of production. We also recommend the use of change in inventory, finished goods, and work in process if the cycle is a long one. I want to emphasize again that it is very important to have a simple, understandable measurement to apply to any given situation. Even though the measurement is important, it is not nearly so important as the participation part of the Scanlon Plan. If you don't get participation, I don't care what measurement you have or how good it is, it just won't move. One strongly needs the other.

This facet of the Scanlon Plan—participation—is to me the most important. Participation is implemented by setting up what we call production committees and a screening committee. Production committees are established throughout the company—including the office and engineering departments as well as the plant. Each major department has a production committee. Small departments may be grouped together in a single production committee. These committees have representation from both management and labor. Management usually appoints as its member the supervisor of the department or some management person in a decision-making capacity in the company. The union members (or employees where a union does not have bargaining rights) get together and elect someone to represent them on this production committee.

In most instances, we do not have balanced representation on these committees, for there are sometimes as many as six union or employee members meeting with one management member, and this comprises the committee. In other cases, the representation in a production committee may be as small as one management member and one labor member. The function of a production committee is to meet at least once a month (or more often if necessary) to discuss ways and means of eliminating waste, easier and better ways of doing the job, the departmental schedules for that month, and anything else that might pertain to the work going through the department in that month. The committee also processes the suggestions brought in by the union or employee side of the committee. These are often given to them by their fellow employees. It is also the duty of one of the committeemen to record the minutes of their meeting.

The job of the union or employee side of the committee is to convince the management member that the suggestions brought in should be tried or adopted. In many cases, a production committeeman will bring in a person who has given him a suggestion for the meeting, so that the individual can more clearly present his idea to the committee. When the production committee is composed of one union and one management member, it is a very good idea for the union member to bring someone into the meeting with him.

An accurate record is kept of the disposition of each suggestion. Some are accepted and put into effect; others are rejected by the committee because both sides agree that this suggestion is not feasible; and in some cases there is a difference of opinion because the union or employee side of the committee feels the suggestion has merit and the management member of the committee feels the opposite. None of these suggestions can be thrown out at this level. There is no voting at these production committees on the acceptance or rejection of a suggestion.

Management reserves the right to accept or reject any suggestions that may come in. In fact, in most cases during the early months of the Plan this is the area where we have the most trouble. It has been very difficult for foremen to adjust themselves to receiving ideas from their people on how the job ought to be done. And I want to point out that the foremen are not reluctant about accepting ideas, but they are quite concerned about what their boss might think of them if too many ideas should come from their department. The feeling seems to be that maybe management might think the foreman is not doing his job. Consequently there is a tendency to reject many of the ideas that come in at this level during the early stages of the Plan. It isn't until the company, and that is top management, convinces the foremen or the supervisors that they are being measured differently than in the past. If the Plan is to work, the company will evaluate its lower management group on the basis that the best foreman or supervisor is the one whose department has the most suggestions. This means that this is a department where the people are not afraid to speak up. They are not afraid to participate and to say just how their job might be done easier and better. The old idea that the boss does all the thinking and the employees just do the work is dead.

It is also the responsibility of the management member of the committee to give the other members in advance of the meeting information about any problems that he might have concerning the operation of his department. For example, he might provide information about the production schedule for the month, about the order in which jobs have to go through, or about special bottlenecks, for example. But a production committee should not get involved in grievances, or in anything that might infringe upon the provisions of the collective bargaining agreement. In many cases the union shop steward may sit in the production-committee meeting held in his area in order to make sure that the functions of the committee are adhered to.

All ideas or suggestions that are accepted and put into effect are contributions to the whole group. No individual award is made for any idea. Also, suggestions are not submitted through a suggestion box but rather are dealt with in an adult fashion by joint-committee discussion of each individual idea. I also want to point out that at the production-committee level we take more pains with a rejected suggestion than one that has been accepted. The reason is that the suggestor whose ideas are accepted and put into effect sees his contribution to the group, but the one whose suggestion has been rejected doesn't know the reason unless he is personally contacted and told why his suggestion was not adopted. You find in most cases that if a person is given the courtesy of a decent answer, he will submit his next good idea to the committee, rather than feeling that proper consideration was not given to his suggestion.

The minutes of the production committee are forwarded as quickly as possible to the screening committee. The composition of the screening committee is generally made up of an equal number of management and union representatives or employees, and its size generally runs between eight and twelve people. On the management side, the representatives should be the top people, and someone like a president or executive vice president of the company chairs the meeting. Other management members are the controller or treasurer, the chief engineer, and the plant manager or plant superintendent. On the union and employee side, the committee is made up of representatives from the areas covered by the production committees. In many situations one, two, or three production committees are included in a group to elect a screening committeeman to represent them from their areas. Also, the president of the local union is a member of the screening committee.

Screening-committee meetings are held at least once a month and their functions are the following: (1) The first order of business is to screen the figures for the previous month and announce the bonus or deficit incurred during that month. (2) The second function of the committee is a discussion by the officials of the company concerning anything that might affect the Plan. Again, I don't mean anything that might conflict with the collective-bargaining agreement but rather the success we are having out in the field with our product, the problems that our sales people are running into in getting new orders, etc. In many instances, the management will bring someone into the meeting who can discuss the serious problems with the committee. (3) The third function of the committee is to screen, through joint discussion, all of the suggestions that have come in from the various production committees. Those which have been accepted and placed into effect at the production-committee level are put into the record; those which have been rejected jointly by the production committee are reviewed; and, finally, decisions are made concerning suggestions on which there occurred a difference of opinion at the production-committee level. All suggestions are judged on their merit and their contribution to all involved, rather than on their effect on some personality down in the plant.

Again, on this committee there isn't any voting on adopting or rejecting a suggestion. Management reserves the right to accept or reject any idea that has been presented. Yet I would venture to say that acceptances of suggestions under the Scanlon Plan has been greater than under any other method. In fact, it is safe to say that most Scanlon Plans that we have installed have a record of better than 90 percent acceptance on suggestions.

In concluding this discussion on the Scanlon Plan, I repeat that you can see that we have no gimmick. And if management people or union representatives feel that there is a formula or some sort of gimmick that you can just drop into a situation and "presto-chango," things are different, then the Scanlon Plan is not for you. This approach involves a mature relationship. It means treating people like adults and not like children. However, if management and labor can agree jointly on the application of these ideals and principles that I have outlined, I can assure you that they will be entering a new kind of relationship and understanding of each other's problems. And the satisfactions gained from a job well done will exceed the value of whatever employee bonuses and company profits the Plan might generate.

CHAPTER 5

THE SCANLON PLAN: ANYONE FOR FREE ENTERPRISE?

Dr. Carl Frost

The Scanlon Plan had its origin in the 1930s. It concentrated on the survival needs of the economic depression and the productivity needs of the war and postwar eras. Kiplinger suggested the Scanlon Plan as the program to "Divvy Your Gross and Double Your Profits."[1] It was hailed by the editor of *Fortune* as "Enterprise for Everyman."[2]

Joe Scanlon, the author of the concept of management and labor cooperation to assure productivity and profitability, had little anticipation or ambition of the Scanlon Plan enduring or being widely implemented. The Massachusetts Institute of Technology, through the keen foresight of Douglas McGregor, invited Scanlon to join its faculty in 1946. (The participative concept exemplified McGregor's assumptions of Theory Y as contrasted to the widely exercised management assumptions of Theory X.) At the same time, McGregor invited six young instructors to introduce social science into the engineering curriculum. I was one of the instructors, and with Joe Scanlon I developed a personal and professional commitment to the Scanlon Plan as it was introduced into several New England organizations. Joe Scanlon died in 1956. Since that time M.I.T.

---

[1] "Divvy Your Gross and Double Your Profits," *Kiplinger Magazine* 2 (December 1948): 31–3.

[2] Russell W. Davenport, "Enterprise for Everyman," *Fortune* 41 (January 1950): 55–9, 152, 157–59.

has limited its interest in the plan to an annual conference conducted by Fred Lesieur.[3]

In 1949, as a part of Michigan State University's aggressive postwar effort to meet the needs of the ambitious returning veterans and to recognize Michigan's rapid change from an agricultural to an industrial economy, I was invited to become a member of the Department of Psychology. MSU President John A. Hannah accepted experimentally the idea of a new faculty member serving the vocationally oriented students and the changing peacetime needs for industrial productivity. President Hannah questioned whether an industrially oriented and involved faculty member could serve organizations in the state of Michigan as successfully as had the prestigious Extension Service of the College of Agriculture over many decades. I agreed to try the experiment for a year.

There were misgivings on and off the campus regarding this commitment to industrial fieldwork and consultation on the Scanlon Plan. The unions were particularly suspicious of a cooperative relationship with management in contrast to their historic adversary role. I suggested in May 1950, after a year's experience, that President Hannah have Michigan State University alumni confidentially investigate and evaluate this fieldwork. The alumni completed the assignment, at which time President Hannah endorsed the program and its continuance.

Since 1950, with the stimulation and demands of both the academic programs Psychology courses and the industrial organizations, the Scanlon Plan has been tested, revised, and restructured into a program for organizational development that has received increasing national and international attention.

In reviewing this twenty-five-year history of Scanlon Plan experience and the research findings on organizational development, we speak with increasing confidence of what the Scanlon Plan is and is not, and for whom the Scanlon Plan process is appropriate and for whom it is not. The principles have become well documented and the process increasingly reliable.

[3]Fred Lesieur, ed., *The Scanlon Plan: A Frontier in Labor Management Cooperation* (Cambridge, Mass.: M.I.T. Press, 1958).

The Scanlon Plan

The Scanlon Plan is an innovative management process for total organization development. It consists of a set of assumptions about human motivation and behavior, general principles for the management of organizations based on these assumptions, and specific procedures for implementing these principles.

Today, many organizations place primary emphasis on such structural issues as who reports to whom, how best to assign people to jobs, and how to maximize efficiency through job design. Only secondary concern is given to people problems. This emphasis has created an implicitly dualistic theory in which one group—management—is the creative, directive force, totally responsible for organizational performance, and a second group workers—exists to carry out the directives of management.

In contrast, the Scanlon Plan puts it all together. It combines the leverage of capital, the skills of managers, the creativity and competence of all employees, and the opportunities of new technology into a system supported by competent participation and equitable sharing of productivity to meet the needs of customers, capital investors, and employees. In the process, an organization fulfills its proper role in the larger economic system: worthwhile employment, worthwhile goods and services, and worthwhile investments.

Experience over these years with many Scanlon Plan operations has demonstrated that an organization must focus on four critical principles:

(1) *Identity:* The extent to which employees are meaningfully informed of the organization's history, competition, customers, objectives, and so forth; identification and ownership of the current compelling need for change; and organizational development of all the employees as resources.

(2) *Participation:* The structured and guaranteed opportunity and responsibility provided all employees to influence the decision process within the company, and to become accu-

rately informed and responsible in their respective areas and roles of competence.

(3) *Equity*: The opportunity for all employees to realize an equitable return by increasing the investment of their resources of ideas, energy, competence, and commitment.

(4) *Managerial Competence*: The inescapable necessity for management itself to establish, grow, and develop increasing professional competence and systems with assured participation from all elements of the organization's human resources. *[Editor's note: The fourth Principle eventually became "Competency" dropping managerial to include all employees.]*

The Scanlon Plan is not a panacea. It is not an incentive system. It is not a substitute for runaway piece-rate systems, for bitter and antagonistic industrial relations, or for incompetent executives or inadequate management systems. It is not for every organization. The Scanlon Plan is not a pat formula or set of procedures which can be mechanistically implemented with the expectation of automatically achieving a totally cooperative and productive system.

Organizational Development Prerequisites to the Scanlon Plan

The Scanlon Plan is a *process* for organizational development. The decision of whether or not to implement a Scanlon Plan requires three steps: (1) a rigorous and honest diagnosis of the organization's current level of functioning, (2) an assessment of the convincing need to change, and (3) an evaluation of the capacity to change. These discussions present the focus of our findings in recent years.

In our work with small companies and large corporations in the United States and with eight small and giant organizations in Europe, I have found the quality of leadership glaringly absent. Management is there, but not leadership! An article by Abraham Zaleznik states the case convincingly.[4] This lack of leadership is conspicuous in the corporation and in union organizations. If we accept the definition of *leader* as that person who is perceived by followers as the best means available for getting them where they want to go at that particular time, then the dynamics of the process of exercising leadership separate the leader from the manager. Many organizations are being well managed by the accepted fiscal criteria in the short term, but they are not being led by long-term criteria, which genuinely act to the advantage of the consumer-public, capital investors, or the total organization of employees.

Mandate

Your Organization As Your Investment. In the exercise of leadership, there is an initial and a singular responsibility of the leader, *vis-à-vis* the chief executive officer, to identify and define the mandate of the organization. The word *mandate* is used advisedly to state the imperatives required of the organization. These are not placed upon the company as the personal desire or prerogative of the chief executive officer, even though it is the CEO's responsibility to articulate them.

The mandate can be divided into only four or at the most five components. First is the mandate to manage the marketplace. From valid and reliable data, the chief executive officer must identify who is the customer and, just as clearly, who is not the customer. The counterpart analysis is obvious: Who is the competitor, and why does that company compete successfully? The imperative quality of that mandate comes from the customers—not the chief executive officer—who insist that they receive the best return on their investment by purchasing that organization's product and/or service. There is no long-lived brand loyalty to a product/service that does not perform, produce superior results, or payoff better than any other prod-

[4]Abraham Zaleznik, "Managers and Leaders: Are They Different?" *Harvard Business Review* 55 (May–June 1977): 67–78.

uct. Moreover, the corollary is obvious: Without customers and more customers, there is no security or tomorrow.

Second is the mandate required to manage the physical resources of facilities, equipment, supplies, utilities, and so forth, for an imperative return on the investment. The capital expenditure has been made and will continue to be made only if the return on the investment is greater than on any alternative investment. The American public and the corporate office—not the chief executive officer—wisely and shrewdly determine their best investments. There are no real subsidies in the private, public, or government sectors for facilities that lack reliable and high levels of return.

Third is the mandate to manage with assured profitability. Profits are a cost of doing business—not a luxury or reward for a few. Both internal and external investors insist upon this level of performance and return on their committed efforts. The organization must generate capital as well as use it. This level of performance and return is demanded by the capitalist economy—not by the chief executive officer.

Fourth is the mandate to manage human resources. Again, it is not the humanity of the chief executive officer that determines this mandate. It is the action of employees who do and will insist that their employment in this organization is the best opportunity for them; otherwise, they will terminate at the earliest opportunity. It is true that some employees, including executives, paint themselves into corporate corners and haven't the courage or ability to leave. Effective management recognizes, discloses, and declares the mandate of the employees at all levels that this company affords them the best employment opportunity and responsibility. In the economic vernacular, employment here offers them the best personal and professional returns on their investments of energy, education, training, expertise, and life.

Fifth is the mandate, not present in every organization, to develop and manage the unique technology required to survive and succeed. The technology is not the fancy of the owner or chief executive officer, but is required to meet the special needs of the customers, investors, and employees if they are going to consider this organization first. The mandate might be expressed by an organization as the imperative to be number one in electronic technology or the best in short-term intensive health care, and so forth.

The clear compelling identification of the mandate in these five areas, documented by the valid and reliable data showing that their fulfillment is imperative, is the initial responsibility of the chief executive officer. To date I have not encountered one organization that has fulfilled this need and expectancy of the organization for its own mandate. We have been shown mission statements, goals, objectives, annual and long-term plans—but not the mandate. We have been shown lengthy platitudinous rhetoric—but no simple and succinct (one page) statement of the convincing imperatives of the marketplace, the capital investors, and the employees.

A particular feature of the mandate is that the chief executive officer does not get involved or include the means of achieving the mandate. This is the responsibility of the immediate staff and succeeding levels of management, in increasing detail and specificity. If chief executive officers are meeting their appropriate responsibilities, they are less competent in the technical implementation and professional expertise of each mandated area. They must be confident and prove to their organizations that there is the competence in their organizations to achieve the mandate as required in each area.

Finding Out about Your Company as Your Investment. Once the mandate is identified, then executive staff members, as a group, are informed and requested to challenge, clarify, and vouch for the validity and reliability of the data supporting the respective mandates of marketing, physical resources, profit, human resources, and technology. If chief executive officers present mandates as their personal edicts rather than as working papers, they will serve neither themselves nor their organizations. In a large corporation, the mandate for any division or operation is completely consistent with the corporate expectancies of the management of these areas. Often, the full disclosure of the corporate expectancies or the chief executive officer's statement with supporting data is surprising to many members of the staff. There is generally wide variability of the awareness and acceptance of the mandate. To *understand* the mandate—not merely to know it—may require several hours and occasions of intensive discussion to avoid polite or traditional acceptance and conformance. To process the mandate appropriately is a supreme test of leadership.

When the executive staff group appears ready, the chief executive officer requests a secret vote on the question: "Do you understand the mandate?" Almost all staff members demur and claim their staffs do not need to vote secretly. "We are frank, open, and ready to declare our position." That is a cop-out. After such an intensive and frank discussion and challenge of the mandate, the integrity of the chief executive officer and of each staff member deserves and demands a secret vote. If there are abstentions or negative votes, it means more data and study are required to support the questioned areas. It remains the responsibility of the chief executive officer to rework and resubmit the data and revised mandate. When the staff members *understand* the mandate and its implications, and a positive vote is secretly and responsibly made, the staff proceeds to the second question.

The second question is a personal confrontation: "Are you able and willing to accept the ownership of the problem?" If the staff members understand the mandate and its implications for them, this is a new question. For example, when a particular corporation set a mandate that doubled the gross profit required with no new product introductions for five years, the controller resigned, or rather took early retirement. In another situation, when a hospital board of directors froze the operating costs for two years, the administrator resigned. There should be genuine soul searching and review of other personal alternatives before the secret vote is taken. The chief executive officer and staff members need to know the result of this vote, too. If it is satisfactory, then the third question is appropriate.

This question concerns the ability and willingness to make a commitment to achieving the mandate. It has three parts.

The first is a challenge to each individual: "Are you personally competent to fulfill your assignment under the mandate?" The inquiry obviously challenges all staff members to decide if this is their best job opportunity. The second part is a challenge to the members of the executive group: "Is there the required competence represented in each other executive member to accomplish the mandate?" Staff members would be foolhardy to join a team which was not competently and completely staffed to achieve the mandate. The third part requires all staff members to declare specifically what they will do differently to assure the fulfillment of the mandate. This declaration is not more of the same but the recognition of a needed change in quality and quantity of personal and professional investment in their assignments. This third part takes place at a specifically set meeting with adequate time for preparation. During discussion of the third part, it becomes obvious to the chief executive officer and all staff members whether each one understands the mandate, is able and willing to accept the ownership of the problem, and has the competence and commitment to fulfill this responsibility. Only after this rigorous confrontation, a third secret vote is appropriately requested by the chief executive officer: "Are you able and willing to make a commitment to the achievement of the mandate?"

Each vote must be prefaced by the admonition that all members now have all the data and therefore should vote responsibly for themselves, their colleagues, and the organization. On several occasions the chief executive officer and/or staff have decided that they were not ready to proceed. Those decisions have proved to be wise. Obviously, under these conditions the preparatory steps toward the formal Scanlon Plan consideration are held in abeyance. In the meantime the organization usually proceeds to develop itself toward readiness to make a commitment.

This mandate process is most challenging. It establishes the bases, principles and operating rules, and disciplined relationships at the top echelon. Unless and until the process is completed satisfactorily with the executive staff, the process is not pursued at lower echelons.

What to Do about Your Investment in the Company. I will describe the process of judging one's investment in the company by exploring the appropriateness of the Scanlon Plan for a particular organization.

The Customer Investor: The processing of the mandate was completed throughout this 1,600-person organization, beginning with the executive staff, then the operating staff, then the supervisors, and then the operating personnel. The mandate was specifically and operationally documented and illustrated for each department.

The product is a widely used consumer product, visible in the marketplace. Consequently, in discussing the market mandate the question was asked of all personnel: "How many of you use our own product?" The response was far less than 50 percent. They were challenged by the conclusion that personally they did not believe their product was their best investment. Why? Was the problem quality? Service? Price?

Obviously, competitors were enjoying their patronage and loyalty. The inroads of this conspicuous competition were documented and quickly recognized as a genuine threat to the employee's own job security.

The Capital Investor: The facts were revealed as to the conspicuous and substantial investment the corporation had made in this facility and equipment and, consequently, the imperative need to operate it continuously and far more profitably.

The economic data on the required return on investment were disclosed, as was the identity of the capital investors. The American public had had confidence in the corporation stock which had made this new facility and technology possible. Would the stock market investors continue to have this confidence?

The alternatives that capital investors can exercise were identified. The less-than-adequate profit position of the industry was discussed candidly and constructively. Applications were made to the corporation and to this specific operation.

The Employee Investor: The employees were asked about their satisfaction with their jobs. There was almost unanimous agreement that their jobs now were the most desirable, best paying, and most promising in the community.

When challenged about their need for more and additional benefits next year, there was complete agreement on expectations. When they were asked how to assure the continuing ability of the corporation to meet these needs, there was less agreement. It was objectively documented that unless significant improvements in efficiencies resulted in greater profitability, there would be insufficient funds in the bank upon which to draw increased checks for salaries and benefits.

In summary, the organization personnel were informed, educated, and then challenged with three primary responsibilities:

(1) All customers should be convinced that they receive the best return on their investment by purchasing this company's product and services;

(2) American citizens who invest in the stock market and corporate officers all should be convinced that they receive the highest return on their investments in the form of money and of production schedules for this division;

(3) All employees should be convinced that they receive the best return on their job; investment of time, energy, know-how, education, and suggestions by employment in this company.

Once this education process was completed in small groups, a secret vote was taken on four questions:

1. Are you convinced that there is a compelling need to change?
2. Is there a genuine potential for improvement?
3. What is in it for you?
4. Do you want to participate in developing a proposal (Scanlon Plan) through an elected Ad-Hoc Committee to achieve this change?

There were 35 negative votes among more than 1,600 employees in an organization that was already the best operation in the corporation. The employees understood the mandate. They were able and willing to accept the problem ownership. They were committed to achieving the mandate of the customers, investors, and employees.

The fulfillment of the fourth question was the election of the Ad Hoc Committee. Each department and shift had a representative. The 75 members were divided into three committees of 25. The Education Committee had the responsibility for documenting the need to change and the reasons the Scanlon Plan was appropriate. The Rules and Regulations Committee had the assignment of handling the elections, terms of office, functions of the Production and Screening Committee that would be formed, and procedures for handling suggestions. The Formula Committee had the assignment of developing the bases and formula for calculating a monthly bonus in such a way that all employees would recognize their accountability under the Scanlon Plan. *[Editor's note: Today most Ad Hoc committees are subdivided into Identity, Participation, Equity, and Competence committees.]*

This process assured the co-authorship of the Scanlon Plan. The Ad Hoc Committee's work was made final in notebook form. Every company should write its own book. An addendum was prepared from all the questions asked during the inquiries. It appeared in the form of "a quiz you cannot fail" with true and false answers and explanations. This quiz ensured that the majority of employees were confronted with the possible issues, concerns, and questions that might arise in their new experience under the Scanlon Plan. There would be few surprises. The final page of the book was a sample ballot for the secret vote. Of course, the preface included the signatures of all Ad Hoc Committee authors.

The Rules and Regulations Committee had established the majority vote required to introduce the plan. It is usual to require a 90 percent majority to document the level of commitment required to assure success.

As the reader can readily comprehend, this process is a demanding organizational education. It assures that the majority of the employees know the organizational realities of the marketplace, the required return on investment of physical resources, the cost of profits, and the appropriate use of human resources. It also declares (in actual percentages) that the employees are or are not able and willing to accept the ownership of the problem and become responsible. Every step is essential. One client decided it could not afford to educate all of its people—only 400 out of 900 employees. The vote failed to meet the required 90 percent majority. Another client did not work patiently and closely enough with the union local. The local union officers were not able and/or willing to accept the ownership of the problem. Consequently, when the vote was taken, the union members followed the entrenched leadership of their local president, as was predictable from a militant history, and an insufficient majority was returned. The process does require time, patience, and sequential steps to build confidence in one another and trust in the operational facts.

Scanlon Plan Principles throughout the Years

Doing the Right Job, and Doing the Job Right. The mandate and its process assure the chief executive officer and all of the employees of "doing the *right job*" (Peter Drucker's definition of effectiveness). The authorship through the Ad Hoc Committee and implementation of the Scanlon Plan through the Production and Screening committees assure the chief executive officer and the employees of "doing the *job right*" (Drucker's definition of efficiency).

The process of doing the right job and doing the job right continues during operations under the Scanlon Plan. The mandate, rules and regulations, and formula are continually reviewed for validity and reliability. Changes are infrequent, but life is change and consequently should be managed by everyone. The changing operational reality of the organization requires periodic review and revision of the Scanlon Plan to serve everyone's best interest and equity.

The leadership of an organization that has been implementing the Scanlon Plan for many years follows basic principles. In the first principle, *identity*, the chief executive officer and staff members recognize the organization's continual historical successes and failures. They must keep the entire organization alert to the need to change in order to manage the marketplace, physical resources, profitability, and human resources. In this process the customers, the investors, and employees have increasing confidence that they get the best return on their investments and that management is serving them well. The company must continually be alert and develop its unique reason for being or it will lose its identity and commitment. Under a Scanlon Plan, management has an additional demand— identification and development of all employees as important resources who are accountable from their first day of indoctrination to the end of their careers.

In the second principle, *participation*, the long term Scanlon Plan company must be sensitive to the increasing employee demand for more accurate and timely information as well as more prompt response to their questions and suggestions. Employees become more able and willing to participate and accept genuine responsibility when the rationality of management's decisions is obvious. When the rationality of the employees' questions, challenges, and suggestions is accepted and acted upon by management, the employees' trust and commitment increase. The process is never permissive. Management, whether it is the supervisor in the Production Committee or the executive in the Screening Committee, must exercise genuine leadership in decision making. When certain organizations experimented recently by delegating the work situation to the employees and reducing supervision, the employees found the situation confusing, unwanted, and unsatisfactory. There is a discipline which the reality of customers, capital investors, and employees demands. Employees expect and respect this discipline from rational management.

The third principle that is always worth guarding and assuring is *equity*. The quality of equity must be assured among all the parties—customers, investors, and employees. When quantitative records of production are made at the expense of safety, quality, or customer service, there is no reason to celebrate with a bonus. Equity is often in the eye of the beholder, so it is essential to assess continuously the perception of all the organization's members—customers, investors, and employees. Are they convinced of equitable return on their investment in the company?

When the Scanlon Plan really becomes established and the organization matures, there is an awesome demand for *competence*, the fourth Scanlon Plan principle. The epitome of this maturity occurs when all employees of staff and line come to their daily assignments with the assurance that every aspect of their jobs is rational. That quality demands the greatest ability up front to manage the marketplace, physical resources, profitability, and human resources. After years of experience, Scanlon Plan management is still striving to achieve this level of effectiveness and efficiency, so every employee considers every management decision rational.

Today, whether the Scanlon Plan is established in a hospital, school, industrial firm, or government agency, its success as an organizational development process must assure that the marketplace (the patient, student, consumer, or public), the capital investors, and the employees realize their best returns by investing in that product and/or service.

The process must identify among all employees the comprehension of the problem (mandate) and the overt (secretly voted—90 percent majority) ability and willingness to accept the ownership of the problem.

The process must identify the ruthless need for competence of all personnel who do make a commitment to achievement of the corporate mandate.

Socialistic Systems versus Capitalist Economies

The free enterprise or capitalist system uniquely affords management this opportunity and responsibility for organizational development. In work with organizations in the European system (Stremmen Steel, Volvo, British Steel, and others), I found that this opportunity is no longer available. Management and the unions, for example, turned over to the British government the responsibility for the steel industry years ago, abdicating their problem-ownership responsibility.

At Volvo, it seems that innovative programs directed toward the quality of working life fail to assure the competitive competence to survive in world markets.[5] The cost of labor in Sweden is the highest in the world, and the employees cannot tell whether Volvo or their government is the benefactor sustaining high employment in a diminishing marketplace. Is it rational to fail to disclose the facts of life? Is it humane not to give people the right and responsibility to earn their survival, security, and success? In the long run, the reality of the competitive marketplace—and not management—is going to decide.

In evaluating our two hundred years of free enterprise we might ask: Is there leadership—or just managership—in American industry and unions today? The criteria of growth and profitability of auto manufacturers suggest conspicuous managership. But escalating costs, sharply rising foreign car sales, and resistance to solving energy resource constraints question the quality of leadership. The reference could be made to many industries and agencies in the United States.

The Scanlon Plan process challenges both the leadership and managership of all industrial and service organizations. It is not the only system. It is not for every organization; in fact, relatively few are able or willing to accept its premises or meet its demands. It requires that every member of the organization, beginning with the chief executive officer, serve the committed investors: the customers, the investors, and the employees. Otherwise, our egos, blind us to our own constituents' needs, and consequently we fail to release that infinite potential of heterogeneity, genius, effort, and commitment for the good of all.

How long will our free enterprise system support our "life, liberty, and pursuit of happiness" in a realistic caring and sharing world that is honest enough, proud enough, creative enough to accept opportunity and responsibility, and not subsidy?

---

[5] Stefan Aguren, Reine Hansson, and K. G. Karlsson, "The Volvo Kalmar Plant: The Impact of New Design on Work Organization," September 1976, The Rationalization Council, SAF LO.

Part II

Equity
Participation

The Plan doesn't mean giving people a "sense of
Participation." Workers don't want that. This plan means
giving them real participation.
—Fred Lesieur

CHAPTER 6

THE FROST/SCANLON PRINCIPLES: UNDERLYING TRUTHS, BEDROCK ASSUMPTIONS

Terry VandeWater

The four Scanlon principles. You've heard of them. But do you really know them?

"Well, I'm not sure," you say. "Does it matter?"

It sure does. Really knowing them means you have a better chance of enjoying everything they promise.

"Like what?"

Like understanding your organization and having a chance to make it better. That matters because you're part of that organization. The better it does the better for you. And the more chance you have to be involved, the better you'll feel about yourself and your work. Using the principles means understanding your company's strengths and weaknesses. And how you can help build upon those strengths, overcome those weaknesses (Identity).

It means working together to come up with the best solutions, best decisions. Being a member of the team, someone who matters (Participation).

It means being treated with dignity and respect. Treating others the same way. Getting a fair, a just return for how you use your skills and abilities, your time and energy (Equity).

And it means becoming better and better at what you do. Making more and more of a difference (Competence).

The Scanlon principles tell us what we and others in our organizations believe at the deepest level. Our underlying truths. Our bedrock assumptions about people and organizing work. Not this month's hot new program replacing last month's hot new program.

No. They're unchanging laws. Laws that govern what we stand for in the work place. The deep roots that nourish everything we do. That helps us stay true to our beliefs.

In this chapter we'll take a closer look at each of the four Scanlon principles. Then how the four principles depend on each other. And, finally, on the importance of dreaming the Scanlon dream and doing the best you can to make it happen.

Identity: Details that define

Identity, the big one. Covered first because **Identity** is where true understanding of participative management begins. The first among equals, **Identity**, paves the way for the other principles. It's the proven place to start.

Of course, all four principles are important. In fact, they're essential to each other. They're a set; needing to work together as one philosophy—that is, a humane approach to managing the way work is done. But **Identity** remains the principle that's the foundation for the rest.

Each of us has an identity, things about us that tell others who and what we are. Maybe some of us drive sporty convertibles. Some of us prefer small pickups. We may like hiking alone. Perhaps some have a passion for golf. Or spend most of their free time reading mysteries. Some may pray five times a day toward Mecca. Maybe some are slim and fit; others are overweight. You get the idea.

What about you? If we knew such things about you, would we be able to have a pretty clear idea what kind of person you are? What you are like? What makes you unlike others?

Well, that's how the principle of **Identity** works in organizations: It's those details that give them their definition. That identifies them. That set them apart. Make them unique. For each organization is unique, has its own set of successes and "could have been better's," its own strengths and "areas that need improvement."

Identity isn't limited to the organization itself, however. It also includes each member of it. Each one's role. What each needs to do for the organization to succeed.

Identity Questions

To help better understand the principle Identity, look at your own company: • What defines it, characterizes it, gives it its identity? • Is your company known as a good place to work? • Are employees aware of the critical business issues that threaten its existence? • Do they feel empowered to do something about them? • Do they understand how their jobs contribute to the organization's success? • Are employees valued as human beings, treated with dignity and respect? • Does your company have a good reputation for its minority hiring and advancement? • Are employees formed into effective teams, both regular work teams and special teams? • Do employees freely share information with each other rather than hoarding it to make themselves look good? • Is your company dedicated to superior customer service? • Does it aim its products and services at distinct parts of the market? • Do employees know who the customers are and what they require? • Do employees know the role others play, like dealers and suppliers? • Does your company face strong competition? • Is it alarmed by rapidly rising costs? • Is it dedicated to strong research, design, and development?

How you answer these questions and others like them should give you a pretty good idea of your company's **Identity**; whether it's known as a place where its people have a deep understanding of what's important and how they are enabled to respond to opportunities to contribute to its success and survival.

Every Scanlon company has at some time or other written a statement about **Identity**. Here are a couple of pretty good ones:

Identity tells who we are as a company, what we do, whom we serve, why we are in business, what our needs are, what our customers' needs are, and what's going in the economy that is important to us.

Identity is all employees at every level and station having the opportunity to understand the business, how they fit into it, how they can be meaningfully involved in helping it achieve its goals and objectives—that is, being sure they are doing what needs to be done and doing it right.

But we can't leave **Identity** quite yet. Two **Identity** "essentials":

1. **Identity** requires literacy. Literacy in this case means having a true picture of reality when it comes to your organization. It means having satisfactory answers to questions like those in the **Identity** questions above or these:

    > What kind of place is this? • What's happening in my organization? • Who am I here? • How do I fit in? • What do I need to do to help my organization survive? • What does the organization expect of me? • What should I expect from the organization? • How do I get the information I need about the organization? • How do I get my ideas known and acted upon? • How will I know if I am doing the right things right?

    Without answers to such questions, it is difficult to work well with others; to solve problems, make good decisions. Anyone kept in such darkness won't be able to see what needs to be done and may, consequently, have little enthusiasm to find out.

2. **Identity** also requires integrity. Integrity means being people genuinely committed to what they say they believe (not

least the Scanlon principles). Put most simply, it means people being true to themselves. Being free of fraud, sticking to commitments.

Participation: Not a mere buzzword

The second principle is **Participation**. Familiar enough word. But with more than one possible meaning. Sometimes it means full-fledged participative management. Other times it has a more general meaning—referring to any way employees work together—like Quality Circles, Kaizen, a suggestion system (even a suggestion box), Six Sigma, Total Quality Management, task teams, or dozens of others.

This chapter seldom uses "**Participation**" in either of these ways. Instead, it uses it mainly as the name of the second Scanlon principle. And when it does so, it spells it with a capital "P".

So as a Scanlon principle, **Participation** is not a mere buzzword as it is in some places. No, it's the name of one of the fundamental building blocks of any truly participative management plan. One of those bedrock assumptions about people and organizing work. An underlying truth.

It's no surprise that **Participation** is somehow about employees working together. And, yes, it often involves "tools" like Kaizen and Six Sigma and suggestion systems. But as one of the Scanlon principles, it has a much broader and deeper meaning. It is all employees' becoming an important part of the total organizational team. It is, as Scanlon people often say, all employees' "owning the problem"—the problem being helping the organization to succeed.

Participation Questions

Again, take a look at your company: If the organization has a suggestion system, is it working well? • If not, is something being done to fix it? • Is there a strong sense of ownership among employees? • Do they understand the critical issues facing the company? • Are they prepared to work together to solve them? • Or are they grumbling about the way things are and waiting for someone else to make it better? • Do you see groups of people working as teams, joining together their strengths, their skills and abilities, each pulling his or her share of the load to get the job done? • Do work team leaders sometimes say, "Well, it's time to do Scanlon. Let's meet to talk about this month's bonus results"? • Does it sometimes seem that's all **Participation** means to them? • Do people help each other without being told to do so? • Do you hear people saying, "I get paid for running my machine; I leave the thinking to the boss. That's what she gets paid for"? • Is the general sense among employees that being participatory is something you talk about but really don't do most of the time? • Do employees believe they can really make a difference? • If so, do they act on it?

How you answer questions like these should give you a pretty good idea of your company's understanding of and commitment to **Participation**. Whether it is people having a truly deep understanding of what **Participation** looks like, whether it is an organization dedicated to the Scanlon approach to managing work.

Here are a couple of pretty good statements others use to tell what the principle **Participation** means for them:

- **Participation** is providing the opportunity to influence decisions and exercising the responsibility to solve problems.
- **Participation** is all employees having the opportunity to work together cooperatively, responsibly to accomplish their shared business goals and objectives (solve "the problem").

Before we move on to the third principle, two **Participation** essentials—one about the invitation to take part, the other about the response to the invitation:

For participative management to really work, employees need to be invited to be involved. Managerial employees are usually responsible for doing the inviting. That's because they are the ones who usually decide what problems are best solved by involving employees. They also decide how much involvement is needed in each case.

The other employees are responsible for accepting the invitation. Those invited must understand, accept, and commit fully to the clear, concise, accurate, and sincere offer to take part. One's no good without the other.

Equity: Fair and square

Like "**Identity**," "**Equity**" is a word not always easy to understand. The problem is that many assume **Equity** means the same as "equal." But the word equal means everyone getting the same amount of something. That's not what **Equity** means. Instead, **Equity** means everyone getting what they earned—some, perhaps, more; others, perhaps, less—fair and square.

Equity has to do with justice, treating everyone fairly. Which doesn't necessarily turn out to be everyone getting the same. **Equity** means not giving anyone special treatment, not unfairly favoring anyone over others. Not being partial to anyone. So think of fairness when you think of **Equity**.

In many Scanlon companies, **Equity** embraces at least employees, customers, and owners (investors). This trio is often shown as a triangle, each side the same length as the other two. One of the sides is labeled customers, another employees, and the third investors. No matter how big—or small—the triangle gets, if the three sides remain as nearly the same length as possible, it means each group is getting its fair share.

But if, say, employees would get more than their share of the returns, their side of the triangle would grow longer than the other two. The triangle would go out of whack. The returns would no longer be equitable. The same would be true if investors or customers got an unfair return. **Equity** would have to be restored. (In some organizations, **Equity** is broadened to include others who contribute to the success—or failure—of the business, like dealers and suppliers and local communities.)

Equity is not about financial returns alone, however. Dignity and respect matter, too. **Equity** says employees will be

treated with no less dignity and respect than that shown to customers and investors.

Equity Questions

How about your company? • Do employees generally
believe they are being treated justly? • Do they value the
contributions their customers and owners (and possibly
dealers, suppliers, local communities, and other partners) make to the organization? • If so, do they agree that
the other partners should, like them, get a fair return on
their investment in the success of the organization? • Does
your organization have a way to measure whether all partners are being fairly rewarded? • Do some partners suffer at the expense of others? • Does the employee bonus
take into consideration the necessity to give other partners a fair return? • Or is it possible that employees would
get a big bonus when customers (for example) are not
being well served? • Or vice versa? • Is the company's pay
scale fair? • Do the leaders of your organization see to it
that employees are treated as its participative philosophy
promises they will be, with dignity and respect? • Does the
organization earnestly strive to be sure its rewards for performance are fair, evenhanded, proper, principled, impartial, appropriate, what is due?

How you answer questions like these should give you a
pretty good idea of your company's understanding of and commitment to **Equity** as it is understood within the Scanlon
philosophy.

Here are a couple of others' actual statements defining
Equity:

- **Equity** is all parts of an organization—not the least employees and their families but also customers, stockholders, suppliers, dealers, local communities, etc.—enjoying a fair and
  just and honest return on their respective investments to

assure the organization's welfare. For employees this should include such non-monetary returns as the rights to be literate, to be involved, to be responsible, and to become increasingly competent.

- **Equity** is the just distribution of the rewards resulting from the performance of the organization among all those who participate as owners of the problem. This means all must share fairly, equitably—good times and bad. It is employees and other stakeholders asking, given the level of my/our performance in relationship to the organization's results, am I receiving a fair reward or too much or too little?

Before we leave **Equity**, it's "essential": If people want to be true to the principle of **Equity**, they must be willing to be accountable. This means their being willing to take responsibility for their own performance and for that of their organization. They can't point at someone else for their lack of performance. For example, if service and product are poor, customers won't get what they deserve. So employees at every level shouldn't be surprised if the employees are held responsible.

Competence: Right job done right

The fourth Scanlon principle is **Competence**. This may be the easiest principle to understand. It is about each employee being able, skilled, qualified, effective, capable, adept, expert, having the necessary know-how.

We all understand it's important to be good at what we do. Which is what competence means. But it's not just doing a job well but also doing the right job. It's doing what needs to be done. And doing it well. For an organization to live up to its promise, everyone, regardless of job or level of responsibility, has to work at **Competence**. We can always improve the way we do our jobs.

Management employees are most often the ones who invite other employees to **Participate**. This is similarly the case with **Competency**: Management employees are usually the ones that invite other employees to take advantage of the tools and training needed to improve **Competency**.

But, as is also the case with **Participation**, invitations to improve **Competency** are of little use if the other employees don't respond positively to them. Without both a sincere invitation and an enthusiastic acceptance of it, **Competency** won't increase as it should.

All employees must be prepared to work with their leaders. To cooperate with them to improve the overall **Competence** of the organization. Be willing to learn on the job and take advantage of every chance to do so. And then to practice their new skills.

But managerial employees themselves must be **Competent** as well in a number of other areas specific to their jobs—from motivating and delegating to coaching and evaluating. And managing change may be the greatest **Competency** challenge of all.

Competence Questions

Do you see the **Competence** principle where you work? • Do people do their jobs with skill and dedication? • If not, is anyone doing anything about it? • If so, is it working? • Are plenty of training and educational opportunities being offered? • If so, are they the right ones? • Do employees welcome these opportunities? • How are the team leaders at delegating? • Are their intentions clear? • Do they take the necessary steps to be sure everyone involved understands the objectives? • Are the levels of responsibility and authority clearly defined? • Do your managers get too much involved in the "how" of doing jobs rather than the "what"? • Is **Competency** adequately rewarded? • Is the organization **Competent** in integrating the principles of **Participation** into the company's culture, making it the way they work hour by hour, day by day? • Or is **Participation** something employees do sometimes (like writing up a suggestion or going to a meeting or being handed a bonus check) but not others?

How you answer questions like these should make it fairly clear how the principle **Competence** is being played out in your company.

A couple of **Competence** definitions to consider:

* **Competence** is knowing how to do the right job right and then doing it right, being accountable to delivering your personal best, and being committed to becoming increasingly effective.

* **Competence** is all employees in their respective areas of responsibility doing what needs to be done in order for the organization to succeed.

An "essential" before we leave **Competence**:

We saw in the first of the definitions of **Competence** that "becoming increasingly effective" requires commitment. Commitment is all employees' having a sense of purpose. It is their being willing to be held accountable for doing their best. It is their being dedicated to doing their best to make the greatest possible contributions. And it means not being withdrawn, detached, and separated from "owning the problem." But hanging in there and getting the right job done right. Identifying personally with their work. Being fully engaged in what they do. Enjoying the good feelings that come from having done the right work well.

The Scanlon Principles: Indivisible
Working together as one

We had to talk about the principles one at a time until now. Taking them separately let us zero in on each one in order to understand each of them better. But that doesn't mean they can be separated from each other in the real world. No, to have success with the Scanlon approach to participation, we must remember that the four principles are indivisible.

Here are the definitions of the principles:

- **Identity**: understanding your company's strengths and weaknesses, how you can help build upon those strengths, overcome those weaknesses.

- **Participation**: working together to come up with the best solutions, best decisions. Being a member of the team, someone who matters.

- **Equity**: being treated with dignity and respect. Treating others the same way. Getting a fair, a just return for how you use your skills and abilities, your time and energy

- **Competence**: becoming better and better at what you do. Making more and more of a difference.

Given those definitions, consider these questions:

Would you and your fellow employees be able to work together "to come up with the best solutions, best decisions" (**Participation**) if you didn't have a clear "understanding [of] your company's strengths and weaknesses, how you can help build upon those strengths, overcome those weaknesses" (**Identity**)?

And would you and the others be as inclined to work together "to come up with the best solutions, best decisions" if you weren't "being treated with dignity and respect" and if you doubted if you could expect "a fair, a just return for how you use your skills and abilities, your time and energy" (**Equity**)?

And would you have confidence that any of this would happen if you and others in your organization weren't dedicated to "becoming better and better at what you do. Making more and more of a difference" (**Competence**)?

So **Identity** tells you what to do; **Participation** shows you the way to do what needs to be done; **Equity** provides you with incentive to do what needs to be done; **Competence** in each of the other three helps you make the most of each of them to get the right work done right. Which makes the circle complete. Or, to put in slightly different words, a clear sense of **Identity** is necessary for effective **Participation**; effective **Par-**

ticipation depends on everyone's being treated **Equitably**; everything depends on everyone's being **Competent**.

Dreaming Great Dreams: Making the most of the principles

People in organizations who respect the Scanlon principles will understand their organizations better. They will build upon strengths and overcome weaknesses. They will work together more effectively to come up with the best solutions. They will be stronger members of the team. They will treat others with greater dignity and respect and expect others to treat them the same way.

They believe that no company can become great without dreaming great dreams. Making the most of the Frost/Scanlon principles is an important way to get closer to its dream.

If this sound like you, terrific! Your company needs people like you. To realize your dream, commitment to the principles must come first, before everything else. Why? Because being grounded in the principles makes it possible to make the best choices about how all work is to be done—what we might call "process". This will move an organization ever closer to realizing the dream of full participation. This is as true for organizations that decide to "renew" their participative management as it is to those new to such an approach. In renewal, too, it is wise for them to start with principles (not process). Review the principles. Rededicate themselves to what they believe and why. Perform the understand-accept-commit drill. Then, finally, check to see how closely their process aligns with the principles.

The principles are primary. Nothing good can be expected to happen without starting at the beginning—namely, at the principles. So look there and then make the most of what the Scanlon principles promise. It's the least—and the most—you can do for yourself and for your company.

CHAPTER 7

THE SIGNIFICANCE OF CARL F. FROST

Richard Frost

In discerning the significance of Carl Frost, there are multiple dimensions that could be argued: fifty years of teaching and consulting; serving organizations on five different continents; working with privately and publicly held companies; being instrumental with companies smaller than 100 and larger than 8,000; having the ability to engage organizations whose primary purpose includes tires, automotive parts, electronics, clothing, silver, casting, furniture, steel, schools, and hospitals; and the longevity of relationships, some of which spanned multiple generations of employees. Each of these elements is significant when considering contributions to employees, organizations, and industrial organizational psychology. However, the true essence of Carl Frost are the values, principles, and processes that are his lasting legacy.

A bridge to a modern world

In 1946, Carl Frost was asked to join the faculty of the Massachusetts Institute of Technology where he had the good fortune of collaborating with Joe Scanlon and Douglas McGregor, among others. During his years at MIT, Carl created a synergy between the disciplines of clinical psychology and organizational culture, resulting in a dynamic understanding of human and organizational theory. This combination was extremely unique at that particular time because up until then 'work' had been understood strictly as a piece-rate culture, not one that engages the potentials of the individual and whole organization. In the two years working with Joe Scanlon, Carl developed an understanding of the principles of Identity, Participation, Equity and Competency that form the basis of the Scanlon Plan.

In 1948, John Hannah, President of what was then Michigan State College, invited Carl to join the psychology department and establish a program of Industrial Organizational Psychology at MSC, with an emphasis of outreach to the businesses of Michigan. Over the next thirty-five years, Carl served as a professor to undergraduate and graduate students at what came to be known as Michigan State University, and as a consultant to businesses and industries. His primary work was within the United States, but there was focused time when he worked in Europe, Korea, Nigeria, and Brazil, further enriching his understanding of both the human enterprise as well as organizational processes. He retired from MSU in 1982.

From 1982 to 1994, Carl formed a consultant group that focused on the Scanlon principles and process. Some of his most dynamic work occurred during this period with hospitals, financial institutions, schools, and traditional business organizations as they considered the principles and processes. Through these efforts, there was a conspicuous sharpening of the importance of leadership competencies required to be effective and efficient in today's changing world.

Values

All individuals have different value sets that they bring to their personal work and, in all cases, an organizational environment. Carl Frost is no different in that regard, but the fidelity to which he has lived them out is his revealing characteristic. His core values are the Christian faith, integrity, and the genuine caring for his fellow human beings. These three are the basis for the life and work for which Carl has lived and shared, both personally and professionally.

The vibrancy of the Christian faith within Carl allowed him to see the value of God-given gifts within each individual and understand their potential. This unique point of reference fueled a constant interest and commitment in the enabling process for all people to become what God intended them to be. As a consequence of the vibrancy of the Christian faith, there is a desire to serve others as they strive toward reaching one's full potential in the service of the Lord. This value was not stated for public view, but was the bedrock with which his life and work were done.

In working with individuals or organizations, the principle of integrity always formed the condition that was essential in order to proceed. Integrity as defined by Carl required complete honesty, transparency, and fidelity to the conversations, decisions, and actions. He felt so strongly about the need for integrity that he never worked on a retainer; rather, he felt that both the client and he should be able to continue with or terminate the relationship at any time. Integrity was always an essential part of the exploration and understanding of the imperatives within any organization. He would ask for honest participation, but when it came time to ask the difficult questions or a power of differential existed, the conversations were always conducted confidentially. This enabled each person to be who they felt they needed to be, with integrity, rather than what someone else thought they should be.

A clinical psychologist by education, Carl keenly understood human behavior and our psychological condition. With this understanding, he lived his life always caring, regardless of stature or position about the people he was with. This genuine caring manifested itself not only as an interest in the work or position of an individual, but also in the way this relationship impacted their lives personally and within the communities in which they lived. Within these caring relationships, Carl was seen as a trusted friend, a confidant regarding important issues, and someone who supported people in times of sorrow as well as joy.

Foundations

In looking at the body of work, there are four foundations that guide the consulting relationships of Carl Frost. They are

1) We are all in the process of becoming
2) Change is a given
3) Reality is the necessary source for understanding
4) Answers are the easy thing—it's the questions which lead us to life-long learning.

These four foundations were the means used to help individuals and organizations understand the imperatives that drive effectiveness and efficiency.

One of the classic statements is that we are all in the process of becoming, with the essence being, "Who are you becoming?" This concept of becoming draws the individual into the understanding that each day or moment is an opportunity to more fully realize one's potential if it is understood, accepted, and committed to. In the early meetings with individuals, it was not uncommon for the question to be asked, "What do you intend to become at this organization?" or "What do you intend to contribute?" For most, the answer was an easy one: a day's work, or the production of a product, but this answer was not satisfactory. The conversation would continue. Were they becoming more knowledgeable, more insightful with their competitor, or with the technology they used, or more profitable for their shareholders? On more than one occasion, the individual would then say that they had never looked at work, or indeed life, in this way.

In Wooster State Hospital, during his years as a clinical psychologist, Carl often would ask his patients, "What day is it?" If the answer provided the correct date, then he would know that the individual understood reality as it really was. This very simple technique proved to be very effective regarding conversations with individuals and organizations as well. Within an organizational culture, the reality was often understood in five dimensions: investor, employee, competition, unique technology and, increasingly important, competent key leadership. If the reality of each of these five dimensions were not understood, the response would provide less than optimal results for the individual and the organization. Additionally, it was not good enough to understand the reality from only one perspective. Understanding the investors' perspective and ignoring the competition or the employee often jeopardized both the short- and long-term viability of the organization. Each dimension demands understanding in order to have a competent response to, "What day is it?"

"If you don't like surprises, you are living in the wrong century." This was a statement in a Motorola advertisement in 1991 and captures the essence that change is a given. For most of us, we are creatures of habit and do not like to understand that we, our relationships, environments and, in fact, the world is changing daily. This principle that change is a given was often stated as one of the compelling reasons as to why organizations needed to look critically at what they were doing, often taking radical measures that allowed them to survive. Carl's understanding of this perspective of change empowered him to help individuals grasp that what was good enough today would not be good enough for tomorrow, and that only by engaging the entire organization would there be the potential for innovation, success, and longevity.

Perhaps the most vexing of the four foundations is the constant questioning. The questions are the vehicle by which the first three points are energized, forever arriving, the means of the journey. This process, when understood, requires the individual to retain objectivity, honesty, and a willingness to look soberly at all aspects of one's life and the decisions one makes.

Carl was able to exert this demanding questioning because of being rooted in his Christian faith, his integrity, and the care that he wove transparently into the fabric of all relationships. These unique relationships of penetrating questions with executives, managers, and employees empowered and enabled a greater sense of reality and a willingness to commit to excellence.

Process

Joe Scanlon was the original author of the concepts of identity, participation, equity and competence with respect to the Scanlon Plan. Carl's contribution to the Scanlon Plan was to bring the understandings of clinical psychology, *The Human Side of Enterprise* (McGregor, McGraw Hill, 1960), the "Integrative Whole" (Follett, a paper given to the Round Tree Lecture Conference, Oxford, 1928), and *Changing Forever* (Frost, MSU Press, 1996).

There is no one method for the implementation of the Scanlon Principles and Plan. Each process engages the core principles of identity, participation, equity, and competence in ways that embrace the uniqueness and authentic understandings of the reality of the people, starting at the top and working through the entire organization. This journey encompasses the values and principles in ways in which each individual has the opportunity and the responsibility to understand that for which they are uniquely qualified for and expected to do, ensuring a commitment to the entire organization. Carl's approach was built as a covenant between the abilities, potentials, and the realities of both the people as individuals and the organization, seeking to assure a more optimal culture by which excellence is constantly pursued.

Carl Frost's essence is that he lives to serve each person and organization through the values, principles, and the dynamic Scanlon process. His engagement with each individual or institution is unique, driven by their gifts, reality, and genuine interest in becoming effective in work and life.

SERVANT-LEADERSHIP AND SCANLON PRINCIPLES

Larry C. Spears

Getting Started

Since 1990 I have traveled around the world and given hundreds of talks on servant-leadership. No matter where I go, or what group I may address, the most frequently asked question is: "How do you go about implementing servant-leadership within organizations?"

It is a very important and fundamental question, as it gets to the nexus point of organizational applications and personal dreams. And yet, I'm afraid that my initial answer to that question is almost always a disappointing one to the questioner, as I usually begin by saying something like: "Well, I don't believe that there is any single way to introduce and practice servant-leadership in organizations. Each organization must find its own pathway. The introduction and implementation of servant-leadership in any organization needs to be as natural and organic a fit as possible in order to grow a strong root that can last for decades. There is no single model or process for putting servant-leadership into organizational practice. Instead, there are many pathways." While there is no easy answer, there are a number of approaches being used today.

The more challenging and pivotal task involves examining some of the different approaches and models that are in use today in servant-led organizations. One of the approaches being used by some servant-led companies involves their use of the Scanlon Plan and its four principles of Equity, Participation, Identity and Competence. And while the Scanlon Plan isn't the only way to harness servant-leadership within organizations, it is clearly a powerful way to do so.

The primary focus of this book is on Scanlon principles and practices. However, within this particular chapter I want to share with you my thoughts on some of the intersecting points between Scanlon thought and servant-leadership, and to focus primarily upon a basic introduction to servant-leadership for those who may not already be familiar with it.

Robert K. Greenleaf and the servant as leader idea

The term *servant-leadership* was first coined in a 1970 essay by Robert K. Greenleaf (1904–1990), entitled *The Servant as Leader*. Greenleaf, a contemporary of Joe Scanlon, was born in Terre Haute, Indiana. He spent most of his organizational life in the field of management research, development, and education at AT&T. Following a forty-year career at AT&T, Greenleaf enjoyed a second career that lasted nearly twenty-five years, during which time he served as an influential consultant to a number of major institutions, including Ohio University, MIT, Ford Foundation, R. K. Mellon Foundation, the Mead Corporation, the American Foundation for Management Research, and Lilly Endowment Inc. In 1964 Greenleaf also founded the Center for Applied Ethics, which was renamed the Robert K. Greenleaf Center in 1985 and is now headquartered in Indiana.

As a lifelong student of how things get done in organizations, Greenleaf distilled his observations in a series of essays and books on the theme of "The Servant as Leader"—the objective of which was to stimulate thought and action for building a better, more caring society.

The idea of the servant as leader came partly out of Greenleaf's half century of experience in working to shape large institutions. However, the event that crystallized Greenleaf's thinking came in the 1960s, when he read Hermann Hesse's short novel *Journey to the East*—an account of a mythical journey by a group of people on a spiritual quest.

After reading this story, Greenleaf concluded that the central meaning of it was that the great leader is first experienced as a servant to others, and that this simple fact is central to his or her greatness. True leadership emerges from those whose primary motivation is a deep desire to help others.

In 1970, at the age of 66, Greenleaf published *The Servant as Leader*, the first of a dozen essays and books on servant-leadership. Since that time, more than a half-million copies of his books and essays have been sold worldwide. Slowly but surely, Greenleaf's servant-leadership writings have made a deep, lasting impression on leaders, educators, and many others who are concerned with issues of leadership, management, service, and personal growth.

What is Servant-Leadership?

In his works, Greenleaf discusses the need for a better approach to leadership, one that puts serving others—including employees, customers, and community—as the number one priority. Servant-leadership emphasizes increased service to others, a holistic approach to work, promoting a sense of community, and the sharing of power in decision making.

Who *is* a servant-leader? Greenleaf said that the servant-leader is one who is a servant first. In *The Servant as Leader* he wrote, "It begins with the natural feeling that one wants to serve, to serve first. Then conscious choice brings one to aspire to lead. The difference manifests itself in the care taken by the servant—first to make sure that other people's highest priority needs are being served. The best test is: Do those served grow as persons; do they, while being served, become healthier, wiser, freer, more autonomous, more likely themselves to become servants? And, what is the effect on the least privileged in society? Will they benefit or at least not be further deprived?" Servant-leadership is a long-term, transformational approach to life and work—in essence, a way of being—that has the potential for creating positive change throughout our society.

A Growing Influence

The servant-leader concept continues to grow in its influence and impact. In fact, we have witnessed an unparalleled explosion of interest and practice of servant-leadership in the past twenty years. In many ways the times are only now beginning to catch up with Robert Greenleaf's visionary call to servant-leadership.

The idea of servant-leadership, now in its fourth decade as a concept bearing that name, continues to create a quiet revolution in workplaces around the world. In countless for-profit and not-for-profit organizations today we are witnessing traditional, autocratic, and hierarchical modes of leadership yielding to a different way of working—one based on teamwork and community, one that seeks to involve others in decision making, one strongly based in ethical and caring behavior, and one that is attempting to enhance the personal growth of workers while improving the caring and quality of our many institutions. This emerging approach to leadership and service is called *servant-leadership*.

The words *servant* and *leader* are usually thought of as being opposites. When two opposites are brought together in a creative and meaningful way, a paradox emerges. The words *servant* and *leader* have been brought together to create the paradoxical idea of servant-leadership. The basic idea of servant-leadership is both logical and intuitive. Since the time of the industrial revolution, managers have tended to view people as objects; institutions have considered workers as cogs within a machine. In the past few decades we have witnessed a shift in that long-held view. Standard practices are shifting toward the ideas put forward by Robert Greenleaf, Joe Scanlon, Stephen Covey, Peter Senge, Carl Frost, Max DePree, Margaret Wheatley, Warren Bennis, and many others who have suggested that there is a better way to lead and manage our organizations. Robert Greenleaf's writings on the subject of servant-leadership helped to get this movement started—as did Joe Scanlon's ideas via the Scanlon Plan—and their views have had a profound and growing effect on many.

Characteristics of the Servant-Leader

After some years of carefully considering Greenleaf's original writings, I have extracted a set of 10 characteristics of the servant-leader that I view as being of critical importance. The following characteristics are central to the development of servant-leaders:

1. *Listening:* Leaders have traditionally been valued for their communication and decision-making skills. While these are also important skills for the servant-leader, they need to be reinforced by a deep commitment to listening intently to others. The servant-leader seeks to identify the will of a group and helps clarify that will. He or she seeks to listen receptively to what is being said (and not said!). Listening also encompasses getting in touch with one's own inner voice and seeking to understand what one's body, spirit, and mind are communicating. Listening, coupled with regular periods of reflection, is essential to the growth of the servant-leader.

2. *Empathy:* The servant-leader strives to understand and empathize with others. People need to be accepted and recognized for their special and unique spirits. One assumes the good intentions of co-workers and does not reject them as people, even while refusing to accept their behavior or performance. The most successful servant-leaders are those who have become skilled empathetic listeners.

3. *Healing:* Learning to heal is a powerful force for transformation and integration. One of the great strengths of servant-leadership is the potential for healing one's self and others. Many people have broken spirits and have suffered from a variety of emotional hurts. Although this is a

part of being human, servant-leaders recognize that they have an opportunity to "help make whole" those with whom they come in contact. In *The Servant as Leader* Greenleaf writes: "There is something subtle communicated to one who is being served and led if, implicit in the compact between servant-leader and led, is the understanding that the search for wholeness is something they share."

4. *Awareness:* General awareness, and especially self-awareness, strengthens the servant-leader. Making a commitment to foster awareness can be scary—you never know what you may discover. Awareness also aids one in understanding issues involving ethics and values. It lends itself to being able to view most situations from a more integrated, holistic position. As Greenleaf observed: "Awareness is not a giver of solace—it is just the opposite. It is a disturber and an awakener. Able leaders are usually sharply awake and reasonably disturbed. They are not seekers after solace. They have their own inner serenity."

5. *Persuasion:* Another characteristic of servant-leaders is a primary reliance on persuasion, rather than using one's positional authority, in making decisions within an organization. The servant-leader seeks to convince others, rather than coerce compliance. This particular element offers one of the clearest distinctions between the traditional authoritarian model and that of servant-leadership. The servant-leader is effective at building consensus within groups. This emphasis on persuasion over coercion probably has its roots within the beliefs of The Religious Society of Friends (Quakers), the denomination with which Robert Greenleaf himself was most closely allied.

6. *Conceptualization:* Servant-leaders seek to nurture their abilities to "dream great dreams." The ability to look at a problem (or an organization) from a conceptualizing perspective means that one must think beyond day-to-day realities. For many managers this is a characteristic that requires discipline and practice. The traditional manager is focused on the need to achieve short-term operational goals. The man-

ager who wishes to also be a servant-leader must stretch his or her thinking to encompass broader-based conceptual thinking. Within organizations, conceptualization is also the proper role of boards of trustees or directors. Unfortunately, boards can sometimes become involved in the day to day operations and fail to provide the visionary concept for an institution. Trustees need to be mostly conceptual in their orientation, staffs need to be mostly operational in their perspective, and the most effective CEOs and leaders probably need to develop both perspectives. Servant-leaders are called to seek a delicate balance between conceptual thinking and a day-to-day focused approach.

7. *Foresight*: Closely related to conceptualization, the ability to foresee the likely outcome of a situation is hard to define, but easy to identify. One knows it when one sees it. Foresight is a characteristic that enables the servant-leader to understand the lessons from the past, the realities of the present, and the likely consequence of a decision for the future. It is also deeply rooted within the intuitive mind. As such, one can conjecture that foresight is the one servant-leader characteristic with which one may be born. All other characteristics can be consciously developed. There hasn't been a great deal written on foresight. It remains a largely unexplored area in leadership studies, but one most deserving of careful attention.

8. *Stewardship*: Peter Block (author of *Stewardship* and *The Empowered Manager*) has defined stewardship as "holding something in trust for another." Robert Greenleaf's view of all institutions was one in which CEOs, staffs, and trustees all played significant roles in holding their institutions in trust for the greater good of society. Servant-leadership, like stewardship, assumes first and foremost a commitment to serving the needs of others. It also emphasizes the use of openness and persuasion rather than control.

9. *Commitment to the growth of people*: Servant-leaders believe that people have an intrinsic value beyond their tangible contributions as workers. As such, the servant-

leader is deeply committed to the growth of each and every individual within his or her institution. The servant-leader recognizes the tremendous responsibility to do everything within his or her power to nurture the personal, professional, and spiritual growth of employees. In practice, this can include (but is not limited to) concrete actions such as making available funds for personal and professional development, taking a personal interest in the ideas and suggestions from everyone, encouraging worker involvement in decision making, and actively assisting laid-off workers to find other employment.

10. *Building community:* The servant-leader senses that much has been lost in recent human history as a result of the shift from local communities to large institutions as the primary shaper of human lives. This awareness causes the servant-leader to seek to identify some means for building community among those who work within a given institution. Servant-leadership suggests that true community can be created among those who work in businesses and other institutions. Greenleaf said: "All that is needed to rebuild community as a viable life form for large numbers of people is for enough servant-leaders to show the way, not by mass movements, but by each servant-leader demonstrating his own unlimited liability for a quite specific community-related group."

These ten characteristics of servant-leadership are by no means exhaustive. However, I believe that they serve to communicate the power and promise that this concept offers to those who are open to its invitation and challenge.

Tracing the Impact of Servant Leadership

1. Organizations

Servant-leadership principles are being applied in significant ways in a half-dozen major areas. The first area has to do with servant-leadership as an institutional philosophy and model.

Servant-leadership crosses all boundaries and is being applied by a wide variety of people working with for-profit businesses; not-for-profit corporations; and churches, universities, health care, and foundations.

Servant-leadership advocates a team-oriented approach to analysis and decision making as a means of strengthening institutions and improving society. It also emphasizes the power of persuasion and seeking consensus, over the old top-down form of leadership. Servant-leadership holds that the primary purpose of a business should be to create a positive impact on its employees and community, rather than using profit as the sole motive.

Many individuals within institutions have adopted servant-leadership as a guiding philosophy. An increasing number of companies have adopted servant-leadership as part of their corporate philosophy or as a foundation for their mission statement. Among the better known companies are: The Toro Company (Minneapolis, Minnesota), Synovus Financial Corporation (Columbus, Georgia), ServiceMaster Company (Downers Grove, Illinois), The Men's Wearhouse (Fremont, California), Southwest Airlines (Dallas, Texas), Starbucks (Seattle, Washington), and TDIndustries (Dallas, Texas).

TDIndustries (TD), one of the earliest practitioners of servant-leadership in the corporate setting, is a Dallas-based heating and plumbing contracting firm that has consistently been included among *Fortune* magazine's annual listing of the *100 Best Companies to Work for in America*. TD's founder, Jack Lowe, Sr., came upon *The Servant as Leader* essay in the early 1970s and began to distribute copies of it to his employees. They were invited to read through the essay and then to gather in small groups to discuss its meaning. The belief that managers should serve their employees became an important value for TDIndustries. Today, any TD Partner who supervises at least one person must go through training in servant-leadership. In addition, all new employees continue to receive a copy of *The Servant as Leader* essay; and TD has developed elaborate training modules designed to encourage the understanding and practice of servant-leadership.

Some businesses and not-for-profits view servant-leadership as an important framework that is helpful and necessary for ensuring the successful and long-term effects of related management and leadership approaches such as continuous quality improvement, systems thinking and the Scanlon Plan. It is suggested that institutions hoping to create meaningful change may be better served in starting with servant-leadership as the foundational understanding, and then building on it through any number of related approaches.

Servant-leadership has influenced many noted writers, thinkers, and leaders. Max DePree, former chairman of the Herman Miller Company and author of *Leadership Is an Art* and *Leadership Jazz* (and a man clearly linked to both servant leadership and Scanlon ideas) has said, "The servanthood of leadership needs to be felt, understood, believed, and practiced." And Peter Senge, author of *The Fifth Discipline*, has said that he tells people "not to bother reading any other book about leadership until you first read Robert Greenleaf's book, *Servant-Leadership*. I believe it is the most singular and useful statement on leadership I've come across." In recent years, a growing number of leaders and readers have rediscovered Robert Greenleaf's own writings through books by DePree, Senge, Covey, Wheatley, Autry, and many other popular writers.

2. Governance

A second major application of servant-leadership is its pivotal role as the theoretical and ethical basis for "trustee education." Greenleaf wrote extensively on servant-leadership as it applies to the roles of boards of directors and trustees within institutions. His essays on these applications are widely distributed among directors of for-profit and not-for-profit organizations. In his essay *Trustees as Servants* Greenleaf urged trustees to ask themselves two central questions: "Whom do you serve?" and "For what purpose?"

Servant-leadership suggests that boards of trustees need to undergo a radical shift in how they approach their roles. Trustees who seek to act as servant-leaders can help to create institutions of great depth and quality. Over the past thirty years, two of America's largest grant-making foundations (Lilly Endowment Inc. and the W. K. Kellogg Foundation) have sought to encourage the development of programs designed to educate and train not-for-profit boards of trustees to function as servant-leaders. John Carver, the noted author on board governance, has also cited servant-leadership as the philosophical foundation upon which his Policy Governance Model® may best operate.

3. Communities

A third application of servant-leadership concerns its deepening role in community leadership organizations across the country. A growing number of community leadership groups are using servant-leadership resources as part of their own education and training efforts. Some have been doing so for more than twenty years.

M. Scott Peck, who wrote about the importance of building true community, wrote the following in *A World Waiting to Be Born:* "In his work on servant-leadership, Greenleaf posited that the world will be saved if it can develop just three truly well-managed, large institutions—one in the private sector, one in the public sector, and one in the nonprofit sector. He believed—and I know—that such excellence in management will be achieved through an organizational culture of civility routinely utilizing the mode of community."

4. Service-Learning

A fourth application involves servant-leadership and experiential education. During the past thirty years experiential education programs of all sorts have sprung up in virtually every college and university—and, increasingly, in secondary schools, too. Experiential education, or "learning by doing," is now a part of most students' educational experience.

Around 1980, a number of educators began to write about the linkage between the servant-leader concept and experiential learning under a new term called "service-learning." It is service-learning that has become a major focus for some experiential education programs in the past two decades.

In 1990 the National Society for Experiential Education (NSEE) published a massive three-volume work called *Combining Service and Learning*, which brought together many articles and papers about service-learning—several dozen of which discuss servant-leadership as the philosophical basis for experiential learning programs.

5. Leadership Education

A fifth application of servant-leadership concerns its use in both formal and informal education and training programs. This is taking place through leadership and management courses in colleges and universities, as well as through corporate training programs. A number of undergraduate and graduate courses on management and leadership incorporate servant-leadership within their course curricula. Several colleges and universities now offer specific courses on servant-leadership. Also, a number of noted leadership authors, including Peter Block, Stephen Covey, Max DePree, and Peter Senge, have acclaimed the servant-leader concept as an overarching framework that is compatible with, and enhancing of, other leadership and management models such as total quality management, systems thinking, and community-building.

In the area of corporate education and training programs, dozens of management and leadership consultants now utilize servant-leadership materials as part of their ongoing work with corporations. Among these companies are Starbucks, The Men's Wearhouse, U.S. Cellular, Synovus Financial, and Southwest Airlines. A number of consultants and educators are now touting the benefits to be gained in building a total quality management approach upon a servant-leadership foundation. Through internal training and education, institutions are discovering that servant-leadership can truly improve how business is developed and conducted, while still successfully turning a profit.

6. Personal Transformation

A sixth application of servant-leadership involves its use in programs relating to personal growth and transformation. Servant-leadership operates at both the institutional and personal levels. For individuals it offers a means to personal growth—spiritually, professionally, emotionally, and intellectually. It has ties to the ideas of M. Scott Peck (*The Road Less Traveled*), Parker Palmer (*The Active Life*), Ann McGee-Cooper (*You Don't Have to Go Home from Work Exhausted!*), and others who have written on expanding human potential. A particular strength of servant-leadership is that it encourages everyone to actively seek opportunities to both serve and lead others, thereby setting up the potential for raising the quality of life throughout society.

For some people, the word *servant* may prompt an initial negative connotation due to the oppression that many people—especially women and people of color—have historically endured. For others, the word *leader* may also carry with it a great deal of unfavorable historical baggage. However, upon further consideration many come to appreciate the inherent nature of what Greenleaf intended by the pairing of *servant* and *leader*. The startling paradox of the term *servant-leadership* serves to prompt new insights.

In an article titled, "Pluralistic Reflections on Servant-Leadership," Juana Bordas has written: "Many women, minorities and people of color have long traditions of servant-leadership in their cultures. Servant-leadership has very old roots in many of the indigenous cultures. Cultures that were holistic, cooperative, communal, intuitive and spiritual. These cultures centered on being guardians of the future and respecting the ancestors who walked before."

Women leaders and authors are writing and speaking about servant-leadership as a leadership philosophy that is most appropriate for both women and men to embrace. In an essay on women and servant-leadership former Stephens College (Columbia, Missouri) President Patsy Sampson wrote: "So-called (service-oriented) feminine characteristics are exactly those which are consonant with the very best qualities of servant-leadership."

A Growing Movement

Interest in the philosophy and practice of servant-leadership is now at an all-time high. Hundreds of articles on servant-leadership have appeared in various magazines, journals, and newspapers over the past decade. Many books on the general subject of leadership have been published that recommend servant-leadership as a more holistic way of being. And, there is a rapidly growing body of literature available on the understanding and practice of servant-leadership.

The Spears Center for Servant-Leadership (www.spears center.org) is an international, not-for-profit educational organization that seeks to encourage the understanding and practice of servant-leadership. The Center's mission is to fundamentally improve the caring and quality of all institutions through servant-leadership.

Bob Greenleaf and Joe Scanlon

Servant leadership is fundamentally a philosophy for life and work. It starts with each individual but also has important applications for organizations. The four Scanlon principles (Equity, Participation, Identity and Competence) serve as the philosophical core for the Scanlon Plan—a particular means for companies to implement those principles. I believe that the place where servant-leadership and Scanlon principles come together is at the beginning—inside the heart-and-mind of each individual seeker who begins by asking him or herself questions like: "What is my greater purpose?" and, "How can I better serve and lead others?" For some people and organizations, the answers to those questions have led them personally to servant-leadership and corporately to become Scanlon companies.

I haven't as of yet, found any evidence that Bob Greenleaf and Joe Scanlon ever met, though I haven't ruled out the possibility. Joe Scanlon and Bob Greenleaf both taught at M.I.T.—Joe in the 1950s and Bob in the 1960s. Both men also had separate connections to Douglas McGregor, who might have provided an opportunity for Greenleaf and Scanlon to have known one another. However, Joe Scanlon died at the relatively young age of 56 in 1956 (Bob Greenleaf was a senior researcher at AT&T at that time) and so these two men probably did not meet, though I think it likely that Bob Greenleaf must have been aware of Joe Scanlon and the Scanlon Plan as he was a closer follower of new and interesting ideas in business.

While Joe and Bob may not have crossed paths, it is clear that their intellectual ideas were in close alignment as far back as the 1930s. In his superb biography of Robert K. Greenleaf *Robert K. Greenleaf: A Life of Servant-Leadership*, Don Frick includes the following observation and excerpt from a 1935 talk by Bob Greenleaf:

> By 1935, Greenleaf was already making the argument that great leaders worked through others and that worker empowerment was good business. Speaking before a gathering of industry professionals, he said, "The advanced thinkers at supervisory levels are beginning to see the possibilities in the idea that an industry that sets the development of the potentialities of its people as one of its primary aims is ensuring the accomplishment of the end and aim of the industry." In that same speech, he offered an idea that presaged by twenty-five years Douglas McGregor's Theory X and Theory Y views of workers and management. The old-fashioned controlling boss described by Greenleaf corresponds to McGregor's Theory X. The Theory Y approach honors workers' capacities.
>
> 'The old hard-boiled boss is rapidly becoming a thing of the past. This negative sort of supervision had as its criterion the discovery of weaknesses and limitations in people, a sort of pessimistic philosophy, for limitations are mighty easy to discover, and when in search of them, many fine qualities may be obscured. . . A search for the capabilities and possibilities in people is gradually supplanting the search for their limitations. It is a more optimistic philosophy. But the basis for such a change in philosophy is far from sentimental, for it is the wise supervisor who realizes that the grist for his mill is contained in the possibilities in people and not in their limitations'.

Back to the future

Why are servant-leadership and Scanlon principles so important today? After all, in our fast-paced world there aren't a whole lot of ideas from a half-century ago that have worn their age very well. For one thing, I would say that over the past half-century there has been an increasing level of dissatisfaction and resultant changes in the workplace. Decade after decade has brought forth a growing number of people inside organizations who expect more of their organizations in terms of caring and encouraging behaviors. While older models are still to be found, I believe that they are slowly-but-surely going the way of the dinosaurs. In their places we find newer organizations that are flatter (not so pyramidal and hierarchical), and where decisions are more often made by teams than by a single individual.

We also find many more servant-leaders working inside large and small organizations today than ever before. Servant-leadership and Scanlon principles are helping to lead this social movement—a worldwide movement that is increasingly more in tune with contemporary organizations and rising expectations. These expectations are now much higher for organizations when it comes to their customers, clients, communities—on both the serving side and the leading side of the equation. As such, organizations and companies that practice servant-leadership and/or Scanlon practices are increasingly found at the top of their particular industries.

Together, servant-leadership and Scanlon ideas are a very natural fit. Some Scanlon companies have an explicit understanding of this and embrace servant-leadership as a philosophical foundation upon which their Scanlon Plan operates. Others may not call what they are doing servant-leadership, but when you talk with them it is clear that they hold to those beliefs and practices. Two fine examples of servant-led Scanlon companies are Thomson-Shore Printing and Landscape Forms, both based in Michigan.

In recent years that has been a kind of cross-fertilization going on between the ideas of Greenleaf and Scanlon/Frost;

and between the Scanlon Leadership Network and The Spears Center. We are drawing energy and ideas from each other in a way that I believe is exciting and full of promise.

How can servant-leadership be beneficial in both personal and professional areas of life? Part of the great appeal of servant-leadership is that it encourages people to simply be who they are, all the time. It also encourages others to be more accepting of their colleagues, family, etc. without feeling a need to change them. That can also be a powerful and healing end-product of servant-leadership.

Both servant-leadership and Scanlon principles are about who we want to be in relation to others, and a deepening expression of the innate desire that many of us have to both serve and to lead others. There is no single way that companies have sought to implement servant-leadership. Servant-leadership is taught and practiced in different ways in various organizations. Those companies which have also adopted the Scanlon Plan have found that there are reproducible learnings and results.

Following in the footsteps of others

The 20th Century produced a number of highly-principled business leaders who seemed to share deep concerns about the industrial age, and who sought to bring to bear their considerable personal insights and visions in order to point the way to those who followed.

Organizational leaders such as Robert Greenleaf, Joe Scanlon, Max DePree, Carl Frost, Warren Bennis and others have gone on to make use of their experiences, and to write about them, with the goal of creating positive change within organizations and society at large. They and many others were innovators who felt called to align their organizational practices with their own spiritual or humanistic beliefs. I feel a deep sense of appreciation for these pioneers, and for the many men and women who now follow in their footsteps.

Those of us who are privileged to carry forward and to expand upon their work in the 21st century are also called to share the heart-and-soul of servant-leadership. Working together, we help to widen the path for those who follow.

CHAPTER 9

THE ROLE OF THE FOLLOWERS

DICK RUCH

The blunt truth: Without followers there can be no leaders. Leaders are absolutely important, because they provide purpose, direction, and resources. Followers are absolutely important in any organization of more than one person, because they do most of the work. Only followers can make excellent quality and service a reality.

Leaders and followers are two sides of the same coin and cannot be considered separately. People who rush to praise CEOs as the be-all and end-all of an organization's success are simply ignoring reality. Leaders are not some elite species who know everything and have all the answers.

The teachings and principles of the Frost/Scanlon process acknowledge that most people serve as both leader and follower, depending on the task and situation. How is that possible? Because the person with the most competence in a given situation should always have the most influence in deciding what needs to be done. Max DePree calls this "roving leadership" since no one person can possibly have the expertise or experience or wisdom to judge all situations. As Peter Drucker has said, "Lots of people need to make decisions if the business is to be dynamic."

Given this reality, especially today when problems and situation have become enormously complex, it is important to define jobs broadly. The best workers go above and beyond the "job description" and you don't want to shackle people who understand the mission and purpose of the organization. I am

115

including not just employees but dealers, suppliers, consultants, designers, architects—anyone who contributes to the success of an organization. Along with the opportunity to participate always comes the obligation to be both accountable and responsible. Yes, you can't have one without the other in a well-run organization.

Leaders who know how to inspire and motivate followers are on a path to enduring success. No person lasts forever, but an organization with motivated and engaged employees will outlast the founders, and has the potential for long life.

Whether or not you are a Christian, Jesus demonstrates to my mind the attributes of a great leader. At the start of a three-year ministry—his "organization"—he recruited a small band of followers now called disciples. Their task was to carry on after he was gone. At the end of three years, Jesus had at most only a few thousand followers (some would say even the twelve deserted him), and yet today there are some two billion followers! The power of committed followers over time is incredible.

For ordinary people like me the opportunity to influence even a handful of people is a wonderful thing, and if those few people influence others, you leave an important legacy, made possible by followers.

General Motors, unlike the Christian church, hasn't fared so well. There are no doubt many perspectives on the struggles of General Motors in recent years. This is mine, as a former employee and consumer of their automobiles.

General Motors is a classic example of a great corporation brought to its knees because it lacked a significant group of followers committed to GM's success. Was this a failure of leadership? Yes! Both the leaders of GM and the leaders of the UAW. Both management and the union leaders failed to recognize the competitive threat of the global economy. In the early years the union under Walter Reuther was relevant and necessary to correct management abuses, but later it became focused on *me* equity rather than *we* equity. This resulted in high paying jobs for a few and the loss of employment for many.

When foreign car makers began to establish manufacturing plants in the U.S., they were careful to keep the union out through location and enlightened personnel policies. They created loyal and committed followers who gave them a significant cost and quality advantage, an advantage not shared by GM. Committed followers enjoy much greater job security (ironically one of the key goals of unions) because they make their companies more productive and much less likely to outsource their jobs.

In the case of GM, the leaders failed to live up to their responsibilities. Of course followers have responsibilities too. In my book *Leaders & Followers*, I wrote about the responsibilities of followers, using examples from people I worked with at Herman Miller. Accepting and carrying out these responsibilities requires competence and commitment by followers. Here is that list of responsibilities:

1. Take responsibility to do the work necessary to achieve the mission.

Howard Johnson was the first person Herman Miller hired in Human Resources. At that time, Herman Miller had just over 500 employees. Before Howard, the human resource function was handled entirely by the line organization. There was no personnel handbook, and this proved to be a blessing. Howard did not preempt the line organization but became a strong advocate for production workers and was especially diligent in responding to their concerns and problems. For the company to succeed during a very high growth period, Howard saw his mission as hiring the people Herman Miller needed. Without any prompting, he accomplished that.

2. Care about the business and choose and be chosen to be part of it.

Duke Aardema was a local truck driver and warehouse worker who had a 43-year career at Herman Miller. After he had worked for 33 years, he said "I plan to help build this company for another 10 years." He did. Duke was someone you could always count on to do whatever needed to be done. Once when his teammates kidded him that while he had joined Herman Miller in the same month as Dick Ruch but hadn't moved up as far, he said, "Well, someone has to hold the ladder." Not only did he have a sense of humor, he had a sharp mind.

3. Welcome accountability and seek results.

Al VanKlompenberg had a long career with Herman Miller as a master upholsterer. He could do any job that required upholstery and always tried to do more than the standard. He said to me one day, "The standard for the Chadwick sofa is 18 a day. I try to do 25."

4. Always seek improvement by challenging what is and being open to influence—always a better way.

For many years, Pep Nagelkirk was the lead model maker at Herman Miller. He was a terrific problem solver for our product designers. He could render virtually any prototype or model required and was especially expert at solving mechanical problems within the scope of the design criteria. He was always after improvement—but only after listening carefully to the description of the problem.

5. Lead when appropriate and take the initiative to influence others (roving leadership).

Bill Wiersma is a capitol equipment technician for Herman Miller specializing in jigs and fixtures. He works with company plant facilities all over the world to provide the necessary jigs and fixtures to produce Herman Miller products. He has a great capacity to find ways to gain acceptance of the process, working with production personnel even in situations where he does not speak the language.

6. Be competent and honest and often have a word of encouragement for others.

Al Pacini was a mail service courier at Herman Miller. You just had to like Al. He always did his job well and was ready with an encouraging word to lift the spirits of the people he met.

7. Go beyond expectations to serve and delight the customer.

Ron Aardema was the first long distance Herman Miller truck driver hired. He didn't just drop off the furniture at the dock but helped the customer receive it and understand what they were getting. He also was a good friend of people in trouble along the highways of America.

8. Develop teamwork by trusting, listening, and communicating.

Diane Bunse was one of Herman Miller's first female supervisors in production. In her job she had to prove herself to a lot of people. Someone once said, "Whatever women do, they have to do twice as well as men to be thought half as good as men. Fortunately this is not difficult." And it wasn't difficult for Diane. Her group was both happy and productive.

9. Anticipate and prevent problems but, when they do occur, accept ownership for solving them.

Gary Miller is Executive Vice President and Chief Development Officer. He may seem an odd choice as an example of a good follower, since by the nature of his job he is also a leader. However as I've said before, every competent employee is both a leader and a follower depending on the situation. A gifted engineer by training, Gary is a wonderful resource to the Herman Miller designers who often want to push the envelope of known technology to create a breakthrough design. When problems occur as they usually do with new technology, Gary accepts the responsibility and either personally solves the problem or finds someone else who can solve it.

10. Commit yourself to lifelong learning.

I define learning with two overlapping components: training and education. Training is learning the "how to" of a skill. Education is the acquisition of general knowledge, thereby developing the powers of reason and judgment.

While formal education is important, in my experience, most jobs provide continuing opportunities to learn for those so motivated. At Herman Miller, Brian Walker is a great example of a person so motivated. After graduating from Michigan State University with high honors in accounting, he worked as an auditor for Arthur Anderson for four years, becoming a C.P.A. in the process. He joined Herman Miller in 1988, became the Chief Financial Officer in 1996, President in 1999, and CEO in 2004. Along the way, he became a strong advocate for EVA (Economic Value Added) as a key performance metric for Herman Miller. With his broad experience in all of Herman Miller's global operations, and the respect of both external and internal audiences, he has both learned a lot and accomplished a lot in a short time. He is an example of a great follower who has become a gifted leader.

Great followers—like great leaders—go way beyond merely living up to their responsibilities. Great followers buy into the mission, purpose, and strategy of their organizations. They understand, accept, and commit themselves to a larger goal and in so doing motivate themselves and others to perform with excellence. This goes far beyond showing up and doing your job competently. There is a huge difference between those who merely comply and those who commit.

With good leaders and good followers, there is the opportunity for every person to make a difference and feel good about his or her contribution to an organization's success. I'll end with a story about leaders learning to be better followers. Herman Miller's annual reports are designed by a gifted graphic designer, Steve Frykholm. One year when I was CEO, the senior officers of the company were debating the relative merits of some directions for the year's annual report. We debated color and type size and kinds of paper and images. For a moment, we had all forgotten we were not graphic designers—we were business people. Eventually we allowed Steve to guide us in our choice. And in the end, we realized that better decisions result when the person with the most competence in a given area exerts the most influence.

INTEGRITY— THE CRITICAL FACTOR

RANDY G. PENNINGTON

The success of any attempt to forge lasting change in individual or organizational performance is enhanced or limited by the integrity of the leader and/or organization. This makes integrity the critical—and often missing—factor in an organization's ability to thrive and compete in a global economy.

Integrity has appeared at or near the top of every list of desirable leadership characteristics for many years. And, its impact has never been greater. The issues organizations will face in a truly global economy—pressure on cost and profit margins, strategy execution, expanding partnerships, and continuous improvement—demand a work place that is fast, flexible, focused, and committed. Integrity is the unifying trait that makes it possible.

Dr. Carl Frost said it well: "The degree and quality of employee participation, accountability, competence, and commitment are determined to a large extent by the presence of, absence of, or uncertainty about integrity."[1]

What is Integrity

For many, the word *integrity* is synonymous with *ethics*. That is a critical piece of it, but integrity goes beyond personal or organizational character to include competence and consistency.

[1] Carl F. Frost, *Changing Forever: The Well Kept Secret of America's Leading Companies*, East Lansing: Michigan State University Press, 1996.

Webster's New World Dictionary defines *integrity as, "the quality or state of being complete; wholeness; the quality or state of being unimpaired; and being of sound moral principle."*

Leaders and organizations adopting this broader definition deliver integrity in their products, services, and relationships. They make every decision: new product design, marketing, business development, employee relations, customer service, sales strategies, accounts payable schedules, contributions to charitable organizations, and everything else that comes up in the organization on the basis of what's right, rather than who's right. They also provide quality products and services while embracing continuous improvement in all performance areas. They maintain a culture where ethical behavior and doing what is right is expected and rewarded. They operate in an open, transparent manner with all constituencies while delivering on promises (implied and explicit) to all constituent groups. And, they comply with the spirit of applicable regulations rather than the minimum requirements, thus insuring accountability for integrity at every level of the organization.

As a result, they experience: enhanced brand loyalty and reputation; increased morale, commitment, and productivity; improved resource utilization; confidence in compliance with laws and regulations; and, more effective response to crisis situations.

What would be different in your organization if every individual could be trusted to act with integrity? What might you be able to save in compliance costs? What might you be able to achieve through increased productivity and performance? How might a reputation for integrity in products, services, and relationships affect customer loyalty?

How Integrity-Driven Leaders and Organizations are Different

All great leaders create focus with clear goals and high expectations. They expect results, and they ensure effective execution of well-designed strategies. Integrity-driven leaders simply approach their leadership responsibilities from a different perspective.

Their power comes from trust rather than fear. They pay attention to relationships as well as results, and they stress credibility rather than control. As a result, they generate confidence from others instead of skepticism and cynicism.

Stephen Carter asserts in his book, *Integrity*, that we admire integrity in our leaders because of their forthrightness, steadfastness, consistency, compassion, and the reliability of their commitments.[2]

We live in a world where trust, confidence, and credibility are the victims of the quest for success at any cost. We are skeptical, and often cynical, about the motives behind the action of others. We have seen a lack of integrity in our elected officials, heroes, and even in the institutions on which we rely to define our society. Integrity lapses are not confined to business and the workplace. Examples can be drawn from our schools, government, religion, and even families.

Leaders and organizations operating with a heightened sense of integrity are no less focused on results. They simply understand that short-term results, without the long-term trust from all stakeholders, create an environment where on-going success is not sustainable.

That makes the quest for integrity—as defined by Webster—the most important goal to which a leader can aspire.

Why Doesn't Everyone Act with Integrity?

The almost universal acknowledgement that integrity is critical to long-term success is put to the test when we see questionable acts in our corporations, government institutions, and even families.

Why would an executive making a great salary with stock options and perks mess it up by alienating staff or manipulating profits? Why would a mid-level manager cook the

[2]Stephen L. Carver, *Integrity*, New York: Basic Books, 1995.

corporate books? Why wouldn't any of us speak up when we saw a co-worker delivering a less than promised product or service?

Why doesn't everyone act with integrity?

Here are five factors that contribute to individuals and organizations delivering less than integrity-driven performance.

1. A culture of competition and winning at all costs. Competition is a way of life in today's world. Businesses and individuals must compete in a global marketplace. For some, it is a matter of perceived survival. For others, it is simply about winning the game—at all costs. Bending the rules becomes legendary whether we're talking about making a profit, producing a product on time, or getting our children accepted into the best schools. Water cooler conversations, promotions, and public recognition confer star status on those who win at any cost.

The stars in any endeavor exhibit a love of competition and winning. But a culture that rewards winning at all costs subtly encourages people to cut corners or push the envelope beyond what is right unless integrity is equally valued. The choice to go along and get along is often easier than standing for one's values and fighting the culture.

2. Poorly designed systems. Systems promote efficiency and consistency. They are also powerful vehicles for developing habits through repetitious behavior. Poorly designed systems can unconsciously promote a lack of integrity. Look around in the place where you work. Must individuals routinely circumvent written policies to accomplish their goals? If so, a culture that accepts less than integrity-driven performance can be forming.

3. The push to do more and more with less and less. The tension created when expectations exceed available resources inspires creativity. But, the line between innovation and a lack of integrity can be blurred when the pressure to produce, results in questionable behavior. Reports of cutting corners, falsifying documentation, and withholding information have appeared as front page news leaving otherwise good people and organizations with a sullied reputation.

4. Blind loyalty. History contains numerous examples where a leader's ability to inspire has clouded the judgment of otherwise well-intentioned individuals. A more likely scenario in today's world is the assumption that all decisions have been thoroughly examined by our leaders. Individuals who carry out any directive without evaluating the consequences can find themselves sacrificing their sense of integrity, their reputation, and in some cases, their freedom.

5. The lure of expedience. Speed drives our world. We complain about the wait to microwave our meals. A two-minute report on the evening news is called an "in-depth analysis." Is it any wonder that we want immediate success? Society reinforces the notion that success is defined by what you have rather than your character. We are told that we deserve it all; we are unsuccessful if we don't have it all, and we should receive it right now.

The lure of expedience is often linked to a win-at-all-costs culture. An out of control desire for external success symbols starts individuals and organizations down a slippery slope in which a return to the standards of integrity is difficult.

Are You Integrity-Driven?

Complete the assessment below to determine if your organization is laying the foundation for integrity in its culture. Rate yourself on a scale of 1 to 5 with "5" being *excellent* and "1" being *needs improvement*.

1. Decisions are made based on "what's right for all parties" and not on   ____
   the basis of tradition, expediency, or political positioning.

2. People at all levels of the organization clearly understand what is   ____
   expected of them in areas of productivity, quality, service, job performance, and integrity.

3. Telling the truth is rewarded. The organization does not shoot messen-   ____
   gers or avoid the truth to protect the illusion of success.

4. Leaders and managers are held accountable for the development of peo-   ____
   ple and the manner in which results are achieved in addition to the
   results themselves.

5. The organization's leaders set a good example of integrity.   ____

6. Individuals are rewarded for their performance that demonstrates   ____
   integrity.

7. The organization deals swiftly with individual performance that vio-   ____
   lates the trust of others.

8. The organization has a reputation for honesty, value, and integrity.   ____

9. Everyone is united behind the common goals of providing quality prod-   ____
   ucts and services to customers in a manner that communicates honesty, value, and integrity.

10. The organization acts responsibly toward the welfare of the commu-   ____
    nity as a whole.

SCORING

If your score is 40 or above, your organization does a terrific
job of demonstrating its integrity. There may be a few areas you
want to fine tune, but you are doing well.

If you scored between 30 and 40, you're doing a good job
overall, but there are probably a few specific areas on which
you should work.

If your organization scored below 30, you should take steps
to immediately improve your performance. Your customers and
your employees will appreciate your effort, and your organization will become more effective.

A culture based on integrity in products, services, and relationships builds trust. And, trust is the competitive advantage

in an environment where cynicism and skepticism rob you of the ability to excel.

Making Integrity a Way of Life

A decision to make integrity the cornerstone of your organization's operation begins with the leader and is driven throughout the organization by performance and execution. Here are seven strategies to help you start and continue your journey.

1. State your expectations clearly. Everyone must understand your expectations and their contribution to driving integrity through every aspect of your operation. Communicate in an open, honest manner so everyone knows their obligation to customers, suppliers, communities, and each other. Avoid hype. Admit that you are constantly working on your own performance, and ask for everyone's commitment to achieving the vision of integrity in products, services, and relationships.

2. Pay attention to structure and processes. Structure and systems create habits that ensure consistency when human breakdowns occur. A seminar participant made the case for aligning structure and processes with these words, "how do they expect us to trust them when the policies say one thing, but we are asked to do something different every day."

3. Everything is ultimately connected. Deceptive marketing practices influence attitudes and behavior in other departments. Allowing disrespectful treatment of employees in one area will eventually affect other areas. The integrity of the whole is called into questions when we see inconsistencies among the various parts. Each area of the business should be evaluated by the following questions: Are we doing what we said we would do? Are we providing what we said we would provide? Are we operating in a manner that builds trust in our products, services, and relationships?

4. Create accountability and rewards. People must see that acting with integrity means something. Deal quickly with those who violate the organization's standards. Fear of consequences can create an environment where individuals work to avoid getting caught. Make honoring commitments and the ability to build trust among diverse groups criteria for promotion. Recognize and reward those who demonstrate their integrity in a difficult situation, even when the result is not as you would have hoped. Behavior that is recognized is repeated.

5. Provide the skills and tools to put principles into practice. Even the best system can malfunction or be improved. People create systems, and good intentions can go awry when either skills or tools are absent.

6. Talk about integrity often. How often do you speak about your organization's key performance results? How often do you speak about the fact that success is ultimately based on the integrity of your products, services, and relationships? Hanging a values statement on the wall and distributing wallet cards are not enough. Very few take the time to stand in the hallway or search their wallets to read the values statement when they face a difficult choice. Don't start a new program. Create stories and legends about those who achieved superior results while modeling integrity. Talk about the challenges of earning and maintaining the trust of others. The more attention leaders give to the value of integrity as a competitive tool the more important it will become in the organization.

7. Welcome bad news. The test of a healthy organization is not the absence of problems. It is the ability to address them in a positive manner. The permission to share bad news without fear of retribution promotes an honest, open environment that continually strives to improve. As good as your organization is today; there is a strong chance that someone is withholding information that can make it even better. Remember—truth is the victim when we value the allusion of success. Integrity-driven leaders and cultures focus on what is real.

FIGURE 1. Exhibit A

Don't forget personal leadership.

Leadership is about the ability to influence—nothing more and nothing less. Leadership has very little to do with position and everything to do with your ability to influence others. Employees, suppliers, customers and the community are watching. They judge the sincerity of our actions very quickly and will take their support elsewhere unless they see integrity in our performance.

Leaders influence others by their decisions and actions at three levels: Personal, Interpersonal, and Organizational (Exhibit A). Leadership development programs often focus on the interpersonal and organizational strategies and techniques. While those are important, we can't underestimate the power of individual choices and behavior. All leadership begins with personal leadership.

Ralph Waldo Emerson once said of a guest, "The louder he spoke of his honor, the faster we counted our spoons." That statement is as relevant today as it was when it was first made in 1860. Who we are—at our core—matters just as much as the ability to communicate, to make good decisions, or to implement sound practices.

Leader or Liar?

Most people have good and honorable intentions. They want to do what's right.

Here is the challenge—we know our intentions while others simply look at our behavior and performance filtered through their lens of perception. We are evaluated on a simple standard of integrity: Did we do what we said we would do?

Organizations and their leaders are faced daily with choices that affect the lives and safety of customers, employees, and suppliers. In our personal lives, choices affect the security, cohesiveness, and survival of our families. In our communities, leaders make decisions that have an impact for generations to come. We may see ourselves as leading and living with integrity, but to others we are simply lying.

The demand for and benefits from integrity—and the trust it produces—will continue to grow. The leader's job is to create an environment that delivers results without sacrificing personal or organizational integrity. There is no program of the month. It is an on-going process that must become a part of the organization's fabric.

Like the gardener who nourishes, cares for, and weeds his crop every day, the quest for integrity cannot be left to chance. It must be front and center in every discussion, decision, and action if the goal is to continually thrive, compete, and succeed.

Part III

Equity
Participation
Identity

"What Day Is It?"
—Dr. Carl Frost

Part III

JEFFERSON, SCANLON, AND OPEN-BOOK MANAGEMENT: A BUSINESS STORY THAT MUST BE TOLD

JOHN SCHUSTER

Those who control the stories that define the culture of a society control its politics and the economy.
—*David Korten,* **The Great Turning: From Empire to Earth Community**

Can you remember the first time you heard about the Scanlon story? It may have been the 70's or 80's, if you are a boomer, or the 90's if you are an X'er or millennial. Remember your excitement and initial curiosity that lead to questions like.

- *"How long has this been going on?"*
- *"What companies are doing this?"*
- *"What results do they get?"*
- *"What are the challenges of maintaining the Scanlon practices?"*
- *"What is the headquarters of the association doing in Michigan, anyway?"*

You most likely remember that as you researched Scanlon, its principles resonated with something in you that yearned to make business a force for social good. Perhaps you had heard about the mondragons in Basque, or the self-managing teams at Volvo, or Ben and Jerry's egalitarian workplace. Depending on how you entered the field of thought for humane and efficient workplaces, through total quality, or an MBA class with an imaginative professor, when you heard about the Scanlon practices you knew right then that they had value. You became a fan. When you dug into it more and saw the results, you became an advocate at some level.

You knew that this was the kind of business story that needs to be told, the real human story of people's work lives and a business leadership steeped in the better angels of our nature.

You perhaps had not realized it fully, but you had become fatigued by the old business story. With Scanlon and other important contributions, you had found a new one more worthy of your best efforts and closer to your sense of what it means to be a person.

I came to Scanlon thinking by having become an early and visible champion of the movement that got named open-book management (OBM). The books I co-authored and the countless workshops and speeches, were part of the movement that swept through the business press in the 90's, and was on the lips of many business people. It has since faded, morphed, and continued under different names. A bit more on that later.

Because of my advocacy and experience, I had the honor in the mid-90's and again in 2004, to be the speaker at the Scanlon Plan's annual meeting, witnessing the Scanlon companies celebrate, educate, share and re-commit to the principles they have put into practice in their companies. I would recommend attending the conference if you never have—it will be good for your soul.

Open-book management (OBM) is closely aligned to Scanlon in many principles and practices: sharing financial information, involving all levels of employees in decision-making, established formulas for sharing financial gains with all employees, and more. Underneath OBM and Scanlon is an invitation by company leaders to all employees to become business thinkers and to contribute, to be corporate citizens. In this way, both philosophies have a strong Jeffersonian bent, a trust in the common worker to be able to rise above self-interest and think and act on behalf of the whole enterprise.

OBM and Scanlon are based on a different story of human enterprise than the dominant one being told across our culture. The dominant story of business is seen every evening on TV: ticker tapes of stock prices sliding by on the bottom inch of the screen, mergers and earnings reports, the latest scandal, a CEO getting hired with a signing bonus the size of Macedonia's GDP, new numbers on growth in Asia. We, as absentee shareholders with our retirement in mutual funds, view the show, or read the *Wall Street Journal*, hoping that whatever shares we hold will rise because of management's strategic moves, the right weather, increasing demand, and our trust in the market.

There is nothing wrong with this story by itself. It is only incomplete.

The Scanlon and OBM story of business, told from the Jeffersonian bottom up, focuses on the workers and their leaders as they strive to serve customers while sharing in the production gains of the real, not abstract, goods and services they provide. Share prices are included along with other measures in this version of the story, as are the lives of real workers and the communities in which they live and work.

So what has happened with OBM?

The good news is it is alive and well. The Scanlon companies can tell you what, if anything, they learned from open-book management practitioners and promoters like myself. The books on OBM have been written. Organizations like the Beyster Institute and the ESOP association, promoting the spread of equity into every worker's hands, disseminate the practices of OBM. There is a community of fans and practitioners who meet on occasion with my former partner, Springfield Manufacturing, at their workshops and conferences. They tell their stories and swap best practices, like the Scanlon companies. It reminds me of different churches with distinct histories and founders, but all heading the same direction by renewing their faith in people doing business in right and inclusive ways.

My firm created a business simulation that teaches financial knowledge using accelerated learning principles in 1992. Fifteen years later it has morphed into insurance versions and utility versions and eight other industry simulations. People enjoy learning finance and accounting through a game. (Some 300,000, by our estimates, have played our simulation in its various forms.) Our most recent version is the medical center game. The cost crisis in healthcare is causing management to train all the clinicians and non-financial types to learn about the financial realities of their workplace.

This on-going legacy of OBM is one of its most encouraging features. More people are learning, like the employees in Scanlon companies, how their company and industry works from an accounting and financial perspective.

As OBM started to fade as a term by 2001, many of its better features were being absorbed across business in the U.S. and elsewhere. While *Inc Magazine* was championing OBM in the mid 90's, and Total Quality Management (TQM) had won the day in terms of teams and participation for improving process, Harvard professors Kaplan and Norton were churning out compelling arguments for sharing financial information with employees while also sensitizing executives to what Deming had been teaching—financial measures are lag indicators, not lead indicators.

Thanks to the work and the huge acceptance of the balanced scorecard across corporate America, far beyond Scanlon and OBM put together, and more on a scale of TQM at its heyday, dashboards and scorecards measuring lead indicators like quality and employee and customer satisfaction have taken their place along side of the financial metrics. Whatever role OBM had in that development, and I know it had some because I was there, it is part of its worthwhile legacy.

The dominant business story runs amok

The dominant business story no longer builds community or provides enough meaning. Perhaps it never did.

We can trace our roots with markets and economics over the centuries and see that it has never been an ideal picture of equal amounts of capital in the hands of large groups of Americans building wealth for the greater good. But in the midst of the ugly stories of robber barons, or earlier stories of brutally taking the land from American Indians and building an economy dependent upon slaves, we have had many good stories.

One such large story was the growth in prosperity post WWII for almost all Americans and the spreading of gains across all the segments of our society. And the early Scanlon plan adoptions in the 50's and 60's, and a bit later in the 70's and 80's, even into the mid 90's, the spread of OBM and of employee ownership plans were important positive sub-stories.

But, let me relate a telling incident that confirms what many of us know in our hearts and that the data now supports—in the last 15 to 20 years there is much about the dominant business story, told so often and so automatically, that is far from healthy.

When I was first promoting open book management and discovering the powerful parallels with my older and wiser Scanlon brothers and sisters, Ben and Jerry's was at the peak of their business iconhood. They had managed, like Anita Roddick at the Body Shop, to make their company stand for a great product and a force for social good. In the early 90's, they conducted a very well-covered, and now hardly mentioned, search for a CEO whose salary would be pegged at seven times the pay of the lowest worker. The press loved this story and its egalitarian and hippie vestiges in a capitalist world.

I was in my initial open-book fervor, accompanied by a dose of naiveté, quite convinced that business had turned a corner on including workers in the equity side of things and that a new kind of widely distributed wealth generation was about to take place across America and beyond. My European, Asian, and Australian consultant friends were inviting me to their countries to show them how it all worked.

I had exposure to many compensation consultants in those days and I remember asking several of them something like, "so are you watching the trend increase to bring executive pay into

greater alignment with their employees', like Ben and Jerry's?" Upon hearing this, they would look at me and do something of a double take, like they couldn't hear what I had
actually asked them because it was so entirely unexpected. And
then, when they realized I was serious, they would gather their
thoughts and say something like, "No . . . er, uh, no, we don't
actually see anything like that."

I had received my first hint of what was to come in the later
90's, and continue up to the present time.

A second hint was the widely read *Dilbert* comic strip series
that made fun of open-book management and the size of executive salaries. *Dilbert's* creator had seen OBM for what it was,
a powerful philosophy and set of methods totally out of step
with some other even more powerful trends that had taken root
and were spreading like kudzu across the business landscape.

Of course, that was the early nineties, with dotcom fever
about to take off, the decoupling of executive pay to their
employees in big companies, and the increase in financial capitalism and its legal magic that creates paper wealth that may
or may not be tied to the making of goods or delivery of services. The beginning of the spiral that bought us Enron and
scandals aplenty was already underway. The era of the rich and
shameless was born. The ghost of Alexander Hamilton had
returned center stage and Jefferson's ghost was backstage.

To be sure, OBM, total quality and Scanlon principles and
just plain old good leadership, were helping companies who
refused to stoop to the fads of the day. These companies, and
any that were lead by leaders with actual value on their minds
and not just financial gain, used their energy to innovate for
customers and create real, not paper, wealth.

But the dominant story had taken off. My idealism and love
of business had a hard time accepting the fact that cowboy
capitalism, reduced social nets, scapegoating the poor, regres-
sive environmental and energy policies, depressing wages and
over-rewarding capital by those who, what a surprise, had the
capital—all these trends had won the day.

So my question to the comp professionals looks incredible
to me in retrospect—how could I have asked it? As wages con-

tinue to be depressed for the working class, as the spectacular run of corporate profit increases quarter after quarter continues, wealth has gushed us to the topmost rungs of the social ladder and the middle and lower rungs have been trickled upon. We are in a clear situation where a rising tide raises all yachts.

What will we do to tell a better story?

The causes for all this are too complex to address in this space. Anyone who brings up "class" issues of haves and have-mores and have-nots is seen as an archaic social relic, or worse, a dangerous perpetrator of anti-market, unpatriotic tripe. One thing I can say is that I have been making a payroll with my partners for 25 years, my customers are all in businesses that I admire, and I mentor CEO's as part of my work. I like every CEO whom I have the privilege to serve.

Alexander Hamilton's ghost may haunt my dreams, but Jefferson's ghost guards my bed at night, thankful that Scanlon and OBM, and this very anthology with great thinkers in the field, still provide his principles with a place to be applied.

The questions we must address

You may be a fan of Scanlon and open book management. You may be aligned through Scanlon thinking with servant leadership, employee ownership, participative management and the engaged workforce. Given the dominant story of business however, we need to ask ourselves some tough questions.

Are the principles and practices begun by Joseph Scanlon powerful enough, will they be spread widely enough, to have a positive impact, not just on the many companies using the Scanlon philosophy, but on a world much in need of a free enterprise story with soul and substance?

Or will the spiritually impoverished dominant business story, the one being over told today, snuff out these human principles and the good things they produce?

The answer to these questions lies in our collective hearts. Do we have the collective vision and courage to tell the better business story? Do we have the moxie to build better companies and a marketplace worthy of us?

The verdict is still out. Each of us has our part to play. OBM may go away entirely some day, as Scanlon may. But the attempt to make business work for all its stakeholders, to align the interest of shareholders, with managers with customers with employees, has to go on. Our humanity makes it so.

Robert K. Greenleaf knew this long ago. He wrote these words in October of 1986:

> *Top leaders . . . have the opportunity to create an atmosphere in which consensual dreams can emerge that have power to guide purpose and decision in ways that make for greatness.*

About eight years later in 1994, I read a poem to Scanlon companies at their annual meeting. The poem ended with words that need to be heeded more than ever, as the dominant business story fails us and threatens to shrivel our hearts and imaginations:

> *The lessons Scanlon folks can teach the business world are ample. Keep going, Scanlon friends, keep open-book truth at your core. We need your courage and shining example.*

Jefferson and Scanlon knew that business could be a place for greatness. Let's make it so.

CHAPTER 12

PROFIT SHARING UNDER COLLECTIVE BARGAINING: THREE CASE STUDIES

Joseph N. Scanlon

[Editor's note: We have included this article from 1948 for two reasons: 1. It is a good example of Scanlon's thinking and was written by Joe Scanlon himself and 2. It is a potent reminder of both how far we have come and how far we have to go.]

In the postwar period of labor unrest considerable attention has been focused on profit-sharing plans as a remedy for current industrial relations ills. Proponents of the idea insist that strikes and low productivity are twin symptoms of an internal maladjustment. The real trouble, they say, lies in the worker's fear of insecurity and his belief that he is being exploited. The solution, so runs the argument, is to hitch the wage earner's interest to the employer's profits. Both thereafter will work together in peace and harmony. And, indeed, this has been the experience in isolated cases; but most schemes have been far less successful. They have failed to show even the most elementary common sense in devising means to create greater worker interest in the welfare of the enterprise.

In a quick check of its records the National Industrial Conference Board reports that of 161 profit-sharing plans surveyed in 1937, about 60 per cent had been abandoned. The Board warned employers against too quick judgment on the advisability of following the profit-sharing movement. Never-

143

theless, profit-sharing plans seem more tempting today than ever before. The reason is simple. Since V-J Day, the wage issue has all but erased other questions affecting labor and management. Union statisticians charge that since the war real wages have fallen while profits have soared. Management, on the other hand, answers, "Yes, we're making money, but with our costs so high, even a small drop in demand can put us in the red." Profit-sharing, then, is thought of as a substitute for a wage increase. And while no national policy has as yet been adopted, unions in general have opposed profit-sharing plans because they have been used as a substitute for a justifiable wage increase—a substitute which amounted to a wage increase with a retriever string attached.

Labor also has a historical objection to profit-sharing. Too often in the past a plan of this kind was introduced as a weapon to combat union organization. And even when this was not the ulterior purpose, the effect upon the minds of the employees was the same, for management conceived and established such plans on a unilateral basis. Quite naturally, union membership viewed with hostility and suspicion a program which weakened the principles of collective bargaining. And in by-passing representatives of the employees, management failed to develop a sense of partnership or participation, indispensable ingredients to the fulfillment of any program to foster greater productive efficiency.

The following case histories of three profit-sharing plans, one a complete success, the other two failures, may well point up the strength and weaknesses inherent in the basic idea, together with some important elements which influence the broad over-all results.

Profit Sharing Plan Number One

In 1936 when the organizing drives were instituted in the mass production industries, the employer already had a well-developed program designed to combat outside organization of his employees. It followed the usual pattern. A company union was set up and functioning. There is little doubt that the company was entirely responsible for this development. Through the company union the employees had been granted all of the advantages in wages, hours, and working conditions gained through collective bargaining processes by the Steelworkers' Organizing Committee in the plants that had been organized.

Nevertheless, early in 1938 an organizing drive conducted by the Steelworkers' Organizing Committee seemed destined to succeed, and they petitioned the National Labor Relations Board for an election. At this juncture the company decided to install a profit-sharing plan. The proposal presented to the company union officials contained the following provisions:

A. If the board of directors decided at their first meeting after the end of each fiscal year that the company had enjoyed a good year, then each employee of the company would share in the profits of the preceding year.

B. Each employee currently employed would receive a bonus of five cents per hour for each hour worked during the preceding year.

C. This agreement would remain in effect only so long as the present bargaining agent represented the employees. In the event of a change in representation, the plan was automatically canceled.

This agreement proved to be a most effective weapon in combatting outside organization. In the National Labor Relations Board election, the employees voted overwhelmingly to continue the company union. They reasoned that if they could secure an increase of 5 cents an hour over and above that being paid in all other basic steel plants in the area, this was more than they could expect to accomplish in a monetary way if they were represented by the Steelworkers' Union.

Beginning with 1938, for six consecutive years the bonus was paid. The employees were well aware of the fact that they were receiving this bonus for staying out of the union. Just as regularly, each year prior to the meeting of the Board of Directors a synthetic organizing threat developed within the ranks of the employees. Pamphlets were distributed and organizers were called in to address meetings. A great deal of excitement was generated. "If you join an outside union," the workers were told, "you will lose your bonus." This pressure campaign never failed to achieve the desired objective. The board of directors always decided that the company had experienced a good year and the bonus was paid. During six years of operation the company has paid out approximately $1,250,000 in bonuses and had received in return the somewhat dubious satisfaction of keeping the union out. No sense of partnership, no joint participation in an effort to increase efficiency, no effort to improve the profit-making possibilities or the competitive position of the company had been developed. The plan was founded on hypocrisy and bad faith and had degenerated into a subtle game of wits.

Early in 1945 the United Steelworkers of America (the old S.W.O.C.) conducted an intensive drive at the properties of the company. It proved successful. A majority of the employees voted in an N.L.R.B. election for the Steelworkers' Union, despite the fact that the company again used the bonus elimination threat as their chief weapon. The union had made a sizable wage demand on the industry and it dwarfed the importance of the 5-cent-per-hour bonus or share of the profits.

The industry refused to grant the demands of the union and a strike ensued. The employees of this company joined in the work stoppage. Agreement was finally reached on the return to work. Not so with this company. The strike here was continued for several additional weeks. The profit-sharing bonus was the stumbling block that prevented a settlement. The company was willing to grant the 18.5-cent-per-hour wage increase, but insisted that the plan must be discontinued. The union contended that wage stabilization was in effect and that the profit-sharing bonus could not be canceled. It had been paid during the entire period of wage stabilization and now was considered a part of the wage structure. The Office of Price Administration had granted the industry price increases to com-

pensate them fully for the general wage increase over their previously existing wage structure.

A compromise settlement was finally reached on the following basis: The profit-sharing plan was continued as originally applied with 5 cents per hour for each hour worked by
every employee during the year. The profits after taxes of the
second lowest year beginning with 1938 through 1944 was
used as the base to determine whether the bonus was payable. This base replaced the original understanding, which left
the matter to the decision of the board of directors. Likewise,
it took the issue out of the area of wage stabilization and
relieved the company of the obligation to pay if profits were
below the agreed-upon level. It is interesting to note that the
base or payable level is approximately one-half of the profit level
maintained during the war years beginning with 1940.

It was pointed out during negotiations that if its purpose
was to increase production and efficiency, this plan as applied
even under ideal conditions had little promise of success. Some
efforts were directed toward the development of a graduated
scale of bonus payment based on the profit level. These efforts,
although looked upon favorably by several individual members of the company's official family, were finally vetoed by a
majority as being unfeasible. Under the presently applied plan
there is no incentive for the employees to do anything other
than hope that a certain fixed minimum profit may accrue at
the end of the fiscal year. They do not know from month to
month whether they are maintaining a profit level sufficiently
high to ensure the payment of the bonus. Even if they did
know, there would be no incentive to increase the base minimum profit level. No relationship has been established between
employee efforts and returns from the plan. If the company's
profits are ten times greater than the base, the bonus share
remains constant at 5 cents per hour. This plan is rightfully catalogued a failure.

This plan, however, should not be charged as a failure
against profit-sharing. It was neither conceived nor designed in
any way to give the employees an opportunity to participate in
a share of the profits of the company. It did not comprehend

the development of a sense of partnership and participation in order to enhance profit-making possibilities. It was an instrument designed for the sole purpose of preventing the employees from joining a bona fide trade union. In this it failed, and the bonus payments remain a monumental evidence of this failure.

Profit-Sharing Plan Number Two

The employees of this company were organized in 1940. Early in 1941 the union won an N.L.R.B. election and was certified as a collective bargaining agency. Negotiations with the company for a collective bargaining agreement began in March of that year and dragged on through July without progress. The company had engaged the services of a well-known law firm to represent them in the negotiations. At no time did any of the company officials participate in the many conferences. The union pressed for a standard agreement; the corps of lawyers representing the company steadfastly refused to accept any of the existing clauses in the standard contract. Their patience exhausted because of the extended delay, the employees engaged in a work stoppage. They charged the company with refusal to bargain in good faith. The strike lasted for three weeks, during which time a great deal of ill will developed. It was settled when a memorandum of agreement covering the basic issues involved was signed, with a stipulation to the effect that the parties were to begin negotiations on the remaining differences within ten days after operations were resumed.

A meeting was scheduled for the seventh day after the strike was settled in order to complete the contract. The union's negotiating committee attending the meeting was surprised to find the lawyers were conspicuously absent. Heretofore they had met exclusively with the company's attorneys; at this meeting they met for the first time with the company president, his assistant, and the plant manager.

The conference got under way and within three hours the remaining issues were disposed of in a satisfactory manner. The atmosphere was friendly and co-operative. At the conclusion of the meeting the company officials informed the union committee that they had decided it was in their best interests to do everything possible to get along with the union. The company president expressed the hope that a sound and friendly relationship might be developed. He frankly admitted that some of his friends in the industry and even his own board had been working on him. They had convinced him that his policy of fighting the union was extremely short-sighted. The union committee met this approach with mixed emotions. They were both pleasantly surprised and deeply suspicious.

Exactly four weeks after the strike settlement, the president of the company called the union committee to his office for a meeting. With a dramatic flourish he read a statement to them. The company had been giving much serious study to the many profit-sharing plans then in effect in American industry. They had now reached a decision. To cement a co-operative relationship with the union and as a gesture of good faith, they had developed a profit-sharing plan and were prepared to install it at once. He explained the details of the plan and its method of operation, so that they would be completely familiar, and so that the committee members could explain them to the union membership. The provisions were as follows:

A. In all good years the company had earned in excess of 4 per cent on its net worth.
B. Beginning with 1941 the employees would participate in a share of all profits above the 4 per cent net worth level.
C. Fifty percent of all profits above this level of earnings would be placed in a pool for distribution to all employees.
D. Each employee would receive a proportionate share applied on a percentage basis to his total earnings during the preceding year's operations.

The sincerity of the management of the company in proposing the plan is undoubted. The wisdom of the move under the existing circumstances is questionable. The union had not even begun to function as such. Its officers had not the slightest idea of how the union affairs should be conducted. The newly elected grievance men had not as yet processed a grievance.

The bitterness and suspicion aroused during the organizational campaign and the subsequent strike were still fresh in the minds not only of the union membership but also of the supervisory force. The rank and file of the employees read into the announcement of the plan all sorts of trickery. They were not convinced that management had suffered a change of heart. "The company was using the plan as a technique to wreck the union. What was a profit anyway? Some wise guy could manipulate the books; every company had two sets anyway. The wage rates were too low. If the company was really honest about the whole business, it would use some of its profits to bring the low rates up. Let's go on a strike and make them give us the money now." These and similar remarks made the rounds of the mill. Although the local union officers and committeemen were convinced that the plan had been offered in good faith, they were too inexperienced to present the case clearly. They did not know enough about their responsibilities, nor did they understand the plan well enough, to fight the tide of doubt and suspicion, so they rode along with the general opposition.

Reports of the reaction to the plan began seeping back to the president's office. He and his official family were first hurt, then angry and resentful. They were almost completely disillusioned. The president's plan had been misinterpreted and completely misunderstood. His immediate reaction was, "To hell with them and the whole damned business. I guess I've been a fool." The relationship with the union developed in a haphazard manner. No further efforts were exerted to make of the profit-sharing plan an instrument that would function properly.

In 1941 the employees received a bonus of 14 percent; in 1942, 11 percent; 1943, 9 percent; in 1944, 12 1/2 percent; in 1945, 7 1/2 percent. Approximately $5,500,000 was paid out in the five-year period.

The situation today is just about the same as it was back in 1941. The same efficiency level has been maintained. As an incentive to induce greater teamwork and productive efficiency, the plan has failed. It has produced no tangible effect whatsoever and is now generally accepted as a part of the general wage structure. As a matter of course, when the share dropped to the 7 1/2-per-cent level in 1945, there was a great deal of griping. This plan can likewise be catalogued a failure.

This plan was never afforded an opportunity to succeed. It had at its inception one of the basic ingredients so necessary for success—sincerity of purpose. From this foundation, with care and effort, it might well have been developed into something extremely worthwhile. However, such consideration was woefully lacking. Confidence and a stable relationship, basic factors necessary for successful development, were conspicuously absent. The timing of the proposal was ill advised. Months of constant effort in order to allay suspicion and bitterness should have preceded the application of the plan. The simple device of announcing a plan developed on a unilateral basis, and then sitting back complacently awaiting results, has seldom achieved the desired objective. This plan not only failed as an instrument of profit sharing, but the impact of its initial reception has so disillusioned the management of this company that they have not recovered from the shock. Its failure haunts every collective bargaining conference, every grievance meeting, and has made it virtually impossible to proceed in the orderly development of a stable, mutually beneficial, collective bargaining relationship.

Profit Sharing Plan Number 3

The employees of this company were organized in 1937 and a satisfactory labor agreement was negotiated within a week following certification of the union as the bargaining agent by the N.L.R.B. The company was a leader in its particular segment of the fabricating industry. Its wage structure was the highest in the community and in the industry; and it had the reputation of being a consistently good profit maker.

The relationship between the union and the company had been a stable, healthy one. In nine years of collective bargaining there had not been a work stoppage of any description. In 1942 a labor-management production committee was set up, and it functioned with much success during the war period.

The labor-management production committee was composed of a subcommittee in each of the five operating departments. The union elected one representative to act on each of the subcommittees and management appointed a representative to serve in like capacity. Their function was to meet at least twice each month to discuss production problems in their particular department and to review all suggestions made by the employees of the department for improvements in productivity and efficiency.

The main committee, which was designated the production and planning committee, consisted of three management representatives—the company president, the general manager, and the auditor—and three union members—the local union president and two members elected by the union membership. Meetings of the committee were held at least once each month, and minutes of the subcommittee meetings were reviewed. All controversial issues which developed in the subcommittee meeting were disposed of by this main committee.

Well pleased with the results of their joint efforts to increase efficiency, and with a sincere desire to continue these efforts during the postwar period, a joint committee made up of management and union representatives began to examine the various types of profit-sharing plans in effect throughout American industry.

The committee's investigation of existing profit-sharing plans began in August 1944 and continued for several months. After a thorough study and a complete analysis of existing plans, they developed one which seemed to fit their particular needs. At this point the joint committee brought their recommendations to the international offices of the union for counsel and review. If the plan was approved, it was to be installed immediately.

Here the committee encountered a serious disappointment. They had developed a straight profit-sharing plan that was not approvable under wage stabilization rules. The problem of producing a temporary plan that would conform to War

Labor Board restrictions was then assigned to the experts of the international union and the president of the company. After weeks of joint study, it was agreed to request N.W.L.B. approval of a plan using as a factor the ratio of labor costs to production values. This ratio had remained fairly constant during the 1938–1944 period. Its high point was 1 to 2.86 and its low point 1 to 2.69, with an average of 1 to 2.77. At this level the company's profit had averaged about 4 percent on net worth. It had not operated in the red over a fourteen-year period. All employees except the president of the company participated in the plan on the basis of 1 per cent increase in earnings for each 1 percent increase in efficiency whether they were on a salary or an hourly rate.

In other words, the percentage of increase in earnings each pay, referred to as a bonus, was equal to the percentage of increase in the ratio of production value to labor cost over the 1944 ratio of 2.77. Had there been a change in the selling price of the items produced, in the cost of materials, or in any factor other than volume of production, a compensating change would have been made in the base on which this bonus was calculated.

The joint operating and administrative committee working with management was given an intensive course of education in the many important factors relating to the business. Controllable cost factors were stressed particularly, in order that all employees might get a clear idea of what they, as a group, could contribute in their efforts to increase productive efficiency. Fixed charges and the impact of greater productivity on unit costs were emphasized. Fuel, material, tools and supplies, delay factors, rejects, salvaged products, better and easier ways of getting the job done—all these and many more problems were tackled. The committee met almost nightly in an effort to make this information available to all employees and to get their suggestions. The problems that had been peculiar to management were now common problems.

A new and improved method of getting material into the shop was developed, reducing unloading cost by 20 per cent. Scrap losses were cut 11 per cent. A bottleneck between the shaping and welding department that had long been a source of expense and difficulty was quickly removed. The bosses were goaded into energetic activities in their efforts to keep ahead of the workers who had their first real opportunity to exercise their know-how and were bent on making good at it. Cost clerks, welders, engineers, and machinists, together with laborers and the plant manager, all had a common interest and were busily engaged as a group in improving that interest. The War Labor Board finally approved the plan. A review of the first nine months of its operation indicates clearly the results attained:

Monthly ratio of labor cost and production value

January	1 to 3.56
February	1 to 2.95[1]
March	1 to 3.98
April	1 to 4.15
May	1 to 3.80
June	1 to 3.50
July	1 to 3.30
August	1 to 3.53
September	1 to 4.41

The change in ratio over this nine-month period was an average of 1 to 3.70, compared with a base ratio in 1944 of 1 to 2.77.

At the end of the first year's operations under this plan, the company's profit was two and one-half times greater than it would have been had the 1 to 2.77 ratio prevailed, and each employee of the company had received a monthly share in the benefits of increased efficiency of approximately 41 percent applied to his base wage rate or salary. At the end of the year, it was mutually decided to change this plan to a straight profit-sharing application. The reasons for the change were that both the union and management recognized factors inherent in the original application that under certain conditions work a hardship for the company. If, for instance, the demand for the prod-

---

[1] Severe snowstorm halted transportation and prevented the men from getting to work.

uct did not permit full production schedules, the employees could maintain their bonus earnings, and, because of constant fixed charges, the company might well suffer losses. The workers' acceptance of this point was possible only because they understood in detail the whole financial picture.

Both parties realized that plant improvements or new equipment installed to improve operating efficiency might drastically affect the ratio of labor costs to sales value. If this situation did arise, it would necessitate a change in the factors in order to protect the company's interests. The local union itself initiated the action for a change to the profit-sharing plan. A series of comparisons tended to show that, had the employees shared in 50 per cent of the profits before taxes during 1945, they would have received approximately 37 per cent on their earnings, a few points below the 41 per cent share accomplished under the labor-cost production value plan. Both the union and management agreed to replace the old plan with the new profit-sharing arrangement effective January 1, 1946. The provisions were:

A. Fifty per cent of the profits before taxes for each month would be paid out as a share on the twentieth day of the succeeding month.

B. The proportionate share figured percentage wise would be applied to the total earnings of each employee for the month in which the profit was earned.

The results achieved in 1946 under the profit-sharing plan were even better than those obtained in 1945. Even though there developed a time lag between a general wage increase in January of 19 cents per hour and an increase in sales price allowed by O.P.A., the employees' share in 1946 averaged out at 54 per cent and the company's profits, before taxes, almost doubled the 1945 figure.

The employees are kept constantly informed of their day-by-day progress. A huge clocklike instrument just inside the main factory entrance records the estimated levels of efficiency being maintained during the current month. One set of hands on the instrument shows the preceding month's levels as compared with the current month.

The results of this joint effort are best exemplified in an action taken by the production committee members of the local union. On discovering that the plant manager, who was also the company president, did not participate on a salary basis but only in the profits, they voluntarily voted him a $12,000-a-year salary, despite the fact that the contract covering the plan did not provide for any change whatsoever and this meant $12,000 less in profits for division.

It is important to note that when the Steelworkers Union made their demand for an 18.5-cent increase per hour in January 1946, causing the shutdown of practically all steel plants, this company was one of the few that maintained operations and applied the increase immediately. In fact the company president was more concerned about the application than were his employees. He reasoned that if they got it one way, they just would not get it the other, and it made little difference to him. He did refuse to deal in half cents, however, and for payroll simplification made it an even 19 cents.

It is pertinent to note that although there has been much controversy over the request of some unions to look at the books, the management of this company invites the union to do so. It was at management's insistence that the following clause was inserted in the profit-sharing agreement: "The United Steelworkers of America, C.I.O., shall have access to the books of the company at any time in order to verify the operating statements."

Two years have elapsed since this provision was placed in the original agreement, yet the union has at no time found it necessary to exercise these rights.

The most interesting factor concerning this plan is that the company is in a highly competitive segment of the steel-fabricating industry. Before adopting the plan, it had been considered the leader in its field. Its wage rates were the highest of nineteen companies surveyed, and since 1930 it had been a consistent profit maker. This marked degree of improvement in productive efficiency was achieved from a level which was considered, cost-wise to be almost perfect. There was no broad area of inefficiency and sloppy management to begin with.

All possible care was exercised in developing this successful plan. A stable union-management relationship predated its application. The plan itself was the product of joint efforts and understanding. A complete sense of partnership and participation was fully developed before the plan was put into operation. The end point was clear and concise. To ensure success, every possible effort was expended in outlining the contribution all employees could make. The workers today know just as much about the company's business as does the boss. They are in every practical sense partners in the venture. The president of the company has stated publicly that the success achieved by this plan would have been impossible without the organization of the employees in a bona fide labor union. He reasons that organized co-operation is most effective, and that to get it he must have organized employees.

The Skeptic's Retort

Much has been written and reported concerning the successes that were achieved with union-management co-operation plans of the prewar period. Studies reveal that practically all the plans were a product of expediency. Most companies and unions that engaged in such programs did so for selfish reasons. The companies involved were generally in a bad way financially, unable to meet competition, and were driven into this type of relationship in an effort to save themselves. Self-preservation and job security were the motivating forces.

Almost without exception, the experts who study profit sharing ask if this type of co-operation could be achieved between union and management in a firm that was operating successfully and making money. Case no. 3 (together with several others that have been developed in the past few years) answers this question satisfactorily. Now these same skeptics are again voicing fears and uncertainties. They are wondering what would happen if profits disappeared and a division was no longer possible. Between the two extremes there is a salient point that they have missed entirely. Whether it is a motivation fostered by a fear for job security or a desire for participation in the benefits of increased efficiency, if the fundamentals of participation and partnership are properly developed, the incentive to produce at the highest possible degree of efficiency is constant.

In any event, success can be achieved only if the employees, through their union, are taken into management's confidence. This is admittedly a broad statement; but let us consider its ramifications. What are the problems affecting the industry, the company, or the plan? The worker would like to know about them. He is anxious to contribute his know-how and intelligence in helping solve these problems. He is not, as a rule, the unthinking, selfish person many people would have us believe. He needs an outline and a proper sense of direction. Granted that a normal evolutionary development has taken him from the area of strife and suspicion, fighting for the very existence of his union, into the area of complete acceptance, a new and different set of constructive activities and responsibilities must replace those he has discarded.

If management expects to gain anything beneficial from these new relationships, it must now devote just as much time and effort in building with the union a complete sense of participation as it has probably spent in the past in fighting the union. As the industrial psychologist might put it, the egoistic needs of the group must be satisfied. Participation and partnership on a democratic basis will furnish these satisfactions.

In all successful plans, whether based on profit sharing or other acceptable factors of measurement, an outline of the future course of the business insofar as it is humanly foreseeable is a prime requisite. Departmental committees, meeting jointly with management, should be given all facts and figures on costs pertaining to their particular departmental operations. This information should deal especially with the costs that are controllable.

Committees should be rotated in order to reach the broadest possible degree of understanding and participation. Each union and management representative on these departmental committees should exercise good judgment in bringing into the meetings from time to time those employees of the department who have the greatest experience and knowledge of the problem outlined for discussion.

The unionization of the workers in many industries in the past ten years must necessarily bring a new approach to this type of problem. Whether or not a union is involved, if profit-sharing plans are to be successful, they must be a product of joint formulation, participation, and responsibility.

Controllable Cost Factors

There has been too much mystery and secrecy in connection with cost factors. The old shibboleth has broken down. The over-emphasis placed on labor costs, inherent in most of the presently applied wage incentive plans, is due for some modification.

The Bureau of Census in its 1939 Census of Manufacturers covering all manufacturing industries showed that the total wage bill in these industries averaged 16 per cent of the plant sales dollar. This figure has undergone some alterations during the war years but it seems unlikely that it has increased above the 20 per cent level. The fact remains that close to 80 per cent of the sales dollar is expended in areas outside the wage bill. There is every indication that in the average plant and industry there necessarily must exist a wide range of costs that lend themselves to worker control. In a general way these factors may seem somewhat broad and indefinite. They will probably include material costs, fuel, power, and general overhead (administrative and factory). Broken down by departments they become more tangible and understandable. Here they may be translated into many subdivided areas of control, such as tools and supplies; fuel consumed; materials wasted; yields, scrap per cent or quality control; impact of greater efficiency on burden costs; delay factors of all descriptions; and impact on costs of processing defective materials.

Few open-hearth workers were aware of the fact that fuel costs per ton were greater than labor costs, that each 1 per cent increase in yields, or the percentage of what came out over what went in, meant a saving of 25 cents per ton; that each hour a furnace was down there was a $45 loss, and that fixed charges were $10 per ton at a certain level of production and could be cut almost in half at double that level.

Few men employed in a rolling mill knew that each hour the mill was down represented a $600 loss. Machine delays and crane delays are costly and represent lowered efficiency. Few employees in a heater plant knew that the burden placed on a heater that sold for $45 was $16.50 when the production level was at 125 units in an eight-hour turn. When they thoroughly understood the impact, not just on labor costs but also on fixed charges, and participated in the over-all benefits, they discovered ways of increasing production to the 200-unit level. When they discovered how costly it was for a defective product to be sent out to the customer and returned, or to require servicing at a far-distant point, they, as a group, exercised much more control over this problem. When they found that a product that was definitely defective in the second operation often went on through fifteen more operations before being scrapped, they had a full knowledge of how costly it was, and reduced this practice to an unbelievable minimum.

Management knows best just what its controllable cost factors are. If a profit-sharing plan is to work successfully, the employees who participate and make it work must have an outline. If they are forced to struggle, with no sense of direction and without a full knowledge of what they can contribute, no worth-while results need be expected. All suggestions designed to increase efficiency should be carefully screened, so that every ounce of know-how available in the working force may be utilized to the best advantage. If this fundamental program is carried out, there should be little need for the fear that is most generally expressed in the question: "What will happen when profits are no longer available to distribute?" If the working force is aware through detailed knowledge of the whole situation that there are no profits for distribution because the company is operating in the red, then they will have a powerful incentive to accomplish the job more efficiently. This background of understanding is most essential to a successful profit-sharing plan.

At about the time when the unions made their last general wage increase demands, there was an influx of proposals from companies suggesting the joint application of various types of profit-sharing plans. In most instances, the unions were forced to reply: "Too little, too late." The time to propose a profit-sharing plan is after the wage increase is granted. It cannot function as a substitute. In a recent example of this approach, typical of many, the president of a fairly large company visited the union office to discuss a plan he had developed. After some exploratory conversation, he outlined his proposal:

A. He did not want to grant a wage increase.
B. His company had never earned over 4 per cent on invested capital.
C. He would divide with his employees 20 per cent of all profits over 6 per cent on invested capital.

Naturally the union was not interested in either the timing or the provisions offered.

Profits, to the average worker, have little significance. The term at best has an unsavory history, one of vague conceptions, subject to all sorts of manipulations by so-called mumbo-jumbo experts. Quite naturally, the worker associates the term with his past experiences. He remembers too well that every time he asked for a wage increase, he discovered to his surprise that the company was losing money. If, in his ignorance, he expressed some disbelief and a lack of understanding, an auditor and an accountant were called in to prove to him that the company was broke.

Conclusion

The analysis of these plans indicates that a sense of participation and partnership is the fundamental prerequisite. If this is fully developed, the type of plan itself is of secondary importance. The employees must be given an opportunity to exercise some degree of control over job security. Their efforts directed toward greater efficiency and productivity must be clearly and directly related to returns. With this foundation the employees of Company C continued to expand and improve their co-operation and efficiency levels even though the method of reward was changed. The substitution of the profit-sharing plan for the one using labor cost ratio to sales value of production in no way influenced the broad over-all results. Hundreds of companies, particularly the smaller ones, caught in the vise of increasingly difficult competition, are looking with greater favor on profit-sharing plans as an answer to their problem. If they are prepared to spend all the time, effort and care necessary for the constructive development of such a plan, they may find their answer. If not, they would be well advised to steer completely clear of the idea of profit-sharing.

CHAPTER 13

SCANLON AND RETAIL STORE PERFORMANCE

K. Dow Scott, Jane Floyd, Philip G. Benson, James W. Bishop

Based on its roots in the 1930s, the Scanlon Plan is often narrowly characterized as a gainsharing program, based on historic labor costs, that is most appropriate for manufacturing companies. However, during the last sixty years Scanlon Plans have been successfully implemented in virtually every industry, and utilize a variety of bonus formulas. What is common among companies that have implemented the Scanlon Plan is their adherence to four fundamental principles that they believe gives their companies a competitive advantage.

These principles were formally articulated by Carl Frost (Frost, Wakeley, and Ruh, 1974; Frost, 1996) and have been refined by numerous companies that have implemented the Scanlon Plan.

Over the years, "Scanlon Companies" and consultants have developed a specific approach for implementing a new Scanlon Plan, or renewing commitment for existing plans. First, there is a widely held belief that a participative leadership approach should be installed participatively. Not only does this approach build commitment for participation, it also helps adapt the plan specifically to the unique characteristics and needs of the organization.

The process often followed has specific steps and has checkpoints to determine levels of commitment. Typically, management explores the potential of the plan for their organization by learning how the plan is designed, how it may affect their company, and what changes will be required to successfully implement the plan. Management attempts to obtain consensus to move forward with the development of the Scanlon Plan. Where unions exist, their leadership is often included in this initial exploration of the Scanlon Principles and Processes.

Next, the senior management team presents to employees the need for such a plan and how the plan will be developed, allowing employees to voice their approval. Usually, some mechanism to judge support for the development of such a plan is used, such as a secret ballot vote. Then, a joint management—employee committee is empowered to develop the plan. Both senior management (representing the investors) and employees must approve a test or trial period for the plan, with employees often giving their approval through a secret ballot.

Finally, the plan is revised as necessary and there is a final approval by senior management and employees to continue use of the plan. Because the markets, competitors and technologies change rapidly today, many companies specify that the plan must be reviewed periodically and redesigned as necessary.

Although the Scanlon Plan was first developed over seventy years ago, Scanlon type programs have only become popular in the 1980s and 90s. Based on a number of surveys (e.g., Markham Scott, and Little, 1992; O'Dell and McAdams, 1987), we estimate that over 15 to 20% of Fortune 500 companies have incentive programs that share the characteristics of a Scanlon Plan for a least one unit within the company. Most work on Scanlon Plans has focused on the manufacturing sector, but we describe here the application of this method in a service organization. Specifically, we describe the implementation of these concepts at a large retailer. Such service applications have been notably absent in the literature on Scanlon Plans (O'Bannon and Pearce, 1999), and this large retailer was motivated to try a different motivation strategy because of sagging sales and loss of market share.

Research Location and Method

The Scanlon Plan was implemented on a trial basis in six stores. Adopting the Scanlon principles and processes at a specific store was voluntary, and required both store management and employee commitment. Each retail store was matched with a control store that closely resembled the store adopting the Scanlon Plan on a number of dimensions (e.g., size, sales volume, and location type). For comparison purposes, comparable data were collected from the control stores at the same points in time.

The goals of the Scanlon Plan are to promote employee ownership perceptions and behavior by:

- Involvement of all store employees in improving business performance,
- Sharing information about business performance and performance goals, and
- Sharing the benefits/consequences of business performance (i.e., shared reward program).

Although the Retailer adapted some of the terminology associated with traditional Scanlon Plans, the fundamental principles of the plan and the process of implementation were carefully followed. The company used both internal and external consultants to help design the plans for each of the six stores, relying heavily on the Scanlon Leadership Network for technical support. The Scanlon Leadership Network is a nonprofit organization, established in 1964, that has been funded by an alliance of companies that have implemented Scanlon Plans.

The size of the stores ranged from 83 to 232 employees; and each store had been in operation at least two years.

Retail store performance was measured on a number of dimensions. First, a customer survey was administered at both the stores where the Scanlon process had been implemented and at the stores used as controls. The customers were asked to rate store friendliness, whether the customer would recommend the store to others, whether the store met their expectations, their loyalty to shopping at the store, and their satisfaction with their shopping experience.

The percentage of employee turnover and the percentage net sales to store plan also were collected. Store turnover ranged from 37.3% to 95%, and net sales percent to plan ranged from 95.5% to 106.2%. These data were collected during the first year the plan was in operation, and the data collected from the comparison stores were for the same time period.

Finally perceptual data were collected from employees concerning their willingness to make suggestions for improvements, to cut costs, and their interest in financial information.

Findings and Discussion

Stores with Scanlon Plans on average received a more favorable response on all customer satisfaction measures of performance than found for control stores. In some cases the difference in scores between stores with and without the Scanlon Plan was substantial. Customers expressed significantly higher levels of satisfaction with their shopping experience and were more likely to have their expectations met in stores with Scanlon Plans than the control stores. Customers indicated that Scanlon stores provided more friendly service and they were more loyal to Scanlon stores than control stores. Scanlon Stores had consistently higher sales performance to sales goals than the control stores. This is particularly impressive since sales are affected by many factors beyond the control of store employees (e.g., economic variables, weather, and changes in customer tastes). Turnover was lower in Scanlon Stores (49%) than in the control stores (63%) by a substantial amount (14%).

Finally, employee willingness to make suggestions is higher in Scanlon Stores (53.2%) than Control Stores (48.3%). Interestingly, employees involved in the implementation of the Scanlon Plan had substantially more favorable response to the question than did employees who were not involved in the implementation of the plan (66.9% and 48.3%, respectively). This same pattern of responses was consistent across the other three questions directed to those involved in the implementation of the plan and employees not directly involved: 1) try to find ways to cut costs (76.8% and 54.9%, respectively), 2) seek out financial information on company performance (59.7% and 36.7%, respectively), and 3) share in the consequences of company financial setbacks (74.0% and 54.6%, respectively).

Although this study does indicate that the Scanlon Plan has a positive impact on retail store performance, there are certain weaknesses inherent in a study of this type. First, there are a limited number of stores that adopted the Scanlon Plan, making statistical comparisons very difficult. Second, stores were not chosen randomly so other store characteristics may have impacted the findings. Third, we are unable to isolate the specific aspects of the Scanlon Plan which contributed to the higher scores on any one of the Scanlon dimensions. As such, there is considerable room to further explore the impact on Scanlon Plan on retail performance data, and customer and employee attitudes.

Conclusions

Our findings support the contribution that Scanlon Plans make to effectiveness of retail stores and to a somewhat lesser degree, to customer satisfaction perceptions. Thus, one need not restrict the use of the Scanlon Plan to manufacturing organizations. Furthermore, employee responses show stronger ownership perceptions among stores that have implemented a Scanlon Plan than those that did not. Not surprisingly, those employees involved in the implementation of the plan had a much more positive response than those who were not involved. This indicates that involvement in the implementation process contributes to employee commitment to the value of the program.

In the course of implementing the Scanlon Plan, the primary internal consultant learned several lessons. First, it is critical to have senior management support and commitment. Second, this is an initiative that cannot be delegated. It also is disruptive to have a store manager leave because the new store manager may not have the same level of commitment or understanding of the program. Third, there will be inherent skepticism among employees that only time and good leadership can overcome. Fourth, it is difficult to recover from false starts. Finally, the Scanlon Plan is not for every store. It is not a panacea, it demands a committed and participative leader, and it can create some turmoil when it is initiated.

Another lesson learned was the importance of having a systematic and participative implementation process. Based on Scanlon methodology a six step process was developed for implementing the plan in the retail stores. These six steps involved:

1. An assessment of the store leader to ensure that he or she would be able to provide the leadership for the Scanlon Plan.

2. An introduction of the Scanlon Plan to store management team and polling them to determine if they thought it would contribute to the success of their store.

3. An introduction of the Scanlon Plan to store employees and polling them to determine if they thought it would contribute to the success of their store.

4. Assembly of a joint employee and management design team to adapt the Scanlon Plan for their store.

5. Having management and employees vote to try the plan for a trial period.

6. At the end of the pilot period, having store management and employees review their experience with the plan, revise it as necessary and assess their commitment to continue the program.

As one can see from this implementation process, a high level of commitment is generated for a plan that impacts productivity. This study is not able to determine what aspect of the plan contributed to their success, such as commitment to participative management, shared reward for meeting goals, or a focus on understanding store performance. Thus, there are several avenues for future research. First, more rigorous research needs to examine what aspects of the Scanlon Plan impact performance. This extension of research is particularly true in the service industry, where store outcomes depend heavily on the service orientation of employees; making traditional views based in formal production methods seem less relevant. Overall, the findings from this study are encouraging, but the use of Scanlon Plans in service companies needs further consideration.

ORGANIZATIONAL CULTURE IN SCANLON FIRMS

CHARLES H. DAVIS

Introduction

Joe Scanlon believed the primary task of management is to create conditions of genuine collaboration. He distained gimmicks and believed cooperation should be a way of life. What did he mean by a way of life?

One definition of "culture" is *the way of life for an entire society.*" If we can understand a society or organization's "culture" we can gain an insight into the way of life . . . values, norms, reward systems, etc. that are the heart of the society or organization. Culture is the vehicle through which individuals coordinate their activities to achieve common goals and expectations. It's *"the way we do things here."* Culture helps individuals understand how their behaviors/priorities fit within their organizations. Culture defines the norms of acceptable conduct.

How are the cultures of firms that practice Scanlon's Principles similar or different from other firms? Do they display a "way of life" that is different? Can the differences be measured? Is it shared by other Scanlon Leaders?

Dr. Carl Frost wrote that the Scanlon Principles help organizations "change forever."

What do Scanlon leaders aspire to change their organizations to? Can it be measured? Do top leadership teams share the same view of where they would like to take their organization? Is it similar or different from the direction other companies are heading? Is there a shared standard of "cultural excellence" among great organizations? Do great organizations share a common vision for change?

To find answers to the these questions, more than 60 Scanlon leaders in nine Scanlon Leadership Network (SLN) member firms participated in an applied research exercise to map their current organizational cultures and identify the cultures they desired for their organizations. Senior managers from SLN member firms mapped their firm's culture using a measurement instrument that was provided by the Hay Group, a global management consultancy active in the areas of performance management, organization effectiveness, and human resource management.

Hay had found that clients with similar strategies could have very different performance results. To explore why organizations obtain such different results, Hay interviewed executives in leading companies throughout the world and discussed the changing nature of work. Hay asked:

- What is your overriding strategic intent?
- How are you structured?
- What are your values?
- How is work organized?
- How are decisions made?
- How are resources allocated?
- What behaviors are encouraged?
- How much power do people have?
- How much risk are they allowed—and do they wish—to take?
- How are they selected and developed?
- How are they rewarded?

Through these intensive interviews Hay discovered four cultural prototypes. Hay maintains that all organizations are a hybrid of these four cultures. Hay used this research to develop a simple and effective way to measure the four cultures.

The Hay Group culture measurement instrument has been used in hundreds of organizations. It is described in the book *People, Performance, and Pay* by Flannery, Hofrichter and Platten. Hay was able to provide benchmark data to SLN members from thousands of leaders in many different industries. Of particular interest to SLN members was Hay's culture data on the firms in *Fortune's* "most admired" list. (Hay conducts the research that Fortune uses to generate the list each year and has obtained culture data from firms on the list.)

The Hay Group was interested in studying SLN companies because Hay had identified a typical work culture profile associated with gainsharing practices and they wanted to see if the Scanlon cultures matched this predicted gainsharing culture.

The Hay Group's conceptual framework for culture is comprised of four operational dimensions (technology, reliability, customers, and flexibility) and four principal cultural models: the process culture, the time-based culture, the network culture, and the functional culture (see Figure 1).

These models show "how organizations are changing from the more traditional hierarchical functional model of work to other models to meet changing business needs" (Shields, 1999). The models "provide a way of characterizing the behaviors that are most important within an organization for supporting the business strategy and achieving the desired results" although few organizations are culturally pure (ibid.).

Methodology for Measuring Culture

In the Hay Group's Target Culture Modeling procedure, each of 56 culture attributes is printed on a small card. Respondents model their firm's current and target culture by rank-ordering the cards from "this organization rewards, encourages, and supports the following Behaviors and Activities" along a continuum from "very frequently/to a great extent/in most parts of the organization" to "very infrequently/to a small extent/in few parts of the organization." Cards are rank-ordered in a forced distribution comprised of seven degrees of agreement, as shown in Figure 2.

Achieving Strategy Through People

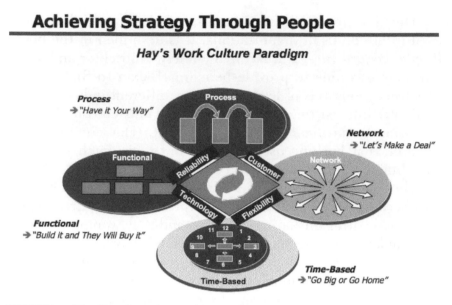

FIGURE 1. The Hay Group's Four Principal Organizational Culture Models
Source: Flannery, Hofrichter & Platten (1996)

Hay's Targeted Culture Modeling Process ^{SM}

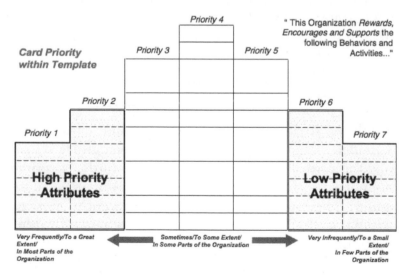

FIGURE 2. The Hay Organizational Culture Model Process

In the forced distribution, five statements best describe the culture in question and five statements are the least descriptive of the culture. The remaining statements are ranked in descending order in columns of seven, ten, twelve, ten, and seven statements respectively.[1] The statements that best describe the culture are scored +3. Statements in subsequent columns are scored +2, +1, 0, −1, −2, and −3 (see Figure 2).

The traditional form of business organization is the Functional model of work culture. It is characterized by administrative hierarchies that control the execution of standardized tasks with consistency, reliability, and efficiency. The five cultural attributes that are most encouraged, supported, and rewarded in the Functional model are:[2]

7. Being highly organized
8. Using proven methods to serve existing markets
18. Maintaining clear lines of authority and accountability
32. Limiting the downside of risk
45. Minimizing unpredictability of business results

According to the Hay Group, many Functional cultures are evolving into Process cultures, which are more flexible and more sensitive to customer satisfaction and product and service quality than Functional cultures. With this change in orientation comes an emphasis on cross-functional team performance around business processes, and location of planning, execution, and control activities close to the customer. Today many manufacturing organizations are trying to become "lean" using methods developed by Toyota. Lean organizations display characteristics of the Hay Process culture. The five cultural attributes that are most encouraged, supported and rewarded in the Process model are:

[1] The position of a statement in a column is not significant.
[2] Numbers refer to the items on the list of 56 cultural attributes in Table 1. The description of the Hay Group's four model cultures is from Flannery, Hofrichter & Platten (1996) and Shields (1999).

4. Maximizing customer satisfaction

6. Demonstrating understanding of the customer's point of view

13. Delivering reliably on commitments to customers

20. Continuously improving operations

46. Gaining the confidence of customers

Examples of firms that have moved to Process cultures are Cabot Corporation, Hallmark Cards, and Harvard Pilgrim Health Care (Flannery, Hofrichter & Platten, 1996).

However, two other models of organizational culture are emerging to replace Functional cultures: the Time-based model and the Network model. The Time-based model emphasizes agility in product and service innovation to capture market opportunities. Firms with Time-based cultures limit managerial hierarchies and develop capabilities around multifunctional individuals. Time-based firms strive to dominate markets in their high-profitability phases and move on to other opportunities when the markets mature (ibid.). The five cultural attributes that are most encouraged, supported and rewarded in Time-based cultures are:

9. Significantly decreasing cycle times

54. Developing new products or services

25. Maintaining a high sense of urgency

27. Capitalizing on windows of opportunity

42. Adapting quickly to changes in the business environment

The Network model emphasizes flexibility and responsiveness to customers. Like the Time-based culture, Network culture firms must match product innovation with market opportunities. However, in Network cultures, work is project-based and involves temporary alliances that bring together competencies from within and outside the firm. Managers in Network cultures are producers who coordinate venture projects based on talented individuals. The entertainment and construction industries provide a good illustration of Network culture (ibid.). The five cultural attributes that are most encouraged, supported and rewarded in Network cultures are:

54. Developing new products or services
27. Capitalizing on windows of opportunity
12. Establishing new ventures or new lines of business
41. Building strategic alliances with other organizations
33. Using resources outside the company to get things done

The Hay Group has also identified an ideal Gainsharing culture. The Gainsharing culture encourages continuous improvement, delegation of decision-making, and rewards for performance. Behavior and activities that are most encouraged, supported and rewarded in the ideal Gainsharing culture are:

14. Being flexible in thinking and approach
20. Continuously improving operations
34. Capitalizing on creativity and innovation
36. Taking initiative
51. Pushing decision-making to the lowest levels

Results of the Culture Study

Results were analyzed using two distinct methodologies. The data were first analyzed by Hay and then by the author. Hay reported the Scanlon results by comparing them to their database using correlations and percentiles. I used a different analytical technique called "Q" which will be explained later.

Hay Results

There is a shared "way of life" or culture in Scanlon organizations. Hay found that current Scanlon cultures map 100% to the Process culture (see Figure 3).

Scanlon Leaders build Process cultures that reliably meet the needs of customers by sharing information, working to-

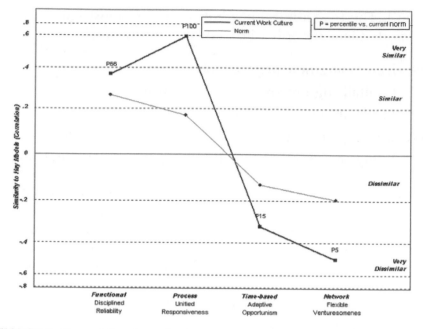

FIGURE 3. Current Scanlon culture

gether to solve problems and by investing in developing the competence of the entire workforce. Many are engaged in lean practices that use "value stream mapping" and other lean techniques to better align with the needs of their customers.

Scanlon organizations share elements of the Functional culture and less of the Time-based and Network cultures than the Hay norms. Most of the Scanlon organizations surveyed are engaged in manufacturing. Historically, most were Traditional culture organizations. Often they embraced Scanlon as a way to change their culture in a more Process direction.

Scanlon Organizations currently share few elements of the Time-based or Network cultures. Scanlon's focus is on building long term relationships with customers, investors and employees. Time-based and Network cultures are not dependent on long term relationships. Group rewards and recognition are stressed in Scanlon/Process cultures as opposed to individual rewards and recognition in the Time-based and Network cultures.

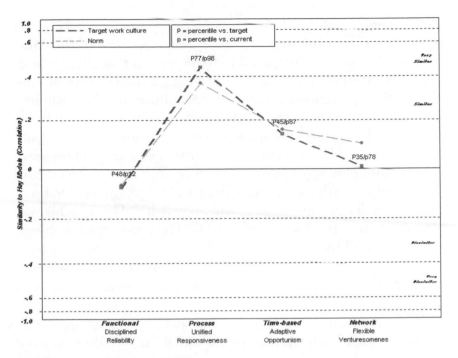

FIGURE 4. Scanlon desired culture

Scanlon Leaders are remarkably similar to other business leaders in what they want their desired culture to be (see Figure 4).

Scanlon leaders do not see much future in the Traditional culture with its rigid structures and hierarchies. The future appears to belong to organizations with a Process culture with elements of the Time-based and Network cultures.

Today's leaders understand that the customer is king, but they need more innovation, flexibility and speed. Their challenge is to create cultures of innovation, flexibility and speed while serving their customers and earning the commitment of employees.

Scanlon Culture Compared to Most Admired Companies

Scanlon Leaders were compared to the "Most Admired Companies." (The Most Admired Companies are Fortune 500 companies recognized by their peers as being the best). Hay has found that one of the distinguishing characteristics of the Most Admired Companies compared to their peers is that the top leaders in the Most Admired Companies have a high degree of consensus (99th percentile) on what their "culture" is. Most Admired Companies can be found with all four cultural preferences. Whatever the culture, the leaders see it the same. Scanlon leaders were in the 87th percentile. In average companies many leaders have blinders on. They do not truly understand the culture of their organizations and they are not in agreement. Dr Frost taught Scanlon leaders to ask "what day is it?" This was his way of making sure they focused on reality. The cooperation between employees and their leaders and the communication that travels up and down Scanlon organizations (and the Most Admired Companies) helps leaders to truly understand the culture or "way of life" in their organizations.

Leaders of the Most Admired Companies and Scanlon leaders were remarkably similar in the attributes of their desired culture (see Figure 5).

The most admired company leaders were only in the 38th percentile on consensus for their target culture. Scanlon leaders were in the 98th percentile!

Same Top 3 Target Attributes

Top Priorities in Target Culture

Target Attributes of the World's Most Admired vs Scanlon Companies	World's Most Admired	Scanlon Companies
	Maximizing customer satisfaction	Maximizing customer satisfaction
	Encouraging teamwork	Encouraging teamwork
	Delivering reliably on commitments to customers	Delivering reliably on commitments to customers
	Rewarding superior performance	Continuously improving operations
	Gaining the confidence of customers	Demonstrating understanding of customer's point of view

FIGURE 5. Top priorities of desired culture: Most Admired companies and Scanlon companies

Q Analysis

The Hay Group's Targeted Culture Modeling procedure resembles Q-sorting but in the Q technique respondents' sorts are factor analyzed rather than aggregating them by averaging the scores. Q analysis identifies shared viewpoints among individuals.

The nine SLN members produced 61 "as is" (current culture) and 61 "to be" (desired culture) sorts. The author factor-analyzed the two sets of data separately using PCQ for Windows, a commercial software package for Q methodology. In each case, the simplest solution was a two-factor solution.[3]

In other words, Scanlon members see two distinct current cultures and two desired cultures. Scores defining each culture are provided in Table 1.

Of the two current cultural models that characterize the SLN member firms that participated in the culture study, one is a version of the Functional culture. Scores are provided in column A of Table 1. Ten SLN respondents from three firms loaded significantly on this factor. Activities and behavior that are most encouraged, supported and rewarded in the Scanlon version of Functional culture are:

2. Supporting the decisions of one's boss
26. Establishing clear job descriptions and requirements
37. Respecting the chain of command
50. Supporting top management decisions
55. Being loyal and committed to the company

This Functional culture obviously values hierarchical control above everything else, including improved performance. It describes a command-and-control organization that is animated and directed entirely by senior management.

The second current Scanlon organizational culture is a version of the Process culture. Thirty-one respondents from six

---

[3]The simplest factor solution is the one with the fewest factors in which the largest number of respondents load significantly on one factor only.

TABLE 1. The 56 attributes in the Hay Group's work culture model and their scores on 9 models of organizational culture

	A	B	C	D	E	F	G	H	I
1 Encouraging teamwork	+1	+2	+3	+3	-2	+3	0	-1	+2
2 Supporting the decisions of one's boss	+3	+1	-2	+2	-1	-3	0	-2	-3
3 Providing secure employment	+2	+2	-1	+2	+2	0	-2	-3	-2
4 Maximizing customer satisfaction	0	+3	+3	+3	+1	+3	-1	0	0
5 Experimenting with new management techniques	-1	-3	0	-1	-3	-1	-2	0	+1
6 Demonstrating understanding of the customer's point of view	-1	+2	+2	+3	0	+2	-1	+1	-1
7 Being highly organized	+1	-2	-1	+1	+3	0	+1	-1	-2
8 Using proven methods to serve existing markets	+2	+2	-1	0	+2	+1	0	-2	-1
9 Significantly decreasing cycle times	0	-2	+1	0	-3	-1	+3	0	+1
10 Providing employees with resources to satisfy customers	0	+1	+2	+2	0	+2	+1	-1	+1
11 Maintaining existing customer accounts	+2	+3	-1	+2	+3	+2	-1	+1	-1
12 Establishing new ventures or new lines of business	-3	-1	+1	-1	-2	0	+1	+2	0
13 Delivering reliably on commitments to customers	0	+3	+3	+3	+1	+3	-1	0	0
14 Being flexible and adaptive in thinking and approach	-2	1	+2	+1	-1	0	+1	+2	+3
15 Using limited resources effectively	+1	0	-1	0	+1	-3	+2	-2	0
16 Selling successfully	0	+1	+1	+1	+1	-1	0	+2	0
17 Promoting one's point of view strongly	+1	-3	-3	-3	-3	-2	-1	0	-3
18 Maintaining clear lines of authority and accountability	+2	-3	-3	+1	+2	0	-3	+1	-3
19 Establishing clear, well-documented work processes	+2	-1	0	+1	+3	+2	-2	-3	+1
20 Continuously improving operations	+1	+1	+3	+2	0	+3	-3	-1	+3
21 Attracting top talent	-2	-2	0	+1	+1	-2	+2	+3	0
22 Treating employees fairly and consistently	+1	+2	+1	+2	+2	+1	0	-2	+1

(continued)

TABLE 1. *Continued*

		A	B	C	D	E	F	G	H	I
23	Rewarding superior performance	−1	0	0	+2	0	0	+2	+1	+1
24	Pioneering new ways of doing things	−3	−1	+2	−1	−1	0	+1	+2	+2
25	Maintaining a high sense of urgency	0	0	0	0	−2	−1	+3	0	−1
26	Establishing clear job descriptions and requirements	+3	−2	−2	+1	+1	−3	−1	−2	−2
27	Capitalizing on windows of opportunity	−2	+1	+1	0	−1	−2	+1	+3	0
28	Applying innovative technology to new situations	−3	0	0	−1	−1	−3	+2	+1	+1
29	Tolerating well-meaning mistakes	0	+1	0	−2	−1	+1	−3	0	+2
30	Responding to customer feedback	+1	+3	+1	+1	0	+2	−2	−1	0
31	Participating in training and continuing education	+1	0	0	0	0	+1	−1	−2	+2
32	Limiting the downside of risks	+2	1	−2	−2	+3	−1	−2	0	−2
33	Using resources outside the company to get things done	−1	−2	−1	−2	0	−2	+1	+3	−1
34	Capitalizing on creativity and innovation	−3	0	+3	0	−3	0	+1	+2	+3
35	Anticipating changes in the business environment	−1	0	0	0	+2	+1	+3	0	0
36	Taking initiative	−2	1	+2	0	−1	0	+2	+1	+3
37	Respecting the chain of command	+3	−1	−3	0	0	−2	−1	−3	−3
38	Organizing jobs around capabilities of individuals	0	0	−2	−2	−3	+1	0	+1	0
39	Increasing decision making speed	−1	0	+1	−1	0	+1	+2	−1	+1
40	Encouraging innovation	−2	1	+2	0	−1	0	+1	+2	+2
41	Building strategic alliances with other organizations	−1	−3	0	−1	−2	−3	0	+3	−1
42	Adapting quickly to changes in the business environment	−3	0	+1	0	0	−1	+2	+3	0
43	Taking action despite uncertainty	−2	0	0	−3	−1	−2	+3	+1	+1
44	Quality checking subordinates work	1	−1	−3	−2	+1	−2	−3	0	−2
45	Minimizing unpredictability of business results	0	−2	−2	−3	+3	−1	0	+1	−2

(*continued*)

TABLE 1. *Continued*

		A	B	C	D	E	F	G	H	I
46	Gaining the confidence of customers	+2	+3	+1	+3	0	+3	−2	−1	−1
47	Encouraging expression of diverse viewpoints	−1	−1	0	−2	−2	+1	−1	0	+2
48	Being precise	1	−2	−3	−1	+2	0	−3	−1	−2
49	Acquiring cross-functional knowledge and skills	0	−1	−1	−2	−2	+2	0	−1	0
50	Supporting top management decisions	+3	+1	−2	+1	+1	−1	−2	0	−3
51	Pushing decision-making to the lowest levels	−1	−1	+2	−3	−1	+1	0	−2	+3
52	Minimizing human error	0	−1	−2	−1	+1	−1	0	−3	−1
53	Finding novel ways to capitalize on skills that people have	−1	−3	−1	−3	−2	0	−1	+1	+2
54	Developing new products or services	−2	+2	+1	−1	+1	0	+3	+2	−1
55	Being loyal and committed to the company	+3	+2	−1	+1	+2	+1	0	−3	+1
56	Achieving budgeted objectives	0	0	−1	−1	0	+2	+1	−1	−1

A: Scanlon Leadership Network "As-Is" Organizational Culture no. 1 (Functional culture)
B: Scanlon Leadership Network "As-Is" Organizational Culture no. 2 (Process culture)
C: Scanlon Leadership Network "To-Be" Organizational Culture no. 1 (Gainsharing culture)
D: Scanlon Leadership Network "To-Be" Organizational Culture no. 2 (Commando culture)
E: Hay Group Functional Organizational Culture
F: Hay Group Process Organizational Culture
G: Hay Group Time-Based Organizational Culture
H: Hay Group Network Organizational Culture
I: Hay Group Ideal Gainsharing Culture

SLN firms loaded significantly on this factor. Complete scores are provided in column B of Table 1. The following cultural attributes are most supported, encouraged and rewarded in the Scanlon version of the Process culture:

4. Maximizing customer satisfaction
11. Maintaining existing customer accounts
13. Delivering reliably on commitments to customers
30. Responding to customer feedback
46. Gaining the confidence of customers

Clearly, the Scanlon version of the Process customer focuses primarily on customers. Some SLN firms have developed considerable customer-centricity. The Scanlon Process culture differs from the Process culture identified by the Hay Group in its greater emphasis on customer-centricity over cross-functional organizational structures.

SLN members identified two target organizational cultures. These are described in columns C and D of Table 1. One of the target cultures is a Scanlon version of the ideal Gainsharing culture as described by the Hay Group. It also has some characteristics of a Time-based culture. Nineteen SLN respondents from six firms loaded significantly on this factor. The following behaviors and activities are most supported, rewarded, and encouraged in the SLN version of the Gainsharing culture:

1. Encouraging teamwork
4. Maximizing customer satisfaction
13. Delivering reliably on commitments to customers
20. Continuously improving operations
34. Capitalizing on creativity and innovation

The second target SLN cultural model is unique. It does not correspond to any of the Hay Group's main organizational cultures or to the ideal Gainsharing culture either. I will call it a "Commando" cultural model because it seeks the benefits of teamwork and customer-centricity while retaining highly centralized executive decision making. Twenty-eight SLN respondents from six firms loaded significantly on this factor. The behaviors and activities that are most encouraged, supported and rewarded in the second SLN target culture are:

1. Encouraging teamwork
4. Maximizing customer satisfaction
6. Demonstrating understanding of the customer's point of view

13. Delivering reliably on commitments to customers

46. Gaining the confidence of customers

The main difference between the two SLN target cultures (Scanlon Gainsharing and Commando) has to do with responsibility for decision-making. The SLN target Gainsharing culture relies on employee empowerment and decentralized decision-making, while the Commando target culture centralizes decision-making at the top and favors employment security as an explicit goal. For example, the Scanlon Gainsharing culture does not reward "supporting the decisions of one's boss" (statement no. 2 is scored –2), while the Commando model does (+2). The SLN Gainsharing culture pushes decisions to the lowest levels (statement 51 is scored +2) while the Commando culture retains central control (–3). The Commando culture model encourages employment security (statement no. 3: +2) and the Process model does not (–2). The Commando culture rewards superior performance (statement 23: +2) and is intolerant of well-meaning mistakes (statement 29: –2). Also, the Commando cultural model is indifferent to creativity and innovation (statement 34 is scored 0) and initiative (statement 36 is scored 0) while the SLN Process model values them highly (+3 and +2 respectively).

The SLN Commando cultural model seems to be saying that the key to competitiveness in the current business climate is a social contract between enlightened senior leadership and workers. According to this contract, if work is properly performed by work teams to produce continuously improved products for current customers, if employees are treated fairly, and if superior performance is rewarded, then the firm can compete and employment security can be provided. But execution of strategies must be disciplined and precise, without internal dissent. This may be how Scanlon leaders perceived their situation in 2004, when many manufacturers saw their customers moving to low-wage production locations, and many executives were wondering if they would have to follow suit to stay in business. Most SLN firms consider that they have already moved toward a Process culture model. If the Process model does not provide sufficient capabilities to overcome the threats of rapid globalization, then which model does? Does a Commando organizational culture provide a foundation for a viable business model, or is it instead a tactical approach to ensuring social cohesion during a time of tension and uncertainty?

Culture Change: moving from one organizational culture to another

The Hay Group's Targeted Culture Modeling procedure provides a useful benchmark for changing specific behaviors and activities that constitute an organizational culture. The complementary procedure described here uses the Q-sort data provided by SLN members to systematically compare a current with a target culture and identify specific actions that organizational leaders need to take. I will illustrate the procedure with case one of the Scanlon Leadership Network member firms, "ABC Co." According to the Q-sort data provided by five of ABC Co.'s senior managers, this firm needs to move from a current Functional culture to a target Gainsharing culture. Using normalized scores from the Q-sort, all 56 cultural attributes are arrayed on two dimensions in Figure 6: as-is (the current culture) is the vertical dimension and to-be (the desired culture) is the horizontal dimension. The resulting four quadrants identify the behaviors that are to be maintained, developed, eliminated, and avoided.

The behaviors in the upper right quadrant are ones that are already strongly encouraged in the current culture and also desired in the target culture. They should therefore be **maintained**. They are:

4. Maximizing customer satisfaction
20. Continuously improving operations
10. Providing employees with resources to satisfy customers

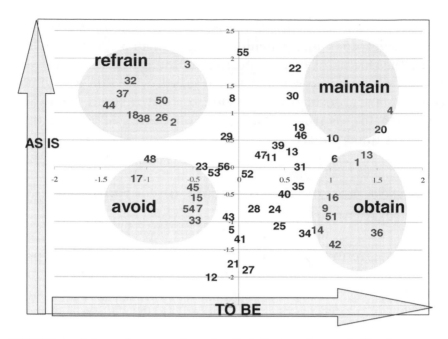

FIGURE 6. Culture change roadmap for ABC Co. Numbers in bold refer to items in the Hay Group's work culture model as listed in Table 1.

The behaviors in the lower right quadrant are not encouraged in the current culture, and they must be developed in the target culture. Therefore they must be **obtained**. They are:

36. Taking initiative
13. Delivering reliably on commitments to customers
 1. Encouraging teamwork
42. Adapting quickly to changes in the business environment
51. Pushing decision-making to the lowest levels
 9. Significantly decreasing cycle times
16. Selling successfully

These behaviors can be developed through rewards, recognition, training, teambuilding, and other organizational development initiatives.

The behaviors in the upper left quadrant are encouraged in the current culture but they are to be discouraged in the target culture. The firm must **refrain** from rewarding or encouraging them. They are, notably,

32. Limiting the downside of risk
37. Respecting the chain of command
44. Quality checking subordinates' work
18. Maintaining clear lines of authority and accountability
38. Organizing jobs around capabilities of individuals
50. Supporting top management decisions
26. Establishing clear job descriptions and requirements
 3. Providing secure employment
 2. Supporting the decisions of one's boss

The behaviors in the lower left-hand quadrant are not encouraged in the current culture and are not desired in the target culture. Leaders must ensure that the firm **avoids** undue encouragement of these behaviors. They include:

 7. Being highly organized
54. Developing new products or services
33. Using resources outside the company to get things done
17. Promoting one's point of view strongly

By identifying the work behaviors and organizational attributes to maintain, obtain, refrain from adopting, and avoid, leaders can provide a relatively high degree of clarity to organizational members, who otherwise might be unsure of how to interpret organizational changes that are expressed in high level statements about mission or strategic intent. In the case of ABC Co., it is clear that a customer-centric orientation is to be maintained and strengthened through new behaviors having to do with teamwork, initiative, and pro-active selling. At the same time, ABC Co. must unlearn a variety of hierarchical administrative behaviors, and it must not allow itself to lose focus by being excessively organized, excessively concerned with individuals' issues, or excessively involved in production of novelty.

Conclusions

There is a shared "way of life" or culture among Scanlon Leaders. It maps with what the Hay Group has identified as a "Process" culture. Organizations with Process cultures compete by reliably meeting the needs of their customers. The emphasis is on long term relationships with investors, customers and employees. Employees are expected to know the needs of their customers. Teams and reward systems like gainsharing emphasize the group over the individual. Most large organizations in Hay's database want to develop Process cultures. The Process culture focus on customers is also shared with "the Most Admired Companies."

However, while leaders want the Process culture, they also are seeking the speed innovation and flexibility inherent in the Time-based and Network cultures. The business press is full of examples of organizations that are outsourcing, insourcing, partnering, rewarding key champions, etc.—all elements of the Networking and Time-based cultures. Can elements of the Time-based and Networking culture be adopted without losing the core Process culture? That is a key challenge facing today's Scanlon leaders. Some Scanlon leaders are also interested in a "Commando" cultural model that is rapid, team-based, management-led, and customer-centric.

Culture change is a significant management challenge. Q methodology provides an effective way for leadership teams to visually map their current and desired cultures. When culture can be visualized it can be discussed providing a valuable mechanism for leaders to build consensus on their current culture and the specific actions they need to take to reach their desired culture.

CHAPTER 15

THE ABC'S OF GAINSHARING: LESSONS FROM THE SCANLON PLAN

PAUL W. DAVIS AND
MAJEL C. MAES

Why Gainsharing?

Today there is increased interest in gainsharing, a management concept that has endured for more than a century. Gainsharing is a guiding management philosophy of at least five organizations that have been featured as one of the"100 Best Companies to Work for in America". Donnelly Corporation, Herman Miller, Beth Israel Hospital, Motorola, and Dana have all credited at least part of their world class performance to their gainsharing systems.[1]

A comprehensive study conducted by the American Compensation Association beginning in 1989 and published in 1994 found companies averaged over $2410 per employee per year in productivity and quality improvements after installing gainsharing. Subsequent ACA research has confirmed the initial findings. After deducting program expenses, and after paying bonuses of 4–5% (median) of base pay per employee per year, they received a 222% return on every dollar paid

---

[1] Robert Levering and Milton Moskowitz, *The 100 Best Companies to Work For In America* (New York: Doubleday, 1993)

out.[2] The financial results are impressive, yet they are only one of the many benefits of gainsharing. Study after study has found that gainsharing programs also improve employee involvement, communication, teamwork, labor relations, and quality.[3]

A 1998 study entitled "Participation, Achievement, Rewards-Creating the Infrastructure For Managing Continuous Improvement ("PAR") conducted by Work In America Institute concluded that "gainsharing, based on a participative work system . . . strengthens the link between pay and performance and mobilizes everyone in the organization to work toward common goals. It can motivate levels of commitment and achievement that are vital to continuous improvement but that cannot be achieved through traditional merit pay systems."[4]

The renewed interest in such an old concept can be attributed to pressures that organizations are now facing. Cost cutting, layoffs, and mergers are considered par for the course. As companies downsize, they seek ways to motivate the remaining employees. As they become flatter and more lean, the old methods of compensation (number of direct reports, etc.) are no longer effective. As competitive pressures increase, they seek ways to increase productivity and quality. After adopting Total Quality Management (TQM) practices, they seek ways to reward and coordinate teams. Unable to afford the high cost of adversarial relationships and ever increasing base wages, union and management leaders look to gainsharing as a way to encourage cooperation within collective bargaining.

[2] Jerry L. McAdams and Elizabeth J. Hawk, *Organizational Performance & Rewards: 663 Experiences in Making the Link* (American Compensation Association and Martiz Inc., 1994)

[3] Schuster, M., Forty Years of Scanlon Plan Research: A Review of the Descriptive and Empirical Literature. International Yearbook of Organizational Democracy, 1, 1983, 53–71.

[4] Jerome M Rosow, Jill Castner-Lotto, and John V. Hickey, *Participation, Achievement, Reward—Creating the Infrastructure For Managing Continuous Improvement* (New York: Work in America Institute, Inc. 1998): p. ix.

What is Gainsharing?

The Japanese have a fable about a crow and a cormorant. In this ancient tale a crow admires the cormorant, a black water bird that can swim in order to catch fish. The crow reasons that because he is a black bird like the cormorant, he too should be able to swim, so he dives into the water only to drown. The fable's lesson is that things that appear to be the same may not be, due to subtle, obscure differences. Those interested in gain-sharing should remember the crow's experience, because gain-sharing systems that at first appear to be identical reveal fundamental differences upon closer scrutiny.

Gainsharing is a generic term with widely different defini-tions. For many, gainsharing is simply a group bonus calcula-tion. For others, gainsharing describes a very sophisticated organizational development strategy. For the purpose of this arti-cle, the term 'gainsharing' will describe any organizational pro-cess designed to increase productivity, quality and financial performance by sharing "rewards" with groups of employees. Furthermore, it will refer to practices that include 1) the estab-lishment of specific goals, targets or baselines, 2) the commu-nication to a group of employees of these goals, targets or baselines, and 3) the sharing of rewards when the goals, tar-gets or baselines are exceeded.

This operational definition of gainsharing will not include discretionary management "bonus" practices such as an annual Christmas bonus because they are not tied to the specific per-formance of the company. In addition, it will not include indi-vidual piecework or merit systems since they reward individuals and not groups. However, profit sharing will be considered a form of gainsharing.

The ABC's of Gainsharing

Most of what is written about gainsharing concerns the mechanics of bonus formulas because various gainsharing sys-tems are typically classified by how the bonus formula is constructed. In these articles Scanlon Plans, Multicost Scanlon Plans, Rucker Plans®, Improshare®, Profit Sharing, etc. are reduced to a paragraph that only an accountant could love. *While the formula is important for gainsharing success it is only one factor among many that differentiate the various approaches.* Recent research indicates bonus formulas may not be the most important factors in gainsharing success.[5] A 1998 American Compensation Association study conducted by the Consortium for Alternative Reward Strategies (CARS) produced these major findings:

1) Differences in plan implementation and support drive effectiveness nearly twice as much as differences in plan design.

2) The strongest driver of culture that supports plan effectiveness is the [general] manager, and through his/her example, the direct supervisors of people.

3) What separates the effective and ineffective plans is how well employees understand the details of the measurements, and what they can do to influence them.

4) How much people think about the plan is a key indicator of effectiveness.

5) Companies are missing the boat by not providing recognition as a part of the Group Incentive plan.[6]

In addition, almost all articles written about the Scanlon Plan's bonus calculation since the 1960's are misleading in documenting Scanlon evolution. They have not kept up with current Scanlon theory or application. While they are valuable as history, they provide little insight for those interested in the current state of the art in gainsharing.

The final reason why the formula approach to describing gainsharing is no longer effective is because it describes fewer and fewer gainsharing applications. Historically, gainsharing

[5] Kim, Dong-One, "Factors Influencing Organizational Performance in Gainsharing Programs," 1994, University of Wisconsin–Madison, unpublished paper.
[6] Jerry McAdams, *Research From the Trenches . . . Making Group Incentives Work* (Consortium for Alternative Reward Strategies IV, 1998).

plans were one-size-fits-all, developed by consultants who trademarked their approaches. Improshare® and Rucker® are two of the most well known. While Improshare® Plans are still being installed, the Rucker® Plan did not survive long after the death of its creator. Today, there are still consultants trying to trademark their approaches but most gainsharing systems are customized to the unique needs of each organization.

A new method of classifying the various gainsharing approaches is needed if the reader truly wants to understand the critical differences and make an informed choice. This article will attempt to help the reader understand the ABC's of gainsharing. This simple device where A = Assumptions, B = Business Literacy, and C = Commitment will help readers understand which gainsharing approach is right for them. If the ABC's can be mastered, the rest of gainsharing (including designing the bonus formula) will be easier. Because there are only two classic approaches that have survived the test of time, Scanlon and Improshare®, they will be used to highlight differences in philosophy and application.

A = Assumptions

All gainsharing systems are developed for some desired end. Typically the motivation may be to produce greater profits, to produce higher quality, or to encourage labor-management cooperation. At the heart of every gainsharing system are assumptions about human motivation and behavior at work. *Gainsharing systems take on specific characteristic based on the assumptions of those who lead, design, and operate them.* These assumptions define the program to a much greater extent than does the method of bonus calculation.

B = Business Literacy

All gainsharing systems claim to increase productivity, profits, or performance. Some are based on the idea that the only thing needed to generate these improvements is more financial motivation, while others stress the importance of teaching employees about the business so that they will know what to improve and how to participate in improving it.

C = Commitment

Gainsharing is a way to change the commitment level of people at work. All gainsharing systems attempt to shift commitment from the individual to a group or organization. The various approaches differ in the size of the group and the level of commitment they attempt to create.

A = Assumptions About Human Motivation

Throughout human history we have sought to harness and control human motivation. We have used a wide range of "motivators" to get people to do what we want. We have used punishment from slavery to starvation and we have used rewards from concubines to precious metals. As society became more civilized, we developed money as the universal form of exchange. With industrialization, we developed a wage system where people work for money that they can then use to purchase desired goods and services.

Despite thousands of years of experimentation, there is still great disagreement about what does and does not motivate. Since motivation is the primary reason organizations install gainsharing, the debate is not academic. Research has produced results that at times seem to contradict what most of us assume is common sense. For example, we have learned through research that money may not be as powerful a motivator as non-monetary rewards. Psychologists have attempted to unwrap the mystery of human motivation, yet there are still wide differences of opinion on: 1) Whether one human being can motivate another: is motivation intrinsic or extrinsic? 2) What motivates people at work? 3) What is the best way for managers to motivate workers? 4) Is money the universal motivator?

Can One Human Being Motivate Another?

All gainsharing systems use some form of incentive or financial reward. So, like the crow, we might assume that all gainsharing philosophies believe deeply in the power of extrinsic motivation. They do not. Scanlon Plans place more of an emphasis on the intrinsic motivation created by participation and education rather than on the extrinsic motivation created by money. Improshare® Plans place more of an emphasis on extrinsic motivation. Alfie Kohn, author of *Punished by Rewards: The Trouble with Gold Stars, Incentive Plans, A's, Praise, and Other Bribes*, argues that the only thing accomplished when we try to motivate others is to destroy the intrinsic motivation in each of us. He quotes one of the foremost management scholars and researchers on human motivation, Frederick Herzberg, who said:

> *Managers do not motivate employees by giving them higher wages, more benefits or new status symbols. Rather employees are motivated by their own inherent need to succeed at a challenging task. The manager's job then, is not to motivate people to get them to achieve; instead, the manager should provide opportunities for people to achieve so they will become motivated.*[7]

Herzberg said this about the typical manager's common sense approach to motivation:

> *Managements have always looked at man as an animal to be manipulated with a carrot and a stick. They found that when a man hurts, he will move to avoid pain—and they say, "We're motivating the employees." Hell, you're not motivating them, you're moving them.*[8]

[7] Alfie Kohn, Punished by Rewards: *The Trouble with Gold Stars, Incentive Plans, A's, Praise, and Other Bribes* (New York: Houghton Mifflin Company, 1993): p. 190.
[8] Lewis Eigen and Jonathan P. Siegel, *The Manager's Book of Quotations* (New York: AMACOM, 1989): p. 271.

What Motivates People at Work?

Researchers and management scholars believe that we each have different needs and, therefore, different motivators. Abraham Maslow predicted that human beings fulfill their needs in a certain order. First, they have a need to eat, sleep, and breathe. He called these physiological needs. When these needs are met, he predicted people would seek to have their security and safety needs met. Maslow believed physiological, security, and safety are lower order needs. When these needs are met, people seek to have their social or affiliation needs met. Next they strive to have their esteem or ego needs met. When all the other needs are met, people seek self-actualization or self-fulfillment. Maslow believed social needs, esteem needs, and self-actualization needs were higher order needs. Lower order needs have more to do with our bodies; higher order needs are related more to our minds.

Frederick Herzberg's work on motivation found that what motivates people is different from what turns them off. He found that working conditions, salary, benefits, status, and security were not motivators. He called them "hygiene factors," and realized they were similar to Maslow's lower order needs. While they have the capacity to turn people off, they have little capacity to turn people on. Hygiene factors are a base from which the higher order needs can be addressed. The "motivators" he discovered were responsibility, achievement, recognition, and satisfaction in the work itself. These he realized were related to Maslow's higher order needs.

Herzberg's research indicates that if we want to motivate workers, we must first make sure that we have a base to work from. The Work In America Institute 'PAR' study agrees: "High levels of performance derived from genuine employee participation generate increased employment stability, which further motivates increasing levels of performance excellence."[9] We must create security by driving out fear, providing insurance, etc. We must provide adequate salary so the need for food and shelter can be met. Once this base is in place, we can help to provide "motivators" by creating organizations that allow the higher order needs for affiliation, esteem, responsibility, recognition, and self-fulfillment to be met.

Managers who accept Herzberg's research would create as part of any gainsharing approach opportunities for employees to have their social needs met (perhaps by having them work in teams). They would design their gainsharing system to encourage responsibility and recognition. They would make sure that everyone has a chance for meaningful achievement at work. They would be careful not to use gainsharing to create greater insecurity (by putting pay at risk). They would not view money as a motivator.

What Can Managers Do to Motivate?

As researchers have explored human motivation at work, they have also studied and written about the nature of management, trying to discover what a manager should or should not do to increase the motivation of the workforce. Managers' assumptions about the nature of people at work have tremendous impact on how they attempt to motivate others. For example, one organization that was exploring gainsharing decided not to pursue the idea further when the President of the organization said, "I do not believe in gainsharing. I grew up in the depression. Having a job is the only gain anyone needs." He assumed his work-

[9]Jerome M Rosow, Jill Castner-Lotto, and John V. Hickey, *Participation, Achievement, Reward—Creating the Infrastructure For Managing Continuous Improvement* (New York: Work in America Institute, Inc. 1998): p. xi.

force shared his views. He believed that their need for security would produce motivation. He clung to his assumptions, even though most of his workforce was younger and had never experienced the depression. He clung to his assumptions even though they are not supported by Herzberg's research.

Managers' assumptions are also influenced by the predominant management gurus of their time. Recent management thought has often been dominated by the work of W. Edwards Deming, Tom Peters, and Stephen Covey. These writers stress the importance of employee involvement and participatory management.

There are those who still follow the theories of Frederick Taylor, one of the earliest and most influential writers about the role of management. Some even credit Taylor with coining the term "gainsharing." His book, *The Principles of Scientific Management*, written in the early 1900's, influenced a generation of managers and launched industrial engineering as a profession. The book explains how to use the principles of scientific management to motivate a steelworker to work harder by offering him more money for loading pig iron. He illustrates with an actual quote from a conversation he had with the steelworker.

> . . . *you will do exactly as this man (manager) tells you tomorrow, from morning till night. When he tells you to pick up a pig and walk, you pick it up and you walk, and when he tells you to sit down and rest, you sit down. You do that straight through the day. And what's more no backtalk. Now a high-priced man does just what he is told to do and no backtalk. Do you understand that? When the man tells you to walk, you walk, when he tells you to sit down, you sit down, and you don't talk back to him.*[10]

Scientific management assumes that some people in an organization are better at thinking while others should simply do what they are told (without talking back). Money and punishment are seen as the most powerful motivators. Workers are viewed as lazy and unwilling to do their best without management intervention. It is assumed that the average worker does

---

[10]Frederick Winslow Taylor, *The Principles of Scientific Management* (1911).

not seek more responsibility and in fact will avoid responsibil ity. Douglas McGregor, the great scholar of organizations, would many years later call these assumptions "Theory X."

Management assumptions are critical to gainsharing success. Assumptions are like lenses in a pair of glasses. They will distort, focus, and alter everything a manager sees. A small Michigan manufacturing company was purchased by a group of investors who had experience with the Scanlon gainsharing system. The investors specialized in turnaround situations. The investors' assumptions about management were not "Theory X." The gainsharing approach they selected was highly participatory and involved the union and the employees in solving company problems. Within three years the company was highly profitable, having carved out a niche by competing head-to-head with the much larger 3M Corporation. The company became so successful that the investors decided to sell, receiving ten times a return on their investment. The Theory X purchasers did not believe in the value of participatory management. Their assumptions distorted their view of the gainsharing system. They saw the bonuses as giving away some of their profits. They saw the frequent meetings required for participation as a waste of time and as a loss of their management power. Within two years, the gainsharing system was in ruins, employee morale was at an all time low, and the new owners were debating moving the plant south to avoid their union.

Today "Taylorism" has fallen out of favor, but its basic assumptions continue to drive many management actions. Theory X managers usually do not support gainsharing if there is an employee involvement component, yet they may embrace gainsharing as a compensation approach. They tend to support gainsharing systems where pay is at risk. In these systems employees are not paid a market wage, but are able to reach market rates or above with the addition of a gainsharing bonus. These assumptions are the same assumptions that drove the Taylor's piecework systems in the early 1900's. The assumptions driving these systems are that money is the primary motivator and employees will not work hard unless their paycheck is at risk. They assume people do not want to work.

They believe management must intervene by designing a more effective carrot if workers are to be motivated to work.

While McGregor studied managers with Theory X assumptions, he also studied managers with quite the opposite assumptions about people. McGregor called these assumptions "Theory Y." These managers assume that workers want to accept more responsibility, actually enjoy work, want to set their own goals, have great ambition, and can be trusted. Today, most modern management practices such as TQM, Teams, Employee Involvement, etc. are based on Theory Y assumptions. Few scholars realize that McGregor developed Theory Y by studying a variety of organizations with Scanlon gainsharing systems. McGregor endorsed Scanlon as Theory Y by writing, "I need only mention the Scanlon (gainsharing) Plan as the outstanding embodiment of these ideas in practice." Donnelly Corporation, a world leader in the automotive glass industry, has had a Scanlon gainsharing system since 1952. Often ranked as one of America's most admired corporations, the company has been a leader in Theory Y management practices. Donnelly CEO Dwane Baumgardner, considered to be one of the top 36 business leaders in America[11] describes the essence of Theory Y management by saying:

> *True motivation is an internal drive that is released by a commitment to worthwhile goals. We believe that everyone has a deep internal desire to have their life make a difference, and they want to be part of a worthwhile endeavor. People will willingly and energetically work creatively toward organizational goals if they believe them to be worthwhile.*[12]

Baumgardner goes on to say:

> *I believe a strong distinction should be made between incentives and motivation. Incentives encourage people to concentrate on the*

[11]Robert H. Rosen, *Leading People: Transforming Business from the Inside Out* (New York: Penguin Group, 1996).

[12]Jerome M. Rosow, Jill Castner-Lotto, and John V. Hickey, *Participation, Achievement, Reward—Creating the Infrastructure For Managing Continuous Improvement* (New York: Work in America Institute, Inc. 1998): p. 55.

reward, not the work to be done. They encourage many nonproductive behaviors. We believe at Donnelly that pay in and of itself is not a strong motivator, but can be a de-motivator.[13]

Is Money the Universal Motivator?

The assumptions behind the Scanlon gainsharing system are congruent with the work of McGregor, Maslow, and Herzberg. Scanlon Systems are based on the assumption that people want to participate and accept responsibility. Other gainsharing systems were developed based on different assumptions about human motivation. Mitchell Fein, the creator of the Improshare® gainsharing, wrote:

> *Herzberg's postulation that money is not a motivator, that the work itself motivates, was sweet music to managers' ears. Not only did workers not accept these notions; neither did management.*[14]

Fein assumes that money is the primary motivator. While Improshare® encourages employee involvement, it is not viewed as the critical component like it is in Scanlon gainsharing systems. Fein cites his own studies, which indicate that the Improshare® system motivates and creates greater productivity without the need for employee involvement. The debate has taken on renewed vigor as a result of the work of the late W. Edwards Deming. Deming, the great quality expert, had very strong feelings about motivation and the role of money as a motivator. He believed in the power of intrinsic motivation. He believed that individual merit pay systems, rewards, punishment, and most of the other motivators used in business were dysfunctional. He believed in Theory Y management. Deming summed up over fifty years of organizational study by saying, "Pay is not a motivator."

If pay is not a motivator, why then is it so common? Voltaire said, "When it is a question of money, everybody is of the same religion." Leavitt writes:

[13] Ibid.
[14] Mitchell Fein, *Improshare: An Alternative to Traditional Managing* (American Institute of Industrial Engineers, 1981): p. 27.

Money incentives have come to occupy a central place because money is a common means for satisfying all sorts of diverse needs in our society and because money may be handled and measured. Money is "real"; it is communicable. Many other means to need-satisfaction are abstract and ephemeral.[15]

Jerry McAdams, in *The Reward Plan Advantage*, takes a pragmatic approach that seeks the middle ground.[16] He does not take the extreme position of Deming or Kohn that all motivation is intrinsic, nor does he endorse the assumptions of Leavitt and Fein that extrinsic monetary rewards are sufficient motivators alone. He believes that a properly designed reward system will avoid the problems of both extremes. McAdams' credibility is enhanced by the fact that he was head researcher in several large-scale studies of alternative reward systems for the American Compensation Association.

Because money is universal, quick and easy it often becomes the only focus of many gainsharing systems. Gainsharing as compensation or a "bonus" is easier to design, communicate, and administer than is a more comprehensive method such as Scanlon. However, Scanlon practitioners have found the real value of financial rewards isn't the money they provide per se, but the way the money helps to focus employees and management on business issues. Scanlon practitioners no longer view Scanlon as simple gainsharing, as a plan, or as a program. They consider Scanlon to be a *Process* for organizational and individual development. Each part of the process is important for success. They believe most gainsharing systems have fatal flaws built into them. Typical gainsharing approaches that consider money to be the only motivator can only motivate when there are bonuses to be paid. They do not provide motivation during tough times, when a company can't pay bonuses but needs motivated employees the most. Many operate much like a lottery. Employees enjoy the opportunity to earn extra money but they believe the bonus is subject to chance. They do not believe they can influence the results. The focus on gainsharing as a pro-

---

[15] Ibid, p. 23.
[16] Jerry L. McAdams, *The Reward Plan Advantage* (San Francisco: Jossey-Bass, 1996).

gram or a plan, instead of a *process or system*, prevents them from adapting and changing which creates built in obsolescence.

There appears to be a basic paradox among gainsharing practitioners. Gainsharing is viewed as a solution for motivating workers by managers who have totally opposite assumptions about what motivates them. Each camp has its own management theorists to justify its assumptions. Each is able to cite objective studies to validate its position. All gainsharing systems are not created equal. Those exploring gainsharing must first determine their own basic assumptions about human motivation and then design a gainsharing process based on those assumptions. If they work with an existing gainsharing process or gainsharing consultant, they must question whether or not the process and the consultant share the same assumptions.

When management assumptions and gainsharing systems match, there is power, synergy and integrity. Gainsharing becomes a way for the manager to manage. When management assumptions and gainsharing don't match, gainsharing is not effective. Gainsharing sends a strong message to the organization about what behaviors are important. Employees are quick to find inconsistencies between what the managers say and what gainsharing rewards. While this is not to say that consistency per se makes gainsharing successful, inconsistencies will soon undermine even the best gainsharing process.

B = Business Literacy

One of the hottest management ideas of the late 1990's was the idea of Business Literacy or "open book management." Authors such as John Case, Jack Stack, and John Schuster have done a wonderful job of documenting the effects literacy training has had on a wide variety of organizations. Stack's own organization, Springfield Remanufacturing Corporation, became one of the most sought after places for a benchmark visit because of its amazing turnaround story.

What these open book managers and/or authors have discovered is the power generated when employees know their business, are provided meaningful information on the performance of their business, are able to influence decisions to improve their business, and are included in the rewards of capitalism. Open book practitioners seek to create companies where every employee is a business person.

Despite the hype, these ideas are not new. Many were developed over half a century ago by Joe Scanlon, the father of gainsharing, and are incorporated in every Scanlon gainsharing process.

The primary Scanlon Principle is called Identity. The Principle of Identity incorporates what writers are today calling Business Literacy. Through a *process* of education all employees are taught about their company, their competitors, and the need to change. Each Scanlon company develops its own *process* to insure Identity. Customer visits, information on competitors, and training on how to read financial reports are all ways that Scanlon companies create Identity. Beth Israel Hospital implemented Identity by sharing hospital information with its employees in three languages (French, Spanish, and English). Wescast Industries, a Canadian company that produces 60% of the engine manifolds in North America, conducts monthly Business Information Meetings and maintains an in-depth company intranet system. Limerick Veterinary Hospital in Limerick, PA created their entire business education process (which they call 'P.A.W.S.') using pet themes. Each company designs an Identity *Process* that fits its industry and size.

C = Commitment

Organizations are changing their commitments to customers, investors and employees. The quality movement has helped world class organizations increase their commitment to customers. Investors led by the large institutions have demanded and received increased commitment to their needs. Paradoxically, during these times of increased commitment to customers and investors, organizations are decreasing their commitment to employees. Many employees work part time, their organizations unable or unwilling to commit to full time employment. Full time employees are told it is impossible for their organizations to commit to lifetime employment. Organizations that have become flatter and leaner cannot even commit to regular advancement for good performers.

While employees are told to expect less organizational commitment, they are asked to commit to new forms of work. They are asked to commit to longer hours and more responsibility. They are expected to commit to being flexible. They are told to commit to lifetime learning to master ever more complex and changing jobs.

Albert Camus said, "Commitment is the soul of work." Johann Goethe said, "Until one is committed, there is hesitancy, the chance to draw back, always ineffectiveness, concerning all acts of initiative (and creation). There is one elementary truth the ignorance of which kills countless ideas and splendid plans: That the moment one definitely commits oneself, then providence moves too."

The various gainsharing approaches differ in the commitment they make and the commitment they seek. Those that are implemented as a compensation strategy commit to pay a bonus when certain performance targets are met. This in and of itself is a major commitment, just like a commitment to meet payroll, to fund benefits, etc. Once an organization commits to gainsharing, it must follow through with the commitment. A bonus can not be promised and then withdrawn later. Most gainsharing systems are self-funding, paying for their administration and the bonuses out of gains or savings, yet even these systems demand organizational commitment. For example, Lincoln Electric had to borrow money to meet bonus commitments. Their system paid a bonus based on productivity gains. Employees improved productivity, yet the company was not profitable. This doesn't happen often, but if it does illustrate the point that a commitment to a bonus is a commitment that must be honored in good times and bad. Many companies avoid that particular scenario by establishing a nominal baseline profit margin, which the company must meet or exceed before any bonus is paid out.

Gainsharing systems such as Scanlon that are fundamentally organizational and individual development systems demand great commitment from employees and their organizations. They demand personal and organizational commitment to participation, to equity, and to increased competency.

Commitment to Participation

Every gainsharing system seeks to alter the commitment of individuals. As a result of gainsharing, individuals are assumed to participate in some way to making the group or organization better. The various approaches differ on how widely to encourage participation and on who is included in the gainsharing group. Some focus only on the production people in an organization and do not include administrative people or managers. Some focus on teams, with each team operating its own bonus system. Some focus on multiple plants or sites. Gainsharing writers call this the "line of sight" issue. People want to be able to influence the results of a bonus. Creating line of sight is a fundamental way of emphasizing the link between performance and reward. It leads clearly from employees' behaviors to achievement, measures them against specific goals, and then uses these measures to determine payoff.[17] The more people included in the gainsharing system, the more difficult this becomes. The less a bonus measure is influenced by participation, the harder it is to explain and to enlist support. For example, employees in a manufacturing operation might feel that they can participate in reducing scrap, yet they may feel they have no control over profits (even though the two measures are related).

Commitment to participation can be built into gainsharing or it can be left to chance. Employees in Scanlon companies are expected to participate by "influencing decisions in their areas of competence." The commitment to participation

[17] Jerome M. Rosow, Jill Castner-Lotto, and John V. Hickey, *Participation, Achievement, Reward—Creating the Infrastructure For Managing Continuous Improvement* (New York: Work in America Institute, Inc. 1998): p. x.

is evident in the way the Scanlon *Process* is implemented. Scanlon is not purchased off-the-shelf from consultants or third parties. They are not implemented unless there is evidence of virtually universal organizational commitment at all levels.

Other gainsharing approaches require little commitment to participate from employees. They are designed by internal or external consultants and then simply communicated to employees. They can be installed quickly. There is no vote. They can be changed quickly and easily. They do not create commitment.

Commitment to Equity

Webster's defines equity as "the quality of being fair or impartial." Scanlon gainsharing systems incorporate this idea of fairness by defining equity as a genuine commitment to accounting for the needs of all constituents including customers, investors and employees. The concept is graphically depicted as an equilateral triangle.

The pursuit of equity is the way the Scanlon gainsharing system holds everyone accountable to the stakeholders. Dwane Baumgardner notes that

> *People often think equity means equality, although that is not the case. Others think it mainly means a bonus, and that is not the case. The principle of Equity means that, among all of the company's stakeholders, there is a fair return for their investment and all issues are dealt with in a spirit of fairness to all—in short, a focus on 'we'*

vs. 'me'. Equity is a balance, and the responsibility for attaining balance is a shared responsibility of all the stakeholders.[18]

Scanlon is the only gainsharing *process* that defines these multiple accountabilities yet the idea is probably as old as time itself. Confucius was reported to have said, "The proper man understands equity, the small man profits."

Dr. Carl Frost, in describing the Scanlon Equity *Process*, said:

> *During the early days of Scanlon and somewhat persistently since, many have defined equity as bonuses. The early days were adversarial. Wages were not nationally uniform or substantial. Too often management permitted and even encouraged the expectation of supplemental income, primarily as a result of productivity improvements, i.e., Improshare®, gainsharing. The use of the word share often suggests difference and division rather than neutrality of benefits that are mutually inclusive rather than exclusive.*[19]

Scanlon companies operationalize the equity concept by creating appropriate reliable databases of customer satisfaction, financial performance, and human resources. There are regular, public occasions where the data is shared and discrepancies between what 'is' and what 'needs to be' are explored. Sometimes, positive discrepancies are noted and sometimes negative discrepancies are found. Frequently, bonus formulas are constructed that take into account the needs of all stakeholders. Spring Engineering and Manufacturing Company even named their Scanlon system the I.C.E. Plan for Investor, Customer, and Employees to emphasize equity. The Scanlon Equity Principle includes many concepts business writers are now calling a "balanced scorecard."

Companies that stress a bonus create employees who are dissatisfied when the bonus cannot be paid. These employ-

---

[18]Jerome M. Rosow, Jill Castner-Lotto, and John V. Hickey, *Participation, Achievement, Reward—Creating the Infrastructure For Managing Continuous Improvement* (New York: Work in America Institute, Inc. 1998): p. 54.

[19]Carl Frost, "Leadership in the New American Workplace," Workbook printed by the Scanlon Leadership Network.

ees are conditioned to expect a bonus. They are not literate to the fact that their investors may be losing money, or that their customers have gone somewhere else. In companies committed to equity, employees know the needs of the other stakeholders and are willing to make sacrifices when necessary. Beth Israel employees, upon discovering that each blood transfusion cost the hospital $200, developed a program to donate their own blood to the center, thus saving the hospital much of that expense. During the recession of the late 1980's, Donnelly paid out no bonus for 3 years, and yet because management believed that the company treated them like equal partners, they accepted a proposal to cut all salaries above $40,000 from 3–17%. Donnelly emerged from the recession with a strong and dedicated workforce. In 2001, Spring Engineering & Manufacturing faced their first ever layoffs, which was a potentially devastating occurrence for this small company. In a spectacular demonstration of employee buy-in, the entire company voted to eliminate their gainsharing bonus in order to save 2 jobs.

Finally it is not necessary and maybe even counterproductive to give money as the gain. Once a bonus check is cashed and the money spent, it is often difficult for employees to know where the money went. Ferro Corporation—Glass Products Division provides its employees with "mall dollars" that they can spend at local businesses. Employees can purchase goods and services from vacations to cars. A new electronic gadget may have more 'trophy value' than does the equivalent in money. Employees remember what items they purchased in mall dollars. Enterprising organizations could even use the mall dollar concept to negotiate favorable exchanges and discounts from merchants. An additional benefit of the concept is that money remains in the local economy.

Other examples include Spring Engineering, which was challenged to find a reward system that would recognize great performance in a positive and motivating but low cost manner. Their ICE Team created a 'Spin the Wheel' system where a division that has met their monthly goals gets a chance to spin a prize wheel for rewards that range from lotto tickets to leave-early/come-in-late passes. A creative approach was taken by Weyburn-Bartel Incorporated, which paid its bonus in meat. Employees signed up for various cuts of beef or seafood that was delivered by refrigerated truck. The system prevented the value of their bonus from being eroded by sales taxes. While these approaches are not for everyone, they show that there are many unique ways to create an equity system.

Commitment to Competency

Business Literacy, Participation, and Theory Y management all require increased employee competency. Employees must learn to do more than what is expected in traditional firms. Motorola's Scanlon philosophy led them to invest over 50 million dollars per year (1990) in employee training and development. Wescast Industries partners with their local community college to offer apprenticeship courses, and will reimburse their employees for these continuing education expenses. Spring Engineering takes it one step further with their Technical Education Academic Manufacturing (TEAM) community college program. TEAM combines applied academic preparation in physics, math, and communication arts with extensive exposure to industry experiences through plant tours, job shadowing, and specialized industry classes. Spring's employees act as mentors and teachers while the students are at their facility. In high-performance work organizations, training also becomes an important component of an employment security strategy.[20] Gainsharing, when utilized as a compensation strategy only, does not identify this type of commitment to increased competency.

Participatory gainsharing requires changes in both managers and employees. Managers must learn how to lead, to listen, and to coach. Employees must learn how to work in teams, control quality, and reduce costs. Both employees and organizations must commit to major investments in time, energy and money to be successful. Scanlon organizations believe the investment is worth the cost. They believe employees are an

[20]Ibid., p. xi.

asset to be developed and not a cost to be reduced. In three separate audits, Motorola calculated a $30 return for every dollar invested in training and development.

At the very least, every gainsharing system must help employees to become competent in understanding the basis of the gainsharing formula that is used. If employees don't understand the calculation, they will not know why they are or are not receiving the bonus. They will view the bonus as some form of lottery in which they hope to win, but in which they have little influence of the outcomes.

Conclusion

Joe Scanlon believed that the health and success of *any* company depended on its ability to create an environment of cooperation and fairness between labor and management. The best way to achieve that, he felt, was by involving employees in the company and giving them an opportunity to share in the rewards gained through their contributions. Gainsharing is a proven, powerful tool to manage an organization if there is an understanding of the basic ABC's of gainsharing. Mistakes are made by those who do not take the time to understand the differences between the various available approaches. Before beginning a gainsharing program, carefully evaluate your Assumptions about motivation. Consider the impact of Business Literacy. Finally consider the level of Commitment your organization will expect and is willing to provide. Once the basic ABC's are mastered, the right gainsharing approach will be much clearer.

Part IV

Equity
Participation
Identity
Competence

*"We cannot become what we need to be
by remaining what we are."*
—Max DePree

CHAPTER 16

SCANLON AND THE LEAN ENTERPRISE

Dwane Baumgardner and Russ Scaffede

The Japanese took Joe Scanlon's ideas concerning worker involvement . . . and the ideas of W. Edwards Deming . . . now people are adopting Japanese management techniques without knowing that many of them were Scanlon's ideas.

—*Warren Bennis*

The Toyota Production System (TPS) is a leadership philosophy and production system that is widely copied but rarely understood. Toyota has been very generous in sharing its methods with others, and there are countless books and articles on the system yet many who study it end up focusing on the tools of the system, and miss the underlying principles and philosophy that make it work.

Americans grab tools. At Toyota, they concentrate on a philosophy. A tool is something you pick up . . . and then put down. A philosophy is a way of life, an on-going thing.

One of the underlying philosophies of Toyota is labor-management cooperation. Today, Toyota is a global industrial giant but in 1950 it was struggling small car manufacturer that came close to bankruptcy. After the war there was demand for the company's trucks but hyper inflation had made money worthless and collections difficult. Kiichiro Toyoda, the founder of Toyota Motor Corp, had a no layoff policy. When he could avoid layoffs no longer, he asked for voluntary pay reductions from his managers and imposed a 10% across the board pay cut to the workers. However it was not enough to keep the company going. Eventually, 1,600 employees were asked to leave, which led to strikes, demonstrations and work stoppages.

To save the company Kiichiro assumed responsibility and resigned even though the problems the company faced were not of his doing. His self-sacrifice bought labor peace. Liker in *The Toyota Way* writes, "His personal sacrifice helped to quell worker dissatisfaction. More workers voluntarily left the company . . . his tremendous personal sacrifice had a profound impact on the history of Toyota. Everyone knew what he did and why. The philosophy of Toyota to this day is to look beyond individual concerns to the long term good of the company as well as to take responsibility for problems."[1]

Kiichiro was a servant-leader willing to sacrifice his own needs for the good of the company. Leaders at Toyota are expected to sacrifice their own needs at times for the good of the group and the organization. By their example they encourage frontline workers to think about the needs of the team and the company. How many CEO's of organizations that wish to be lean would be willing to emulate Kiichiro?

Toyota was not the only Japanese company experiencing labor problems in the post war period. Strikes and work stoppages were common. A group of Japanese Executives decided to see what they could do to improve labor-management in Japan. According to Yasuo Kuwahara, Professor and Editor of the *Ko-jien Dictionary*,

"In February 1955, a few management leaders gathered in Keizai Doyukai (Japanese Association of Corporate Executives) and established the Japan Productivity Center (JPC). Some managers involved in establishing the JPC were deeply impressed by the productivity movement in Europe in the 1950s and wanted to import that idea into Japan.

Labor-management cooperation to restore the economy was progressing in the United Kingdom, Germany (West), and other European countries, financed in part by collateral loans provided through the Marshall Plan. In Japan, the United States offered the

[1] Liker, Jeffrey. *The Toyota Way: 14 Management Principles From The World's Greatest Manufacturer*, New York: McGraw-Hill, 2004.

financial resources of Foreign Operation Association (FOA) through the Ministry of International Trade and Industry (the present Ministry of Economy and Industry), and it was these funds that helped the establishment of the JPC. Founders of the JPC supported the productivity movement because they believed that a proper balance between efficiency and democracy was a prerequisite for the development of stable labor-management relations.

The JPC adopted three principles for the productivity movement: (1) productivity increase should eventually expand employment (through the expansion of the macro-economy); (2) the means of increasing productivity should be studied jointly by labor and management through consultation; and (3) the fruits of productivity increases should be distributed fairly among labor, management, and consumers in accordance with national economic conditions.

The JPC organized several tripartite research groups to study productivity-increasing methods in the United States and Europe. These included labor-and-management groups from the steel industry, they were a strong contribution to increasing the international competitiveness of the Japanese industries, as was the quality control movement encouraged by Dr. Deming and total quality control (TQC) and zero defect (ZD) movements established in following years. The Scanlon Plan was one of the innovative ideas introduced and tested in the same period.

Although the Scanlon Plan seems to have lost its direct impact in the 1970s, the basic innovative idea of the plan has been well inherited and deeply rooted in Japanese industry.[2]"

The JPC's three principles created a firm foundation from which Japan was able to build strong industries. Principle #1 created growth. Principle #2 created a cooperative relationship with labor and Principle #3 created equity between all the major stakeholders. The same three principles are practiced by Toyota and are inherent in every Scanlon organization.

The term "Lean Enterprise" was coined by James Wolmack in his book *The Machine that Changed the World* to describe a Japanese way of producing automobiles. Based on his

[2]Personal correspondence with Paul Davis, President of the Scanlon Leadership Network

research the Japanese produced better automobiles, with less automation, in less space, faster, and at less cost than automobile producers in Europe and America. Wolmack later discovered that much of the positive Japanese results could be attributed to one Japanese automaker . . . Toyota.

Business Leaders throughout the world are adopting ideas either created or perfected by Toyota. Sakichi Toyoda created the idea of intelligent machines that could not produce defects (jidoka). (He invented a loom that stopped when a thread broke. Other looms continued to produce defective materials until an operator shut them down.)

His son Kiichiro Toyota created the idea of "Just in Time" saving space and money. He also developed the company's motto and philosophy of "Good thinking=Good Products." This motto is more than a simple slogan. It is Toyota's belief in the scientific method. Steven Spear and Kent Bowen have called the scientific method "the DNA of the Toyota Production System."[3]

The first step in the scientific method is to observe what is happening. Toyota teaches leaders to do this observation where the work is actually being done (Genchi Genbutsu). Rather than read reports Toyota expects leaders to observe for themselves what is going on. Often observation provides a better understanding of reality than reading a report. Step 2 is to form a hypothesis to explain what is happening. The third step is to use the hypothesis to predict what will happen if a change is made. The forth step is to perform experiments to test the hypothesis. Dr. Edward Deming who taught the Japanese his quality methods, taught the scientific method as a Plan, Do, Check, Act cycle (PDCA). PDCA is done consistently over time is a foundation principle of the Toyota Production System.

The scientific method is a belief in cause and effect. The understanding of cause and effect coupled with the ability to set goals are what psychologists call "Achievement oriented thinking." Goal setting at Toyota is done with a system called "Hoshin Kanri." Individuals, who understand cause and effect and who

---

[3]Spear, Steven and Kent Bowen. "Decoding the DNA of the Toyota Production System," *Harvard Business Review*, Reprint 99509.

have the ability to set realistic goals outperform individuals who believe in luck, chance, fate and magic. Organizations like Toyota with many achievement oriented individuals are very competitive in the marketplace. Achievement oriented individuals have confidence in their ability to adapt to change. Toyota captured that confidence in a document called the Toyota Spirit.

"We strive to decide our own fate. We act with self-reliance, trusting in our own abilities. We accept responsibility for our own conduct and for maintaining and improving the skills that enable us to produce added value."

Eiji Toyota a younger cousin to Sakichi and a Taiichi Ohno a loom mechanic who rose to become a Toyota Executive Vice President studied the Ford production system. At the time Ford was the leader in manufacturing and work organization. Eiji and Taciichi adopted ideas like "Standardized Work" but rejected the way Ford treated his workers.

According to Ford . . .

"Today's standardization . . . is the necessary foundation on which tomorrow's improvement will be based. If you think of "standardization" as the best you know today, but which is to be improved tomorrow-you get somewhere. But if you think of standards as confining then progress stops"

Eiji and Taiichi saw that Ford was at best paternalistic and at other times violent towards his employees. (Ford hired thugs to beat up union sympathizers). The average worker was told what to do, and how to do it. There was no trust between labor and management. Eiiji and Taiichi believed that the average worker is closest to the work and understands it better than anyone else. They viewed workers as intelligent partners in the Toyota production system. This view is a fundamental principle of the TPS and every Scanlon Plan.

Many employers have industrial engineers develop standardized work. This often leads to a dysfunctional game played between workers and engineers to control the standards. Eiiji and Taiichi taught line employees to create standardized work and gave them control of the system. They developed Kaizen events where employees were able to solve problems working together with their leaders.

They also knew that Toyota could not adopt the same mass production system in Japan that Ford had developed in Detroit. They needed to be able to make small numbers of different cars, while the Ford system was designed to make large numbers of a single type of car. This led to a large number of Toyota tools from rapid die changes to cellular manufacturing. All of these TPS tools helped to create better products, at a lower price, with increased flexibility.

The heart of the TPS system is a philosophy of committed cooperative people working consistently together to provide value for customers. It is not the tools.

The unstated philosophy of the TPS is:

- People are Toyota's greatest assets and the source for innovation and waste reduction.
- People closest to the work know it best
- The scientific method (PDCA) is the best way to solve problems
- Cooperation between labor and management is critical for success
- Leaders are servants to the workers
- Everyone must work to produce value for the customer
- Tools can change as better tools are discovered

The Donnelly Story

The authors have years of experience in Scanlon and Toyota organizations. The remainder of this chapter attempts to capture how both systems came together at Donnelly.

Donnelly (now Magna-Donnelly) is the world's leading manufacture of automotive mirrors. Donnelly helped to create the

Scanlon Leadership Network and had a Scanlon Plan for over 50 years. Widely benchmarked for their participative systems Donnelly pioneered the use of teams in industry, had no time clocks, and a no lay-off policy. Donnelly employees even decided their pay increases through their "Equity" process. Harvard wrote "Participative Management at Work" about Donnelly's Scanlon Plan in 1977.[4] Donnelly was considered one of the top ten best places to work in America.

Despite high levels of employee involvement, Donnelly struggled in supplying Honda. Honda's quality and efficiency demands could not be met and Donnelly was put on notice to improve or they would lose the business. In approximately two years, after implementing lean systems at their Grand Haven facility Donnelly was able to reduce defects by 80%, cut scrap by fifty percent, and increase productivity by 29 percent.

The road to lean was rocky. Employee moral was low and there were several attempts to unionize the plant. Outside experts were brought in to do "Kaizen" events.

Liker in *Becoming Lean* describes the reaction of one associate:

> "How can someone who is Japanese, who doesn't even know our language, understand our process in a few hours? They would throw out riddles like: 'I wouldn't want to cook in a dirty kitchen.' We didn't need riddles. We knew the place needed to be cleaned up, but management wouldn't listen to us. They didn't want us to spend the money."[5]

According to Liker many of the suggestions made by the outside consultants were the same ones that had been made by the employees but were never implemented under their Scanlon suggestion system called "IDEAS". Employees became even more frustrated when they saw the outsiders getting credit for their ideas.

[4]"Participative Management at Work: An Interview with John Donnelly", *Harvard Business Review*, January–February 1977.
[5]Liker, Jeffrey, Editor. *Becoming Lean: Inside Stories of U. S. Manufacturers*, Portland: Productivity Press, 1998.-

Eventually, Donnelly hired Russ Scaffede who had direct experience of the TPS system at Georgetown. Russ hired Art Smalley who also had Toyota experience and together they developed the Donnelly Production System based on the TPS.

Donnelly's production system was illustrated as a house (see Figure 1). Employees were expected to be able to draw the house and to explain each major part.

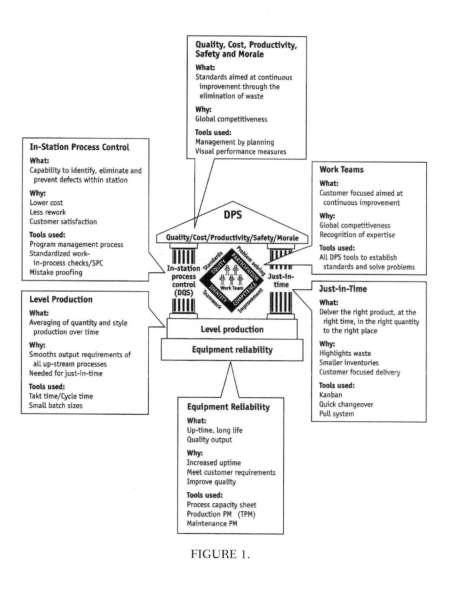

FIGURE 1.

At the center of the house were work teams and the E.P.I.C. leadership Principles of Equity, Participation, Competence and Identity. People truly were the center of the house and the philosophy. They were trained in lean systems and were involved in making their workplaces more efficient.

Goals were made clear using a "Hoshin" process Donnelly called "Management by Planning." This enabled all workers to understand how their goals and objectives related to corporate goals.

A "lean simulation" was developed that taught front-line workers lean concepts in a hands-on way.[6] Workers learned how inventory and work-in-process impacted a balance sheet. Further training taught workers how to compute "takt" times and to develop "standardized work" for their areas. Worker ideas were heard and implemented.

Lean and Scanlon are successful because they are based on universal Principles. Both recognize that the committed cooperation of the average worker is key to the success of the organization. Philosophy and beliefs are more important in both systems than are the tools associated with the systems. Scanlon is more about trust than gainsharing. Lean is more about involvement than rapid die changes, or continuous flow. The Principles of each system are illustrated in Figure 2.

Together Scanlon and lean will produce highly participative and efficient organizations. Both systems have stood the test of time providing a proven roadmap for leaders who wish to create organizations that provide worthwhile employment, produce worthwhile products/services and generate worthwhile investment returns.

---

[6]See The Lean Sim Machine at http://www.scanlonleader.org

Universal Success Principles

Leading in an Age of Lean

	Scanlon Principles	Lean Enterprise Principles
Purpose	Do we share a common understanding accompanied by support and commitment of the fundamental purpose and core values of the company, and have we institutionalized a process that ensures daily operating practices consistent with our purpose and core values?	Exceed customer expectations by eliminating waste through a process of continuous improvement where people and teams including suppliers and customers are engaged in the process together and constantly striving for perfection. Do we believe that the process of becoming lean as permeating every part of our business and requiring a relentless pursuit to eliminate waste as a core value?
Business Reality	Do we understand the business reality we face at a sufficient depth that there is widespread agreement fir a compelling need for change with a genuine potential for improvement, and have we institutionalized a process for education that ensures a highly business-literate workforce on an ongoing basis?	Waste exists is all parts of the business and it is critical to eliminate this waste and change the system to be successful. If we understand "Cost = Sales Price - Profit" and cost is the only controllable, then are we understanding lean principles as the enabler for a "War-on-Waste"?
Right Job	Have we defined the right job (personal, workteam, department, division and total company) that needs to be done to support achieving sustained outstanding company performance, and have we institutionalized a deployment process that ensures broad organization alignment and transparency and an ability to change quickly with changing business conditions?	Have we developed a vision of our long-term lean system philosophies? Have we developed an implementation plan and dedicated the resources to accomplish the task? Have we developed the cascading annual planning and review process to align all the organization for improvement?
Job Right	Have we defined the criteria we will use to determine if progress is being made at the rate needed to achieve outstanding company performance, and have we institutionalized a process for ensuring a disciplined execution of all plans?	Progress with continuous improvement can only be measured against results associated with standardized and improving processes. Have we identified the right metrics for success (safety, quality, cost, productivity, delivery, and morale)? Is the entire organization aligned with our lean principles/values?
Participation	Do we share a belief that the fundamental source of competitive advantage for achieving sustained outstanding company performance is based on tapping the full creativity and commitment of all the people along with achieving a synergy through teamwork, and have we institutionalized an organization framework and process for making this happen?	Recognize that becoming lean is a process that is done "with" people and not "to" people. A total commitment to people and teams is an absolutely essential part of the process. Do we see lean principles as the main enabler to accomplish meaningful, inspiring participation?
Equity	Do we share a belief that fair treatment of all stakeholders is essential in order to achieve sustained outstanding company performance and that only the stakeholders can judge whether or not they are being treated fairly, and have we institutionalized a process for ensuring fair treatment?	Recognize the need to achieve a fair and balanced return for all the key stakeholders (customers, shareholders, employees & suppliers). Work closely with suppliers to eliminate waste in the total value chain and treat suppliers with respect as long term partners.
Competence	Do we share a belief that we are all in a state of learning and that a commitment to continuous becoming and improvement at the personal, professional and organizational level is a critical necessity to competitive advantage and achieving sustained outstanding company performance, and have we institutionalized a process for continuous learning and improvement at the personal, professional and organizational level?	• Develop leaders who understand and live the lean enterprise philosophy • Are we developing a process for continuous learning, refining personal and organization understanding of the lean tools and the applications of these tools through supportive reviews?

FIGURE 2.

SCANLON, SIX SIGMA, and INNOVATION

Praveen Gupta

Six Sigma, is a quality methodology developed by Motorola in the late 1980s, (while they were a member of the Scanlon Leadership Network). Six Sigma has become synonymous with quality improvement and today it is often linked with Lean initiatives. Six Sigma, as implemented by Motorola successfully from 1987–1992 resulted in cumulative savings for Motorola of more than $2 billion. During this time the author worked at Motorola University with those that created Six-Sigma as a philosophy and a set of tools.

The success of Motorola's six sigma program served as a catalyst for many other organizations to embrace Six-Sigma. General Electric with Jack Welch as its champion was the most well known. However, many of the companies that used Six-Sigma as a tool did not understand the participative innovative Scanlon culture of Motorola which nourished and enabled the philosophy of Six-Sigma to work.

Many executives wonder whether their company should commit to Six Sigma. For management to evaluate Six Sigma for their company, they must consider the benefits and cost of implementing the methodology. To determine the potential benefits of Six Sigma, management must first understand the cost breakdown of their operations. The cost of providing a service or producing a product must be considered based on industry benchmarks. The cost of poor quality in terms of internal and external failures and the cost of inspection, test or verification must be reviewed. Unless the facts about company

227

performance are known, it will be hard to identify opportunities for applying Six Sigma.

For management to commit to launching a Six Sigma initiative, questions that must be answered include: What can Six Sigma do for my company in both the short and long term? How much will it cost? The following Table analyzes the need for Six Sigma implementation for different-sized companies.

TABLE SIX SIGMA IMPLEMENTATION ANALYSIS:

Number of employees	100	500	1000
Annual sales (millions)	10	50	100
Cost of implementing Six Sigma ($millions)	0.5	1.5	3
Cost of poor quality at 20% of sales (millions)	2	10	20
Expected number of projects for improvement	10–20	30–60	60–80
Minimum number of projects to be identified for 100% return on investment.	5–10	15–30	30–40

Once the implementation of Six Sigma becomes an economically viable strategy, management must consider giving it the highest priority. Any competing initiative, conflicting priority or strategic initiative in progress must be clearly identified. Besides economic viability, other Six Sigma success factors must be addressed. Critical factors are:

- Commitment to implement Six Sigma
- Active participation by executive leadership, including the chief executive
- Aggressive innovation improvement goals driving the organization
- Decision making based on facts, not emotions
- A performance measurement system
- Employee engagement/participation

Understanding Six Sigma

Uncertainty about initiating Six Sigma comes from several unknowns including the effort involved, level of financial commitment, potential for success and the fear of failure. One way to overcome the initial reservations is to establish SMART (specific, measurable, attainable, realistic and tangible) goals. Thinking positively about how to achieve these specific goals and how to benefit from using Six Sigma in terms of awareness, cultural change, focus on quality, savings and profitability will expedite the decision making process. The executives' enthusiasm, managers' motivation and employees' engagement will ensure success of the Six Sigma initiative.

Why would a company pursue Six Sigma? Studies have shown that when companies have implemented Six Sigma methodology, they have improved their processes by as much as 100%. Traditionally people seem satisfied with 99% performance. At a 99% performance rate, one could expect the following:

- 20,000 lost articles of mail per hour
- 2 short or long landings at major airports each day
- 200,000 wrong drug prescriptions each year

Six Sigma implies 3.4 defects per million opportunities, i.e. an almost perfect work. Six Sigma initiatives require passionate commitment of all employees to achieve dramatic results. Improvement in quality increases employee and customer satisfaction, improves profitability and enhances the reputation of the company.

Improvement is achieved by establishing projects that can be completed within three to five months demonstrating a sense of urgency. The Six Sigma methodology utilized for attacking the opportunity for improvement is called DMAIC (Define, Measure, Analyze, Improve, and Control). The following table summarizes DMAIC:

STEPS	ACTIONS	RESULTS
Define	Identify the opportunity for significant improvement, define its scope, and develop a charter to achieve savings	A clearly defined project, cost benefit analysis, identify necessary resources, good understanding of the baseline process, critical to quality characteristics, and a plan to achieve results.
Measure	Identify key process measure Establish performance baseline Understand variation in the baseline process	Statistical analysis of the process Prioritized list of process parameters needing attention Performance baseline, and expected performance level
Analyze	Investigate for root cause, or Understand sources of variation inconsistencies	Identification of highly correlated causes or process variables, and sources of variation
Improve	Develop and evaluate alternative solutions, and select the best one, optimization	Identify necessary process changes to achieve desired improvement, and remove roadblocks to implement changes
Control	Implement control methods to maintain new performance level, and identify new opportunities	Realize benefits of improved process, recognition of teams, and renewal of the Six Sigma initiative

The profitability equation has two elements: cost of goods sold, and price of goods sold. The price of goods is determined by capacity, quality, demand, and reputation. The cost of goods includes cost of material, processes, equipment and people. To improve profitability one needs to increase sales and reduce costs. Typically, excessive costs include factors such as inefficiencies, rejects, rework, scrap, process inefficiencies, maintenance and other support operations. The reduction in cost of goods to be sold improves the price of sales. So one needs to look for opportunities in the area of cost of goods. Opportunities are manifested in the form of waste of resources in terms of time, equipment, material, facility and maintenance. So the first step in implementing Six Sigma in a company is to identify opportunities for improvement by estimating waste of

resources, be it material, people, machine, or space. To identify opportunities one needs to have some measurements to
assess whether or not the expected process or business objectives were met. Once the opportunities have been identified,
their impact can be assessed, and the opportunities prioritized as shown below:

PROJECT DESCRIPTION	PERFORMANCE IMPACT—LOW(1), MEDIUM(3), HIGH (9)	POTENTIAL SAVINGS (ANNUALIZED)	RANKING
Increase molding process yield	High reject rate, low throughput (9)	$300,000	2
Streamline sales process	Delays in getting order to factory (9)	$100,000	4
Streamline assembly process	Low throughput (9)	$150,000	3
Streamline ware-house operations	High inventory levels (9)	$500,000	1

Six Sigma consists of four key components: Intent, Methodology, Tools, and Measurements. It is critical that leadership
understands Six Sigma in its entirety. Executive commitment to
Six Sigma without taking time to understand it first, can be
called a weak link at best. The intent of Six Sigma is to achieve
a lot of improvement very fast that forces innovative reengineering of operations. The methodology is customer centric and
focuses on improving processes to achieve desired results. Tools
utilized in the methodology are simple, except some advanced
statistical methods which are rarely used. Measurements are
used to monitor performance levels ensuring that the methodology works. In the current Six Sigma environment, the methodology has become a project based institutionalization of
process improvement. Considering the failures of well known
corporations that tried Six Sigma it is important to understand what really made it work was leadership, goal setting and
measurement. Leadership emphasizes the Scanlon E.P.I.C. cultural aspects of Six Sigma, goal setting is a process for aggres-

sive improvement, and measurement is a verification of the improvement.

Six Sigma measurements consist of identifying Customer Critical characteristics. Evaluating performance at a given process step, or for a product, calculating process capability, determining the probability of success and then transforming the process or product in terms of sigma level. Correspondingly for a given sigma level, there is an unacceptable level of performance that adversely affects profitability.

In order to determine the performance level, the process defect rate is normalized per the process output that is called a unit. The unit is a discrete measure of output that can be counted, verified and measured. For example, in an assembly process each board assembled could be a unit. Similarly, each board coming out of the wave soldering or the reflow process is a unit. Unit is used to estimate the quality of the process output in terms of defects per unit, percent yield or the first pass yield.

Defects per unit are defined as a ratio of total number of defects observed in the inspected or verified units over the total number of units processed or built.

$$\text{Defects per unit (DPU)} = \frac{\text{Total number of defects}}{\text{Total number of units verified}}$$

One needs to differentiate between the 'defect' and the 'defective unit'. One defective unit may contain many defects. The goal is to count all the defects.

Having unacceptable DPU, one needs to understand the process step, where in the process the defect occurs, and the root cause of the defect. The root cause could be any part or process that could result in defects. Root causes are really opportunities where things can go wrong. Opportunities become critical when comparing products of various complexities and while solving the process problems. Defects per Million Opportunities (DPMO) is a measurement that normalizes the reject rate based on opportunities instead of units.

Defects per Million Opportunities

$$= \frac{\text{Total number of defects} \times 1,000,000}{\begin{array}{c}\text{Total number of units verified } *\\ \text{average number of opportunities in a unit}\end{array}}$$

To understand the relationship between DPU and DPMO, one can restate the above formula as follows:

Defects per Million Opportunities

$$= \frac{\text{DPU} \times 1,000,000}{\text{Average number of opportunities per unit}}$$

The above formulae work in case of assembly or service processes where things could be counted. Units or opportunities and defects or errors are countable items. In case of continuous processes, where variation is measured, one needs to use the probabilities of producing rejects and then apply the above formula. These probabilities must consider an expected shift in process means that has been established at 1.5 sigma. Based on the 1.5 Sigma shift, probabilities are calculated, and converted into the DPMO measurement.

After calculating DPMO, using an established z-distribution table or software, sigma level can be calculated. The following table shows DPMO and related probabilities:

DPMO	SIGMA LEVEL
66,810	3
6210	4
233	5
3.4	6

Many people believe that they can buy Six Sigma certification and get some marketing advantage. By documenting a few more procedures, they can achieve Six Sigma recognition. However they are wrong.

Aggressive goal setting is fundamental to Six Sigma. As we know, Six Sigma is associated with breakthrough improvement. For a process to move from its current state of three Sigma to four Sigma, a 90 percent (10 times) improvement is needed. To achieve Six Sigma level performance, about 20,000 times improvement is needed.

Six Sigma is not for the faint of heart. One must have vision, guts, courage and wisdom to achieve such monumental improvement. However, it is important to remember that to quickly benefit from it; Six Sigma must be applied to customer-critical aspects of products or services. One must apply Six Sigma in every process, not necessarily to everything in the process.

One of the subtle cultural aspects of a successful Six Sigma journey is driving out fear. Deming has emphasized that driving out fear is critical to bringing out the best in people. Scanlon showed that sharing information (Identity) builds trust. Cooperation between employees and managers in Scanlon organizations drives out fear. Employees are encouraged to take risks, learn from mistakes and accomplish breakthrough results. Six Sigma was used to achieve market leadership and the highest profit in the industry at Motorola. Focusing on sales and costs alleviated the employees' fear of failure and of losing their jobs. Six Sigma meant more capacity for growth, helping to create a positive environment where Motorola was considered one of the best places to work in America.

Communicating Six Sigma

A direct announcement of commitment to Six Sigma from the chief executive is the first critical step toward efficient communication for a companywide implementation. If the Six Sigma initiative is evolving from a department or a division, some level of communication about the strategy is also important. Many companies start the Six Sigma initiative with a set of projects. In such cases, a straightforward memo is enough to keep communication flowing among the employees who are part of the projects. However, communication from top management is still the best source for informing employees of the intent and evolving plans of the new company-wide initiative. The absence of communication may cause employees to fear or resent the Six-Sigma initiative.

For company-wide communication, a much broader approach can be taken. In addition to top management memos and announcements, press releases, publicity brochures or pamphlets describing Six Sigma in context with the corporation are prepared. Trinkets like lapel pins, mugs, shirts, sweaters or caps may be distributed. A video of the personal message from the chief executive can be shown or the announcement in a multi-facility corporation may be broadcast through a satellite link. An even better demonstration of management interest in the new initiative is a live Six Sigma presentation to the employees.

Companies track key business performance measurements through scorecards and dashboards. The scorecards, such as the balanced scorecard or the Six Sigma business scorecard provide the methodology, while various software providers offer dashboards. Dashboards are a collection of meters or gages with color codes for good, bad and questionable performance, simultaneously showing multiple measurements. Companies also plot multiple charts on a page to achieve the same purpose. These charts are called 5-up, 4-up or 3-up charts, depending upon the number of charts per page. One of the distinct aspects of the Six Sigma charts is that an axis may be a log scale due to dramatic improvement, reducing defective parts per million opportunities from several thousands to a few (i.e., more than 60,000 to less than 10, and a goal line).

Six Sigma for Executives

Corporations try to develop in-house expertise to implement Six Sigma. But outside help can prevent a wrong start, and facilitate development of a corporate vision and strategic plan. A project leader (sponsor) and a Black Belt are designated to lead the effort. (Six-Sigma expertise is often designated as green, yellow or black belt. Black belts have the highest competency in six sigma methods). They'll develop a business model; identify growth and profit streams, and list opportunities for improvement. These opportunities are prioritized and used to define various projects, which are then converted into an opportunity for improvement. Costs, savings, probability of success and time for completion are used to prioritize projects. The prioritizing criteria can vary from one company to another, depending upon the business objectives.

Passionate executive commitment must come with the correct understanding of the intent of Six Sigma and with effective executive support of the initiative. To create passionate commitment, leadership must learn certain tools and skills. There are 10 tools that constitute a minimal set of Six Sigma tools an executive must become familiar with to solve a problem or lead employees to solve problems. Four important business tools include employee recognition, process thinking, business scorecards and management review. Three important Six Sigma process tools include statistical thinking, Six Sigma methodology and rate of improvement. Three improvement tools are process mapping, the Pareto principle, and cause and effect diagrams. These tools and skills are listed in the table below (extracted from *The Six Sigma Performance Handbook* (McGraw-Hill Professional, 2004).

With the help of these key executive tools, executives can steer their Six Sigma or similar corporate performance improvement initiatives in the right direction, and guide them to achieve bottom line results. Otherwise, the Six Sigma implementation may fail.

Moving from Control to Perfection (PDCA to 4P's)

Today, PDCA has become a fundamental tenet of quality management. All the emphasis on process thinking is based on the PDCA cycle, be it ISO 9001, ISO/TS 16949, Six Sigma, TQM or SPC. PDCA is a closed-loop engineering application, or a feedback diagram for the quality process. In fact, if you con-

Key Executive Tools

Tool/Concept	Type	What (Description)	When (Applicability)
Employee Recognition	B	Process of recognizing exceptional improvement activities and employees	To inspire dramatic improvement and employee innovation
Process Thinking	B	Understanding business is a collection of processes (4p Model)	Helps understand business processes and how to lead them for improvement
Six Sigma Business Scorecard	B	A corporate performance measurement system balanced for growth and profitability	Learning to achieve improvement in performance and profitability
Management Review	B	Role of internal audits, corrective action and operations management review	Monthly feedback to the management team for necessary adjustment to achieve growth and profitability
Statistical Thinking	P	Understanding random and assignable variation	Helps in determining degree of adjustment or type of actions to be taken
Six Sigma Overview	P	Understanding of Intent, Impact, DMAIC and Requirements	Decision making, specifically when committing to Six Sigma
Rate of Improvement	P	Differences between incremental and dramatic improvement	Achieve dramatic process improvement reducing waste and achieving profitability
Process Mapping	I	Flow charts used to understand information flow, value streams to profitability	Identify disconnects in the business and opportunity for improvement
Pareto Principle	I	A graphical tool to prioritize commitments based on added valued	When deciding about what to work on first
Cause and Effect Analysis	I	Understanding causative relationship between performance and processes	Identify root cause of problems and remedial actions

Legend: B—Business, P—Six Sigma Process, I—Improvement
Ref: *The Six Sigma Performance Handbook*

sider the evolution of quality from in-line, on-line, off-line and quality management to the best-in-class, PDCA has held up pretty well.

The PDCA cycle provides a feedback mechanism for continual quality improvement, which is similar to an engineering feedback model. The four elements of PDCA equate to the four states of a process.

In the PDCA model, "plan" implies defining a process, "do" refers to doing tasks as planned, "check" means verifying acceptance, and "act" entails containment, disposition and correction. Though prevention was intended, it rarely occurred. Quality management systems of the past, including TQM, have emphasized process thinking using PDCA to ensure shipment of acceptable product to the customer. The sampling plans were designed to determine quantities of the product to check. In other words, the "check" step has become synonymous with "inspection" in many businesses. An inspection phase was added to weed out unacceptable product.

In practice, "act" has become the weakest link. The input to "act" comes from "check," which provides inadequate and insufficient feedback for action. The data available from "check" for analysis in most companies appears to be the attribute type. It's like counting the number of OKs, although acting on this number has been difficult. Therefore, typical root cause analysis for the rare "not OKs" has been the operator. Most companies have a problem with poor root cause analysis and recurring problems leads them to question the current PDCA model.

The PDCA model was most likely developed to manage product disposition through process control, which led to the development of workmanship standards with upper specification limits (USL) and lower specification limits (LSL). The system of limits was actually developed to verify the product, but the concept was passed on to process and design personnel. This started the concept of limits, leading to an increase in variability. At this point, Deming tried to reduce excessive variability, while Taguchi tried to avoid it by focusing on targeting in the design phase. Deming focused on reducing variation using statistical tools. Taguchi promoted the concept of "robust" engineering.

The four P's of process management

The "preparation" step represents assurance of good inputs to the process. The inputs consist of Ishikawa's 4 M's. The goal is to ensure that these 4 Ms are delivered as inputs to the process. The "perform" step implies that the process is well-defined, mistake-proofed and understood for consistent and effective execution. The "perfect" step ensures that the process is performing as planned and that the process output is on target. If the process output isn't on target, the gap in the "perfect" step must be recognized. The "progress" step leads to improvement in the process and its outputs if variation around the target is reduced. By continually applying the 4-P cycle, companies can reengineer a process to achieve desired results by the customer through a better process instead of a better inspection of the product.

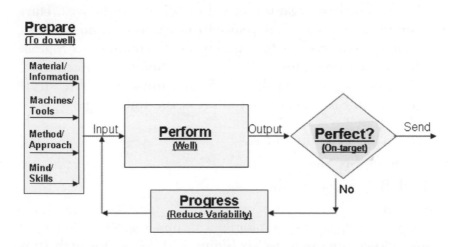

Below is a comparison between the PDCA and the 4 P's. The main difference lies in moving from product control to design control. Because design affects most of the cost factors, it makes sense to control design. Besides, it's easier to achieve a faster improvement by controlling design, than by controlling a process within limits.

ATTRIBUTE	PDCA	4 P's
Date of development	1920s	Present
Intended objective	Acceptable output and improvement	Accelerate process improvement
Constraints	Specification limits	Target
Expected outcome	Acceptable output through inspection	Robust output and improved process capability
Perceived source of problem	Operator	Design
Perceived actions	Development of inspection plans	Improvement through innovation
Typical performance	Quality control	Quality engineering

Sustaining Six Sigma

Company leadership faces challenges, because they feel the need to renew their organizations through new initiatives. Having one initiative year after year can prove to be a boring task for leadership, as well as for employees. Sustaining Six Sigma, just like earlier programs, is a challenge. Some resources must be allocated to renewing the Six Sigma initiatives. The strategy to sustain Six Sigma must address the following:

- Leadership commitment
- Managing Six Sigma
- Black Belt accountability
- Innovation

Leadership commitment to Six Sigma is reflected through strategic actions, personal behavior, continual review of progress and expectations from the management team. Strategic actions must include tactics for realizing sizeable business performance improvement in terms of growth and profitability. Personal commitment to using Six Sigma for improvement throughout the corporation, and compensation incentives proportionate with the improvement rate must also be maintained. Just supporting the Six Sigma initiative and achieving lots of improvement very fast isn't enough. Personal involvement through sharing Six Sigma-related experiences with employees is a great way to motivate the troops.

Managing Six Sigma implies integrating the initiative in the business management system for standardization, audits, remedial actions and performance review. That means, standardizing Six Sigma through various procedures or documents. The procedures must address Six Sigma in process-yield or performance-improvement goals, application of DMAIC, implementation of Six Sigma measurements including defects per unit (DPU), defects per million opportunities (DPMO) and sigma levels. Once standardized through documentation, training and practice, internal audits should review compliance and effectiveness of the Six Sigma implementation. Any inconsistencies or inattention to the Six Sigma practices must be addressed promptly through the root cause analysis and corrective action system. Leadership should then review Six Sigma effectiveness, including the use of DMAIC and the improvement results. If it's determined the Six Sigma initiative isn't producing the desired results against established goals, a highly visible and systemic remedial action must be initiated.

Six Sigma Black Belts are the change agents for corporate performance improvement. That's why the role of Black Belt must be defined. Six Sigma Black Belts aren't supposed to be the statisticians roaming around trying to conduct design of experiments.

They are not improvement Nazis doing Six Sigma to workers. Instead, the Black Belts must be working business leaders facilitating dramatic improvement by reducing waste using Six Sigma intelligently with the cooperation of people closest to the work. In other words, Six Sigma isn't for every project, for every problem and for all the time. Six Sigma thinking is for everybody, Six Sigma measurements are for all managers and Six Sigma projects are for specific opportunities that need significant improvement for directly affecting the bottom line. Black Belts must be continually scouting for such bottom line opportunities and driving the improvement through intellectual participation of employees. Intellectual participation implies enlisting their ideas in developing innovative solutions to achieve great improvement very fast. Black Belts must hold themselves accountable for of the amount of improvement Six Sigma generates and report success of projects. Black Belts must identify areas or challenges in completing projects and remedy barriers to the improvement.

Innovation has been unintentionally excluded from Six Sigma vocabulary. Great improvement can't happen very fast without innovative thinking and attitude. In simple terms, innovation means doing things differently. Black Belts must realize they can't achieve much improvement very fast by doing the same thing over and over, or by fine-tuning existing processes. They must explore new possibilities, eliminate nonvalue-added activities and make processes more efficient. Innovation can no longer be seen as an art only performed by some elite individuals. Innovation must become everybody's overriding responsibility. In today's competitive global environment, the word acceptable isn't acceptable anymore. Businesses must make excellence elementary, thinking a must-do activity and innovation a standard process.

Measuring Performance Improvement

Would implementing Lean or Six Sigma fix all problems of a company? Implementing Lean/Six Sigma may bring the cost of delivering services or goods in line with the expected margins. Cost reduction must not be confused with performance optimization, which implies concurrently balancing multiple factors to achieve profitable growth. Corporations must visibly demonstrate simultaneous commitment to growth and profit with the same vigor. If a company commits to growth at any cost, it'll grow waste faster, too. On the other hand, a company that commits to profit without growth will eventually not be profitable at all. A corporation must analyze all value streams leading to growth and profitability, and then establish a strategy and an action plan to achieve profitable growth. This would include monitoring multiple factors affecting growth and cost.

The following table lists various factors that must be addressed to achieve profitable growth:

KEY GROWTH FACTORS	KEY PROFIT FACTORS
Employee recognition	Supplier responsiveness
Customer service	Process-quality improvement (Six Sigma)
Idea management or innovation	Cycle-time reduction (lean)
Rate of improvement (Six Sigma)	Material costs
Revenue growth	SG&A cost

Extracted from *Six Sigma Business Scorecard* (McGraw Hill, 2003)

For companies that have outsourced manufacturing to meet some randomly established quarterly numbers, the probable outcome is continual outsourcing at higher rates. Sometimes, outsourcing appears to be giving up. It's like "Since I can't fix a problem, and I can't handle the feeling of disappointment at my inability to solve the problem I will just give up." Instead, leadership should be measuring performance in terms of business growth, job creation and return on investment for all stake holders, including employees.

Employee Participation

Employees form a critical group of stakeholders because the work many hours and years, and they invest their savings in the company. The five types of management styles that a company can deploy include Authoritative, Paternalistic, Consultative, Participative, and Partnership.[1] Typically, the management style is characterized by the way in which managers make decisions, and use their power. The participative management style promotes relationship, values, and healthy interaction among organization members. Members in an organization are considered partners who work cordially toward common goals, and demonstrate mutual trust and respect. In

[1] Robert and Paul Doyle, *Gain Management*, New York: AMACOM, 1992.

Scanlon system, partnership becomes an organizing principle at all levels. Irrespective of position in the organization, partnership is about performance. Decisions are made with the understanding that excellence in performance is a result of innovative thinking and voluntary collaboration among members. Truly productive teamwork comes as a result of personal commitment given by partners towards common goals without fear. Such a system produces commitment to excellence, so strong that everyone understands that without such an arrangement, everyone would fail collectively.

Implementing Six Sigma successfully requires a participative style of management, where employees stake their ownership through goal setting, and by sharing gains realized from the initiatives. Bob Galvin, former Chairman and CEO of Motorola, promoted the Participative Management Program (PMP) while driving improvement in the company. (PMP was Motorola's Scanlon Plan). Employees set stretch goals, which they mostly achieved to improve by a factor of ten times in five years. The employee gains emboldened the leadership to set higher standards of excellence in 1986 to ten times in two years leading to Six Sigma in five years. As a result, the company doubled its sales with same number of employees, and everyone benefited from Motorola's success.

Six Sigma requires dramatic improvement, which cannot be achieved without employees' active participation. In the knowledge age, employees' intellectual participation has become even more important not only to achieve Six Sigma level performance, but to stay competitive. Companies must establish a system to continually seek employee ideas to improve process, products and services innovatively. Such a continual dramatic improvement can not be achieved by a select few, irrespective of their expertise.

Companies that have implemented Six Sigma successfully, find their employees experience achievement, influence, fairness, and trust. They like the challenge, and security Six Sigma provides in their workplace. Given the opportunity to practice Six Sigma as it was created at Motorola, employees respond with creativity, productivity, loyalty and commitment.

EMPLOYEE INVOLVEMENT AND SCANLON

M. Peter Scontrino

Every other year an international survey research company asks this question of a representative sample of employees in the United States: *Sufficient effort is made to get the opinions and thinking of the people who work here.* For the past few survey administrations the percent of employees who responded favorably to this question has hovered around 40%. Three out of five employees believe that their employers, their managers, and their supervisors are not devoting enough time, energy, and organization resources to soliciting their ideas and opinions. The results also suggest that employees would like to have their opinions and thoughts solicited—that is, they would like an opportunity to be more involved. Research now shows that involvement is necessary for employees to feel connected or engaged in their work, for customers to be satisfied and for investors to receive greater returns.

In a Conference Board study conducted in 2004:

- 40% of workers felt disconnected from their employers.
- Two out of every three workers did not identify with or feel motivated to drive their employer's business goals and objectives.
- 25% of employees were just "showing up to collect a paycheck."[1]

[1] Press Release: "U.S. Job Satisfaction Keeps Falling, The Conference Board Reports," Feb. 28, 2005.

A study by the Forum for People Performance Management and Measurement at Northwestern University concluded: Organizations with engaged employees have customers who use their products more, and increased customer usage leads to higher levels of customer satisfaction. In addition, satisfied employees see their positive attitudes transferred directly to satisfied customers.[2]

Daniel Dennison at the University of Michigan has shown that high involvement cultures produce a three times greater ROI than organizations with low involvement cultures.[3]

Do employees really have that many ideas? The evidence is overwhelming that the answer is, "Yes." Recently we conducted an employee survey for an organization that is well managed, is known for soliciting and valuing employee input, and is regarded in the community as a good place to work. Over 900 of the company's 1,100 employees offered one hundred and three pages of single spaced suggestions covering every facet of the business.

Employees in Scanlon Companies have contributed cost savings ideas that have saved millions of dollars. National Manufacturing's Scanlon suggestion system processed over 13,000 suggestions that generated over $40 million in employee bonuses and returned over $13 million back to National. A front-line employee at Cerdec with one suggestion found a way to save his company a million dollars a year. A suggestion from several Magna Donnelly employees for a new product resulted in the creation of a billion dollar a year new industry!

Definition of Employee Involvement

The second Frost-Scanlon Principle is participation. Participation is defined as the opportunity, which only management can provide, and the responsibility, which only employees can

[2]Press Release: "Purdue research links employee satisfaction, profit," September 13, 2004.
[3]Dennison, Daniel. *Corporate Culture and Organizational Effectiveness*, New York: John Wiley & Sons, 1990.

accept, to influence decisions in their areas of competence. Participation is based on these facts:

- Each employee is the expert at his or her job (competence).
- Employees have ideas for improving the organization.
- Management must create processes to allow employees to give life to their ideas (participative management).

Employee involvement (EI) and Participative Management are the processes which give life to the Principle of participation. EI is synonymous with employee empowerment, engagement and participation. Participative Management (PM) is the opposite side of the same coin. PM is synonymous with participative leadership, consultative management and servant leadership. Employee involvement cannot occur without participative management.

The Frost definition of participation includes a number of key concepts.

1. Structure—EI processes require structure. Employees need a process or mechanism to voice their ideas and concerns. Later in this chapter we will identify the different structures that organizations are using to engage their employees.

2. Opportunity—EI represents an invitation to participate. It is wrong to assume that employees can be compelled to participate. They can be required to attend EI events, but their heads and hearts can only be volunteered when they receive a sincere invitation from a manager they trust. This is why PM is critical for EI to be successful.

3. Creativity—EI is based on a belief that employees' are experts at their jobs and have insights and observations about things that are not always obvious to their managers and supervisors. D.J. DePree (the founder of Herman Miller) became a servant/Scanlon leader when he learned at the funeral of the company's millwright that the millwright was an accomplished poet. Did he have a poet working for him, who was also a millwright or was he a millwright who was also a poet? DePree concluded that

either people are ordinary or they are extraordinary. In a road to Damascus type transformation he vowed from that point on to treat people as if they are extraordinary. His son Hugh would later write "The difference at Herman Miller is not the lengthened shadow of one man, nor the talents of an elite group of managers. The difference is the energy beamed from thousands of unique contributions by people who understand, accept and are committed to the idea that they can make a difference."

4. Input—EI promises employees that their message will be heard. It is not a promise of blind acceptance of ideas and suggestions. While it is assumed the person closest to the work knows their job best competence is the determining factor. Scanlon companies do not encourage Participation for Participation's sake alone. The reason for Participation is to allow competence at any level to be heard.

Unlimited Potential

Human beings are inquisitive, creative, and questioning by nature. Imagine what would happen in your organization if that energy were released in a controlled, orderly fashion. That is the potential of EI. What could your organization do with a 6% performance improvement?

The term Employee Involvement encompasses a number of different approaches to engaging employees. Some of the different approaches include:

- Structured suggestion systems
- Labor management cooperation
- Quality Control Circles
- Joint shop floor committees
- Work teams
- Ad-hoc teams and task forces
- Production committees and screening committees

- Survey feedback
- Information meetings
- Cells
- Kaizen events

Whatever the mechanism used to encourage EI, it is important that EI system help employees solve work problems. Donnelly encouraged EI by asking their employees the following ten questions:

1. What made you mad today?
2. What took too long?
3. What was the cause of any complaints?
4. What was misunderstood?
5. What cost too much?
6. What was wasted?
7. What was too complicated?
8. What is just plain silly?
9. What job took too many people?
10. What job involved too many actions?

Scanlon and Employee Involvement

Scanlon's Plan is best known as a gainsharing scheme but from the very beginning Scanlon was interested in creating gains as well as sharing them. EI was the primary method Joe Scanlon used to increase productivity and efficiency to create the gains that would later be shared.

The structure of the early Scanlon plans was very straightforward. Each department or unit had a production committee. The production committee included a supervisor and a small group of employees elected by their peers. The production committee's job was "to meet at least monthly and discuss ways and means of eliminating waste, easier and better ways of doing the job, the departmental schedules and any thing else that might pertain to the work going through the department." The production committee also processed suggestions brought to them by employees in their department. Management reserved the right to accept or reject any suggestions. Suggestions that were accepted were implemented. Minutes were taken which were shared with the "Screening committee."

One person from each production committee sat on an organization wide screening committee which also included management from each functional area. The screening committee had three primary jobs.

The first was to report the bonus. Was it on track? Was there a deficit? The second job of the Screening Committee was a discussion by company leaders about anything that might affect the plan. The third function was to screen all suggestions—those approved, and those rejected by the production committees.

The first published example of the production and screening committee model was the Adamson Company. Under the first year of the Scanlon Plan using these two committees the average bonus, based on productivity improvements, was 41%. The productivity enhancing ideas were generated via production committees and implemented via the screening committee.[4]

There is nothing radical about the production committee and screening committee structure. In theory supervisors and managers are always interested in employee ideas. However there was something about Scanlon's plan that was revolutionary leading to articles in *Life*, *Time* and *Fortune* magazines. Scanlon was both a dreamer and a realist. His dream was to create better workplaces where "together we can achieve the impossible." However, his experience in organizations led him to conclude, that often ideas are withheld, or ignored. Structures and systems are needed if EI is going to work.

One of the forces acting against employee involvement is the belief of some supervisors that they should be the source

[4]Schulz, George, P. "Worker Participation on Production Problems," In Lesieur, F. The Scanlon Plan—A Frontier in Labor-Management Cooperation. Cambridge, Massachusetts: MIT Press, 1958: 55

of all ideas. In Scanlon's system all ideas are tracked and there is accountability. Supervisors can not just forget or lose ideas they do not like.

Another reason ideas are withheld, is the reward system associated with suggestions. When management gives money to individuals for ideas, it is easy to inadvertently sow discontent. The idea could have been based on someone else's idea. The idea might require others to implement. Individual rewards serve to limit the cooperation needed to get the idea submitted, evaluated and implemented. Scanlon solved this problem by creating a group bonus system.

In any organization it is difficult to find the time to "drain the swamp when you are fighting alligators."

Scanlon's committee structure and regular meetings make constant improvement a scheduled regular event. In some organizations managers make a habit of postponing or avoiding decisions. In other organizations the right people needed to get decisions made are not at the meetings. Scanlon's system prevents this from happening. Decisions get made.

Today the wide spread sharing of information that occurs in the production and screening committees is called the Identity Principle. Scanlon's production and screening committee system creates a very effective and efficient communication mechanism focused on performance. It allows all the various parts of an organization to understand each other's needs and to work together while still solving problems at the lowest possible level.

Two other aspects of the system deserve noting. First, management maintains their authority to approve or reject suggestions. Scanlon did not use leaderless teams. Managers have a critical participative management role. They are appointed to serve on the committees by top company leaders and are accountable to those leaders. Scanlon's system is not an abdication of leadership or management authority.

The second aspect worth noting is the worker EI system is representative. Employees elect representatives to serve on the committees. This creates another form of EI in Scanlon Plans— a democratic form with elections and a responsibility to represent an area or function while at the same time working for the good of the entire organization.

The net effect of the structure and systems of EI that Scanlon created is to create real participation . . . not a feeling of participation or a feeling of teamwork but real teamwork. Robert T. Golembiewski in *Men, Management, and Morality*, perhaps said it best—:

> "Various bastardized "participation plans" do exist. Often they attempt to get without giving and must take their place in the storehouse of gimmicks that might or (might not) work in the short run and are likely to fail in the longer run. The Scanlon Plan, in contrast, attempts to exploit the possibilities of participation AND distribute the benefits among all. It does not pussyfoot."[5]

The Scanlon EI committee structure continues to be used today. It is the structure that Watermark Credit Union chose for their Scanlon Plan in 2006 (the first in the financial services industry.) However, Scanlon Plans today uses many different forms of EI. In a study of the various forms of participation used in seventeen Scanlon Companies, Dr. Dow Scott discovered the forms of participation shown in Figure 1.[6]

Scanlon companies also use facility-wide problem solving meetings, production committees, Kaizen events Quality Circles, newsletters and focus groups to encourage EI.

Those who develop EI programs in organizations eventually face the question, "Is participation mandatory?" Most employees want to participate and voluntarily commit, but there are others who only want to "do their job and go home." Scanlon companies today have concluded that some forms of participation are mandatory (like attendance) while others are elective. EI is like a staircase. On the bottom steps participation is mandatory but as the employee climbs higher participation becomes more elective. Employees are encouraged to participate at higher and higher levels. EI encourages increased

[5]Golembiewski, Robert. *Men, Management, and Morality: Toward a New Organizational Ethic*. Piscataway: Transaction Pub., 1988.
[6]Scott, Dow. Report prepared for the Scanlon Leadership Network.

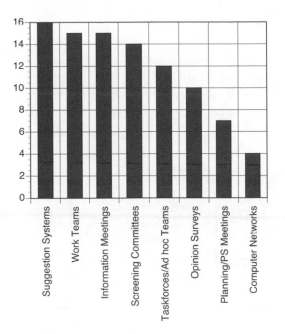

FIGURE 1. Forms of Participation

development as it provides opportunities for development. The Scanlon Participation Model is shown in Figure 2.

How Are EI Cultures Created?

What is the best way to create "a non-pussyfooting EI process?" Scanlon companies since the 1960's have used a process called "The Scanlon Roadmap" developed by Dr. William Greenwood and Dr. Carl Frost. Their process can be better understood based on the results of a study done in the 1940's.

The Pajama Factory

In 1948 Lester Coch and John R. P. French, Jr. published an article titled, "Overcoming Resistance to Change." This article represents a milestone in the employee involvement arena.

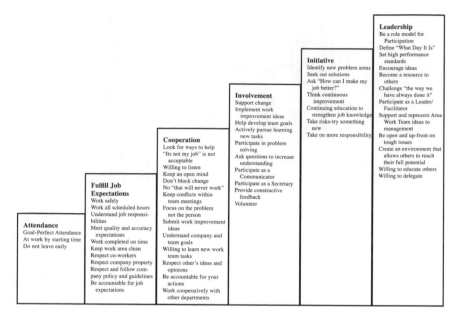

FIGURE 2. Scanlon Participation Model

The authors were interested in the root cause or causes of productivity drops at the Harwood Manufacturing Corporation in Virginia. The plant produced pajamas. Whenever the plant changed methods or jobs, there was a significant drop in productivity. The drop in productivity was accompanied by increases in employee turnover and aggression. The plant managers were at a complete loss to determine the cause or causes of the productivity drop. They asked the authors to study the situation to see if they could identify any causes.

The authors determined that the changes in work procedures themselves were not the problem. The root cause was the employees' resistance to the changes. To overcome this resistance, the authors designed a series of experiments with employee problem solving teams. In one experiment the authors had three different conditions: no participation, some participation, and total participation. The authors found a strong correlation between the degree of participation and the successful implementation of the change. The total participation group attained a productivity level that was 14% higher than the pre-change level. Plus there was no turnover in that group during the forty days following the experiment. This contrasts with the no participation group that made no improvements after the change and was actually disbanded thirty-two days after the experiment.[7]

The Scanlon Roadmap for Change

The Pajama study taught change agents that the best way to prevent resistance to change is to involve employees in changes that impact them The Scanlon roadmap starts with the top leader of an organization developing a "mandate for change." The mandate explains why change is needed and it is shared first with the top leadership group. Often EI is assumed to be only for those at the lower levels of an organization but all levels of organizations want to be involved—to be heard—to use their competencies—to influence decisions that impact them.

The top leader describes the mandate and involves her reports by asking them questions like "is the mandate compelling?" "Do you agree that change is needed?" "Are we ready, able and willing to develop a Scanlon Plan to help us meet our mandate?" A secret ballot vote is then held and the Scanlon Roadmap is not continued if there is not unanimous support. Top leaders do not often allow their subordinates to "vote." Voting is not the norm even in Scanlon organizations for most activities. However, the roadmap vote allows the top leader to know if there is true support of the leadership team for the mandate. In one Scanlon Company the entrepreneurial leader conducted the secret vote and found his team voted not to install a Scanlon Plan. The leader was furious. When he asked his team why they did not want to pursue a Scanlon Plan, he was told that the timing was not right . . . that the team needed

[7]Coch, Lester and French, John R. P., Jr. "Overcoming resistance to change." *Human Relations*, 1948, 11, 512–532.

to focus on several major quality initiatives first. They told him the next year they would fully supported a Scanlon Plan and they did.

Often the vote surfaces issues in the top team. They may not believe their leader is committed to staying in the organization. Members of the team may want to purse other opportunities. There may be ill will from past change efforts. Aligning the top team before others are involved takes time, but greatly increases the odds of success. If the top team can't agree on the need to change or Scanlon as a process, the decision is made before a lot of resources are spent or expectations of employees are raised.

Once the top team agrees to support the mandate and the Scanlon Roadmap process the mandate is shared with the rest of the management team down to the front-line supervisors. Middle managers and supervisors are usually the last to be offered true opportunities for EI. Often they are expected to support decisions that they have had no role in creating, simply because they are managers. The Scanlon Roadmap gives them a chance to learn why change is needed, and to be involved in the decision to proceed or not to proceed with Scanlon. Like the top-level team they are given an opportunity through a secret ballot to voice their support or concerns.

Assuming that the managers are supportive they take the mandate to the employees. Employees are asked to support the creation of a design team to create a unique Scanlon Plan for their organization.

Usually a Scanlon Plan is not created unless at least 80% of the employees vote to proceed. The mandate, information meetings, and vote generate great commitment from employees. At Sears one employee became sick with the flu the day of the vote and was rushed to the emergency room. She called in her vote from the emergency room because she wanted it to be unanimous.

The design team is a cross-section of the organization with some members appointed by top management and many elected to represent their department, shift or unit. Design team members have an incredible (non-pussyfoot) EI experience. They meet with other members of their organization to discuss the mandate and to develop a plan to keep everyone informed, involved accountable and continually improving. As they draft the plan they share their deliberations with the rest of the organization through minutes of their meetings. Research conducted at Sears has shown the importance of the design team as catalyst in increasing the commitment of all employees.

When the plan is finished it is presented to the entire organization. Questions are answered and a vote to install the plan for a trial period is taken. The plan is usually not implemented unless 80–90% of all employees vote for it. During the trial period (usually 1–2 years) the plan may be adjusted. Most Scanlon companies will then vote to make the plan a permanent way of life. The Roadmap process demands a high level of EI/PM from all levels of the organization. For the top leader it requires her involvement in developing the mandate for change and aligning the leadership team. For the managers it requires that they study the mandate and the Scanlon Plan and make a nearly unanimous informed decision to proceed. It requires them to understand why change is needed and to be able to articulate the mandate to their reports. For the average employee it requires at least three votes . . . a vote to create a design team, a vote to install the plan for a trial period, and a vote to make the Scanlon Plan permanent. For design team members it requires them to understand the mandate for change, to understand the Scanlon Process, to represent their function or area and to work with other members of the team to design a workable plan. It also requires them to be the chief spokespeople and advocates of the plan when it is presented back to the organization.

Hugh DePree, former CEO of Herman Miller, wrote: "People need to be needed, want to be productive, need to be responsible, have the right to know, need and want to own the problem. The Scanlon plan can answer such needs."[8]

---

[8]DePree, Hugh. *Business as Unusual*, Zeeland: Herman Miller, 1986.

Organizational Democracy and EI/PM

Scanlon's structures and the roadmap change process used to create them mirror many of the structures and processes found in democratic organizations. The mandate serves some of the same functions the declaration of independence served by explaining why change is needed. The design team serves many of the same functions as the constitutional convention—a representative group that designs a Plan-Constitution that explains how we will work together. The production committees are like local or state governments-focused on local needs and the screening committee is like a federal government—focused on the needs of the whole.

The most democratic of all Scanlon organizations was Donnelly through their "Equity Structure." Employees elected to the Donnelly committee made decisions regarding policies, and fairness—even recommending pay increases.

Scanlon EI/PM beliefs practices and structures led Katz and Kahn to write "Scanlon . . . boldest attempt at employee participation in the United States. Its leadership model approaches the democratic values held by non-industry institutions."[9]

The Scanlon Principles and Processes create organizations where leaders can practice participative management and where employees are meaningfully involved. Fundamental to Joe Scanlon was the belief that "Together we can achieve the impossible."

[9]Katz, D. and Kahn, R. L. *The Social Psychology of Organizations*. New York: Wiley, 1966.

DO SCANLON PLANS FAIL, OR DO MANAGERS PLAN TO FAIL?

Paul Davis

If Scanlon Plans are so good, why haven't more organizations adopted them? If Scanlon Plans work so well, why do some organizations drop their plans?

Variations of these two questions are frequently directed towards those who practice Scanlon/EPIC Leadership and those who are exploring implementing a Scanlon Plan. They are legitimate questions.

The first question has to do with the popularity of Scanlon/EPIC ideas, while the second question has to do with their effectiveness.

Why Aren't Scanlon Plans More Popular?

When someone discovers the Principles, Plans and tools called "Scanlon" they tap into a body of knowledge that has been growing since the 1930's. The sheer size and range of the knowledge can be confusing. Like the story of the three blind men who when asked to describe an elephant could only describe the part they were touching as a tree or a leaf or a snake those exploring Scanlon often miss how the parts fit together. Those who try to explain "Scanlon" often describe only one small part by saying it is a gainsharing system, or an employee involvement system, or it is a set of Principles or it is a written Plan.

259

All of these answers are true, yet they fail to capture the total essence of what we call Scanlon/EPIC Leadership.

Scanlon is a set of assumptions about the nature of people (Theory Y) that require servant-leaders to follow the EPIC Principles. In addition, there are some Scanlon Leaders who follow a participative roadmap to create a Scanlon Plan. The Scanlon Plan is an industrial constitution participatively created that explains how the Principles will be implemented. There are servant-leaders who do not follow the EPIC Principles and there are servant-leaders who follow the Scanlon Principles but do not follow the "roadmap" to create a Scanlon Plan. When someone questions the success of Scanlon they are often looking at the part of the elephant that is the Scanlon Plan.

An organization can practice the EPIC Principles without going through the process of developing a Scanlon Plan. Organizations that create a Scanlon Plan, with its multiple secret ballot votes, and high level of employee involvement are rarer than organizations that practice one or all of the EPIC Principles.

Further adding to the confusion about Scanlon Plans is the lack of a central authority or database on Scanlon Plans. Improshare™ and Rucker™ plans were trademarked by their creators. Joe Scanlon preferred to share his ideas with the world. He did not trademark his approach. Joe and later Scanlon consultants encouraged their clients to give their Scanlon Plans unique names. The Scanlon Plan at Motorola was called "Participative Management;" at Donnelly it was called "Equity;" and at Beth Israel, "Prepare/21". Unless the Scanlon connection is explained, researchers and practitioners do not know that these plans are Scanlon Plans.

Time magazine on September 26, 1955 wrote that Joe Scanlon was "the most sought after consultant in America." For almost ten years, Joe Scanlon had offered a radical new way to lead organizations. *Life* magazine on December 23, 1946 in an article entitled "Every man a Capitalist" popularized Joe's ideas. This led to an article in *Fortune* in January 1950, entitled "Enterprise for Everyman." With Scanlon's ideas featured in both the business and popular press the Scanlon Plan was well known. Some writers estimated that there were over 500 companies with

Scanlon Plans, a number widely cited in research papers about Scanlon. The basis for the number has proven impossible to verify. Scanlon Plans were created in Canada, England, Germany, Japan, Australia and India in addition to the United States. The Massachusetts Institute of Technology (MIT) and Michigan State University (MSU) were major Scanlon learning centers sponsoring research and Scanlon Conferences.

What is clear is that the Scanlon Plan never became "Enterprise for Everyman" and did not make "Everyman a capitalist." The Plans did not live up to the expectations writers had for them to totally transform our capitalistic system. Upon Joe's death in 1956, Dr. Carl Frost and Fred Lesieur became the most prolific Scanlon Plan consultants creating Scanlon Plans in organizations like Herman Miller, Donnelly, Motorola, Wolverine Worldwide, Beth Israel Hospital, Dana, and National Manufacturing. At one point five of the top fifty best places to work in America had Scanlon Plans. While the number of companies with Scanlon Plans probably never exceeded 500 companies their influence in business has been greater than their numbers would indicate.

Unlike management fads, the Scanlon/EPIC Principles did not disappear. They can be found in organizations that practice labor management cooperation, employee involvement, open-book management, servant-leadership, gainsharing, goalsharing, and lean systems. They continue to be refined. An association of Scanlon companies was formed in 1964. Today the Scanlon Leadership Network and its supporting Scanlon Foundation continue to sponsor Scanlon related conferences and research.

Ideas that began to take shape with Joe Scanlon in the 1930's are considered world class and business best practices today. *Training* Magazine in a special millennium issue wrote:

"The 20th Century has been a hothouse of management fads . . . In the meantime one truly big idea has bubbled along since the 1940's, never receiving the accolades we regularly bestow on more modest insights. And it's surprising considering this one has all the elements of a blockbuster. Its watchwords read like an abstract of

50 years' worth of business hot buttons: Employee Participation, management-labor cooperation, collaborative problem-solving, teamwork, trust, gainsharing, open-book management and servant leadership. But you probably won't recognize one of the best-kept secrets in the management world: The Scanlon Plan."

How did Scanlon "get lost in the shuffle?"

Charles Conrad, who founded Thermatron, was fond of comparing Scanlon to aspirin. It took over forty years before aspirin was generally accepted. He believed that Scanlon, like aspirin, would take a long time to become accepted and then would become ubiquitous. While Scanlon/EPIC Plans have yet to become ubiquitous ideas pioneered by Scanlon companies—like teamwork or labor/management cooperation—are no longer considered radical and are considered elements of today's high performance organizations. It is a tribute to Scanlon's genius that many of his ideas are now widely accepted and applied in organizations. One scholar has estimated that 15% of larger organizations in 2006 are practicing the EPIC Principles based on his readings of mission statements and annual reports. In Senate Report 104-259 it was estimated that over 30,000 employers (about 75%) were practicing some form of employee involvement. Teamwork, suggestion systems, and kaizen events, are now considered normal practices in most organizations.

While the number of organizations that have embraced one or more of the EPIC Leadership Principles has increased, the number of organizations with Scanlon Plans has not. Many of the classic Scanlon companies like Atwood, Herman Miller, National Manufacturing and Magna-Donnelly have abandoned their Scanlon Plans (although some still follow the EPIC Principles). Traditionally Scanlon Plans have been installed in manufacturing organizations and manufacturing is in decline in the United States. This can explain some decline in the number of Scanlon Plans, but not all.

Scanlon Plans are built on the assumption that employees, investors and customers are key stakeholders that are "committed" to the organization where they work, invest and shop. In the fast paced "flat" world of today is this concept relevant? Do employees want to commit to their organizations? Do customers care who delivers their products or services? Do investors even need to know the organizations where they invest? The Scanlon Plan builds long-term relationships in organizations. In a world of short term focus and commitments a Scanlon Plan may be a tough sell.

Frederick Reichheld author of "the Loyalty Effect" writes "on average U.S. Corporations now lose half their customers in five years, half their employees in four, and half their investors in less than one." In a recent poll by the Gallup organization of American workers, only 28% are "engaged" or actively committed to their organizations. Fifty-four percent are not engaged and 17% are actively disengaged. Gallup estimates that the actively disengaged group alone cost 350 billion dollars per year in lost productivity. Disloyal customers according to Reichheld "stunt corporate performance by 25 to 50 percent." All customer retention programs are based on the fact that it is often much more profitable to retain a loyal customer than to find a new one. Warren Buffet invests in organizations for the long haul, but many investors do not. During a Scanlon Leadership Retreat Max DePree said, "There is no longer a moral obligation to the investor." He went on to say that in the past investors were committed to the companies where they invested, but today obtaining money was "like buying bent metal." There are obligations to meet monetary commitments to investors, but there is no moral obligation. Today many of the more successful Scanlon companies are privately held companies where investor commitment is visible or they are publicly held companies where the original Scanlon investors control the voting stock.

Studies conducted by Sears show that wealth creation for them begins with employees who are committed to the company. Committed employees provide better service for customers, who then buy more products and services creating wealth for the investors. Studies conducted by Hay of the most admired companies in America show that the predominant culture of these great organizations is a culture where employees are encouraged and supported in serving customers. The most admired companies have discovered the old fashioned way how to create wealth: Committed employees serving loyal customers, supported by dedicated investors—the Scanlon Way.

Why Do Some Scanlon Plans Fail?

The Second question—why do some Scanlon Plans fail?—is easier to determine. Dr. Steve Markham has estimated that approximately forty percent of Scanlon plans "fail" and are discontinued.

The primary reasons plan are discontinued are:

1) Change in Leadership
2) Mergers or Acquisitions
3) Changes in Business Fundamentals
4) The Plan is Perceived to no Longer Provide Value

Changes in Leadership

Leadership is the Achilles' heel of the Scanlon Plan. Leaders who understand the EPIC Principles find the Scanlon Plan provides systems for helping them serve their organizations. For example, every Scanlon Plan has a system for practicing Identity or communicating business realities. A leader uses this system to help those in the organization understand what change is needed and why. The Participation or employee involvement system provides leaders with ideas for improvement. A leader can easily use the Participation system to focus the organization on specific ideas for improvement. For example she can say, "We need to find one million dollars of cost savings in six weeks." Requests like this are common in the Scanlon experience, and often the organization responds. The Equity system identifies the key stakeholders, and balances their needs. The leader can use this system to help his/her organization understand why customers are unhappy, why the investors are restless, etc.

However, a new leader must take the time to study and understand the Scanlon process she has inherited. Often a new leader arrives with the belief that she must create change by removing old systems and practices including Scanlon. Because Scanlon is not widely practiced and is not well known in the popular management press today, new leaders often do not understand what Scanlon is and how to use their Scanlon process effectively. They see meetings, but do not understand their purpose. They see money being spent on bonuses but do not see the savings the bonus system may have generated. They may see hundreds of ideas for small improvements, but could be looking for the one idea that creates a "home run."

Authoritarian leaders do not like the Scanlon process because it disperses power and may limit their ability to rule by fiat. They end the Scanlon plan or let it die by neglect because they simply do not believe in employee involvement. Often in a time of crisis they believe that involvement may take too long or may not produce the hard decisions (like layoffs) that are needed for organizational survival and effectiveness. Scanlon/EPIC produces employees who want to be treated fairly (Equity), want to be involved in decision making (Participation), understand what is going on (Identity), and are committed to continuous improvement (Competence). The culture created by the EPIC Principles serves much like a giant flywheel in the organization. Once started, it is difficult to stop. Once started it serves to regulate the speed of the organization. Employees expect to be informed and believe they should be involved in making the tough decisions that impact them even in times of crisis.

The Sears Scanlon Process, the Plan at Herman Miller and the Plan at Lorin were discontinued when new top leaders arrived. Often new leaders bring with them ideas for change which may not include the Scanlon Plan.

Mergers or Acquisitions

Scanlon Plans are installed in a highly participative manner. Before a plan is implemented there are a number of secret ballot votes. Typically plans are not implemented without a supermajority (80% or higher) of employees voting for the plan. When a merger or acquisition brings new people into the organization who did not share the work of creating the plan, or who are not committed to the plan, it is put at risk.

When Beth Israel Hospital merged with Deaconess Hospital, Beth Israel's Prepare/21 (Scanlon Plan) ended. The intent was to recreate the plan for the entire organization once the merger was completed, but it never happened. If the company with the Scanlon Plan is merged into a company without a Scanlon Plan the odds are the parent will not keep the Scanlon Plan. This happens even when the Scanlon process may be the reason that a company has done well.

American Tape had a successful Scanlon Plan. The United Auto Workers (U.A.W.) and the leadership of the plant used the Scanlon process to create a high performance company that was able to compete with 3M in the highly competitive tape business. Quality increased and net after tax income increased 50%. The investors who used the Scanlon process to improve American Tape eventually sought a buyer who they assumed would continue the Scanlon Plan. They even rejected a higher offer from another company because it would have resulted in a major downsizing of their loyal workforce. They sold to a Korean Company, who they later discovered did not believe in employee involvement, sharing information, or paying a bonus. The Scanlon Plan was ended.

Atwood Mobile Products had one of the most successful Scanlon Plans of its time. Seth Atwood wrote, "The adoption of the Scanlon Plan was the most important business decision made in over fifty active years. I'm totally convinced that the money spent as a result of the plan was a fraction of the money saved. Furthermore, the total reorientation of all employees was profound. All employees participated in trying to improve the success of the company. Instead of viewing management as the enemy, the company employees were able to work together with management towards the goal of outperforming the competition." Atwood was sold and the new owner eventually ended the Scanlon Plan that had made Atwood so successful.

Dick Dufner, former CFO of the American Tape Company believes that this kind of failure of Scanlon has to do with whether or not leadership views Scanlon/EPIC Leadership as an investment or as a cost:

"The investment view recognizes there are tremendous, though probably not specifically quantifiable, benefits which far outweigh the outlays involved. Those who view it as a cost believe it is nothing more than a cost of doing business which must be controlled or eliminated. They do not consider the not-so-obvious benefits that far outweigh costs. The cost-benefit ratio is not only unseen, it is never even perceived."

Changes in Business Fundamentals

The Scanlon Process can help an organization compete but it does not isolate an organization from the business cycle or fundamental competitive challenges. One Scanlon organization used their Scanlon process to reduce costs and improve efficiency producing materials from ancient underground seawater. Unfortunately a competitor was able to mine the same material and ship it from Asia to North America at a fraction of the cost it took the Scanlon company to extract the material here.

Scanlon has traditionally been most prevalent in manufacturing. At the time this is being written, North American manufacturing is under intense competitive pressure from China. Manufactures are being forced to locate in China to supply customers already in China, to seek new customers, and to lower costs. Scanlon organizations are not immune to the pressures other organizations face to relocate or to outsource. Some organizations like Wescast Industries have taken their Scanlon process with them. Wescast has been implementing a Scanlon process in Hungary as it seeks to break out of North America to serve new customers in Europe.

However, other Scanlon organizations like Westling Remanufacturing, Sligh Furniture, Martin Marietta, Westan, etc abandoned their Scanlon Plans when their businesses fundamentally changed or when they went bankrupt.

The Plan No Longer Provides Value

Scanlon Plans are installed to increase productivity and to improve employee relations. Parker Pen's traditional Scanlon Plan was ended because as it was designed it was no longer providing value to Parker Pen. The Equity formula was based on a ratio of sales to labor. Over the years through automation and creative problem solving, the cost of labor was reduced to the point where it was not as great a concern as was quality. Parker Pen could have changed their Equity formula which was no longer focusing the organization on the right job, but instead they chose to end their Scanlon Plan.

Most often it is management that ends a Scanlon Plan because it is no longer perceived as adding value, but sometimes employees may discontinue a Scanlon Plan. Xaloy industries had a very successful Scanlon Plan for over ten years. Every three years their plan required over 80% of the employees to approve the plan for it to be continued. The plan received votes of over 90% to continue several times. Eventually, however, the plan was voted out when it failed to garner a supermajority vote. A minority of employees were able to vote out the plan. These employees were upset with changes management had made to their health care plan and eliminating the Scanlon Plan was a way for them to vote their displeasure. (Note: most Scanlon Plans do not require a supermajority vote after the trial period of the first plan. Scanlon/EPIC at that time becomes a permanent way of doing business and is no longer subject to a vote).

Scanlon/EPIC has Better Results than Other Management Philosophies

This chapter began with an estimate of a 60% success rate for Scanlon Plans. No one would buy a car that only started 60% of the time, nor would we ever fly if we had a 40% chance of crashing. Why would rational business leaders invest in Scanlon/EPIC with these odds?

The reason is that most organizational change efforts do not succeed. Consider these statistics reported in a white paper from the consulting firm ODR:

- Fewer than 50 percent of companies undergoing restructuring, de-layering, and/or downsizing realize lower costs or higher productivity as a result of those changes.[1]

- About 80 percent of Total Quality Management (TQM) initiatives fail to achieve tangible results.[2]

- Roughly 90 percent of Business Process Reengineering (BPR) initiatives fail to produce breakthrough results.[3]

- Approximately 30 percent of all mergers and acquisitions fail outright, while most fail to realize expected synergies.[4]

- Between 55 percent and 90 percent of all technology initiatives fail to achieve their objectives because human and organizational problems are not adequately addressed.[5]

Managers embrace the latest quick fix. When that quick fix fails the next quick fix appears to offer hope. Dr. Steve Markham has determined that even with a 60% success rate, Scanlon is *almost twice* as successful as Total Quality Management (TQM).

Reengineering was an idea widely attempted, with many books written about it. Today it has taken its place in the dustbin of history with even its creator admitting it failed to deliver. Authors and consultants continue to produce books and studies. Leaders read the books and attempt to apply the ideas.

---

[1] C. E. Schneier, G. Shaw, and R. W. Beatty, "Companies' Attempts to Improve Performance While Containing Costs: Quick Fix Versus Lasting Change," *Human Resource Planning*, 1992, 15 (no. 3), 1–25.

[2] A. T. Kearney, study cited in Business Intelligence's report entitled "Maintaining and Sustaining Radical Change," 1977.

[3] Ibid.

[4] R. Mauer, "Transforming Resistance," *Human Resources Focus*, 1, October 1997, p. 9.

[5] D. J. Kabot, "Information Technology to Manage Next Dynamic," in Berger and Sikora (Eds.), *The Change Management Handbook*, New York: Irwin Professional Publishing, 1994, p. 221.

However, "management by best seller" rarely provides the results promised.

Independent researchers have studied Scanlon/EPIC extensively for over seventy years. It has stood the test of time.

The American Productivity Center and the American Compensation Association found "100 percent of all firms with Scanlon Plans report they are having a positive or very positive impact on productivity. Scanlon Plans produce the most consistent pattern of high ratings."

Few other leadership ideas have been subjected to the same testing rigor as have Scanlon/EPIC nor can they claim the same results.

In Conclusion

The odds of success with Scanlon are simply greater than the odds of success with untested approaches. Even when plans are discontinued they are rarely discontinued because they have failed to increase employee satisfaction, customer satisfaction or financial performance. A study of Scanlon companies conducted by Jerry McAdams (lead researcher in the Consortium for Alternative Reward Strategies Research) showed over a 125% return to organizations that install Scanlon Plans.

The question should not be "Why do Scanlon Plans fail?" but "Why do managers plan to fail?" by adopting unproven, untested approaches. *Time* Magazine in an editorial about Scanlon in 1955 wrote, "As far as I am concerned, Joe has the answer to the future for American free-enterprise capitalism." Scanlon/E.P.I.C. Leadership still provides an answer for leaders seeking a better way.

CHAPTER 20

SCANLON SUCCESS STORIES

Tony Adolfi

1. Top-To-Bottom Communication Fuels Participation at Nicholas Plastics

Sparked by a driving need in the automotive industry to reduce costs, Nicholas Plastics Incorporated joined the Scanlon Leadership Network in 1997 to improve Lean Manufacturing and boost employee participation. The company's management first attended a Scanlon Conference, liked what they saw and followed up. Nicholas Plastics, headquartered in Allendale, Michigan, is a family-owned, full-service profile extruder and molder of precision parts, specializing in complete extrusion molding design and engineering services for the appliance, automotive and office furniture industries.

"I look back and think that our involvement in Scanlon and its principles has created a common vehicle for communication with our employees and our customers," said Carl Brown, Executive Vice President and Chief Operating Officer. "It's the best organization I know of that incorporates total employee participation and involvement in the business," he added. Nicholas Plastics holds regular Operating Team meetings where employees and management review the status of the business and any other company issues. The company is grouped into five teams that run different parts of the business, from which representatives are sent to Operating Team meetings. Each team separately holds its own meetings and maintains programs for improving productivity, housekeeping and other areas of the business. Nicholas Plastics gives employees the authority to spend money up to a certain amount on necessary improvements resulting from team meetings.

"We've gone beyond the traditional suggestion system to incorporating Lean Principles," said Brown. "We depend on the small teams to identify changes in our processes," he added. "I don't know of any other organization than the Scanlon Leadership Network that promotes and sponsors networking among shop floor people and executives. Personally, I think it's outstanding." In keeping with the Scanlon Principles, employees are recognized and rewarded for their creativity, innovation and participation.

The four Principles of Identity, Participation, Equity and Competence have also helped Nicholas Plastics set the desired tone of the workplace.

"We want everyone to feel like an owner," said Brown. "It's important to us that people feel responsible for their activities because our customers expect perfection. However, we deal with tools and equipment that don't always yield perfection, so we rely heavily on the human element. Scanlon helps us meet those customer expectations and deliver the high quality products they desire," he added. Nicholas Plastics has invested aggressively in developing new materials, new products, new processes and innovations to meet the changing needs of customers and ensure a competitive position in the markets it serves.

"Everything we do is measured by how well we service our customers, our employees and our communities," said Brown. "We pride ourselves on our ability to meet the changing requirements of our customers.

"A lot of things are subtle," he added, "but from top to bottom, communication and employee participation play a huge role here and lays the groundwork for all that we do."

2. Rooted Values Preserve Small Business Feel at Landscape Forms Despite Growth

Founded by charismatic entrepreneur John Chipman in 1969, Landscape Forms was practicing Scanlon Principles well before it joined the Scanlon Leadership Network more than a decade later. Landscape Forms implemented its Scanlon Plan, Quality, Understanding, Education, Service/Safety and Teamwork (QUEST), in 1981 to help create the "small business feel" in a growing workplace. Chipman wanted to have the same personal influence on the company as when it was smaller years before.

The Kalamazoo, Michigan company, which designs, develops, manufactures and markets proprietary site furniture and amenities for exterior and nonresidential spaces, began primarily as a landscaping business, but were repeatedly faced with slow winter seasons that forced yearly layoffs due to the nature of the industry.

The Scanlon Principle of Competence at Landscape Forms, mainly the company's ability to train new employees each spring, eventually spawned the creation of a new furniture design division that would carry them through the winter.

"Every year we were starting our busiest season with a raw crew," said Becky Fulgoni, Vice President for People. "It was hard to maintain the desired level of quality and keep any semblance of continuity when we were constantly starting over with new people," she added. Landscape Forms was looking for a way to keep its employees busy during the winter so it could move forward rather than starting fresh each spring. "It's a unique story," said Fulgoni. "Normally people don't start businesses to give people work—there's usually a strong financial influence." After that their furniture business took off, she said and it is now the company's main source of revenue.

"Scanlon has allowed us to keep both customers and employees engaged in our business," said Fulgoni. "It has also let us attract the kind of people we want to work with and those who are interested in working for us. It has held us together. While we lack a professional organization to join, we've been lucky to be a part of Scanlon Leadership Network which has served as a networking outlet where we can learn and exchange ideas. The Scanlon Network has filled that role for us."

In addition to Competence, the Identity Principle is key to Landscape Forms' success. "Because our competitive advantage is design, we have to be on the cutting edge," explained Fulgoni. "Being in an environment that's constantly changing, Scanlon has helped with the idea of change and knowing your identity," she added.

Some of the programs launched as a result of Scanlon include quarterly company-wide theme meetings that educate employees on a variety of topics, such as personal health, respect for diversity and customer service. For the personal health meeting, an employee from a local hospital visited to discuss nutrition tips.

"John Chipman had some pretty strong ideas of how people should be treated in a business environment," said Fulgoni. "Instead of establishing arbitrary programs, he wanted that closeness among employees to be part of underlying values," she added. Today those wishes are still inherent in Landscape Forms' culture.

"It's hard to pick out things that are just done as part of our Scanlon Plan," explained Fulgoni. "With everything we do we try to make sure it's influenced by Scanlon Principles," she added. "To me, Scanlon has to be part of the way you work. It's like doing a heart exam—you can't take the heart out without killing the patient. Likewise, if you take something and call it doing Scanlon you're separating it from your real goal.

"We don't want to do things here just because they have a Scanlon label—otherwise, we'd be taking away from what we do, which is making beautiful furniture for people." That was their intention from the beginning, said Fulgoni: to create and maintain a culture defined by intrinsic Scanlon beliefs and Principles.

"Scanlon lets us integrate those founding ideas and principles—they're not just memories and history."

3. Scanlon Spawns both Personal and Financial Growth at Wescast

From a family-owned company in rural Ontario, to the world's largest supplier of exhaust manifolds for passenger cars and light trucks, Wescast lndustries Inc. has used its Scanlon Plan, Helping Everyone Achieve Rewards Together (HEART), to expand its operations, increase productivity and facilitate positive communication among employees. Since adopting HEART in 1989, Wescast has sought to continually engage and empower its people. "In the late 1980s Wescast was at a crossroads," said John Leitch, Director, Machining Operations. "Business was growing, but we had some productivity and management-labor relations issues," he added. "We needed to find a better way to run the business, so we explored various management systems and determined there was a compelling need to change. It was then that we began our Roadmap to Scanlon."

Today, Wescast, with Corporate Headquarters in Brantford, Ontario, designs, develops, casts and machines high quality iron exhaust components for automotive manufacturers at production facilities in North America, Asia and Europe. "I believe that much of the North American growth Wescast has achieved is a result of our people systems, which are a product of the Scanlon Principles and Process," said Leitch.

The Scanlon Principles support a number of Wescast initiatives. A new two-and a-half day leadership training program was rolled out during 2003–2004. Advanced Communications training helped build interpersonal and conflict resolution skills using a simple, easy-to-understand model. Wescast has also implemented Six Sigma, as well as other Lean Manufacturing tools, to help improve operations.

In addition to its employee education and communication programs, Wescast has encouraged growth by applying Scanlon to its sales and marketing functions. Wescast was the first known company to develop a sales force Scanlon Plan.

Wescast's original HEART Plan, while effective for operational metrics such as scrap rate, safety, efficiency, up-time and other manufacturing issues, was not specific to sales and marketing. The company was growing and becoming more complex, facing issues of globalization, product diversification, increasingly tougher customer demands and other factors. Wescast believed it would be more successful if a new HEART Plan included objectives, measurables, accountability and rewards that more closely fit the company's sales and marketing functions.

Guided by the Scanlon Implementation Roadmap, Wescast's Sales Leadership Team worked with Scanlon Steward and Consultant Bill Greenwood to create a detailed, customized HEART Roadmap, which won Wescast a Gold Medal Best Practices award in 2003. "Over the years a lot of the pieces of Scanlon have become embedded in our culture," said Kerry Pletch, Organizational Effectiveness Specialist. "We do many things that are Scanlon based, and sometimes we don't even realize it," she added. "The principles and processes just make sense."

"We apply Scanlon's four Principles every single day." Wescast Industries originally began as a family owned company in rural Ontario and is now the world's largest supplier of exhaust manifolds for passenger cars and light trucks said Leitch. "We practice Identity when we share with our employees as much information as we can about our business, our competitors and the business environment. We provide training and development to give them the skills they need to do their jobs—Competence. And, when they understand the business climate and have the skill sets to make improvements, they participate at a much higher level. The result: everybody wins through Equity. Our company does better, our employees do better and the customer is satisfied. "When we hire people from outside of the company, they often tell us they've never experienced a workplace like Wescast's," added Leitch. "Many companies don't do these sorts of things, but here it's the way we do business."

Today, Wescast's greatest challenge is global competition. "We certainly want to equip our people with the necessary skills and knowledge to succeed on a global basis," said Leitch. "As we enter new geographic markets in Europe and Asia, our challenge and opportunity will be to continue to take advantage of the Scanlon Principles and really engage our entire workforce."

4. Employee Participation Improves SGS Tool Product, Profitability

Family-owned SGS Tool Company of Munroe Falls, Ohio, a manufacturer of solid carbide rotary tools, joined the Scanlon Leadership Network in 1998 to encourage a more participative management approach and to keep the company moving forward by networking with others who share similar values.

Now well versed in the Network's Principles, SGS has used its Scanlon Plan, Together Everyone Acquires More (TEAM), to formalize employee participation, its suggestion system and its Gainsharing program, and to strengthen leadership training. Since joining Scanlon, SGS has also established teams for quality improvement, production methods and safety. Since the implementation of TEAM, employee involvement has improved not only the product but also profitability.

"We were into the whole involvement journey long before we joined Scanlon," said Marge Holata, Director of Associate Involvement. "But we needed something more to take us to the next level. It turned out Scanlon provided the momentum we needed," she added. Holata, who takes care of day-to-day organizational change and development at SGS and is devoted full-time to the company's Scanlon Plan.

"The number of resources we dedicate to Scanlon always impresses people," she said. "All companies have coordinators, but they often have other roles, too. This underscores the importance we place on continuous improvement." SGS employees were supportive of Scanlon from the beginning, when they passed the Plan by an overwhelming majority vote.

"Most employees really want to be involved—we have a lot fewer people now that simply do their jobs and go home," said Holata, who receives more requests to attend Scanlon's Annual Conference than she has space for. With 350 total associates, Holata can only take about 25 to the Conference each year.

"The Annual Conference gets people to understand the four principles in a hands-on environment," she added. "You just can't put a price on that experience." For Holata and many others at SGS, Scanlon's Annual Conference epitomizes employee involvement.

In 2003 SGS began making a video to chronicle its Conference experiences, and in 2004 the company won a Silver Medal Best Practices award for its second Conference video, entitled *Scanlon at SGS: Past, Present and Future*.

"With four separate manufacturing plants and three support buildings, it's too much to have the whole group visit each site to discuss their experiences," said Holata. When participants return they use the video to share what they have learned in an attempt to bring the Conference to their colleagues. "Now those who can't travel to the Conference can still see what it's all about." In 2004 SGS was also recognized for its dedication to employee participation and continuing education opportunities with two other Best Practices Medals: a Bronze for its in-house computer classes offered free to employees on weekends, and a Gold Medal for its revamped TEAM Plan.

The TEAM Gainsharing Plan, implemented in July, 2003, was created by a cross functional team of SGS associates with the help of a Scanlon consultant. TEAM, which is based on specific measurables such as Overall Equipment Effectiveness, Scrap, Spending and Customer Service, replaced SGS' previous profit sharing plan.

"At SGS employees take a true ownership in the company," said Holata. "They understand how they affect business because they have access to those key measurables, which reflect their own work," she added.

SGS' Associate Integrated Management (AIM) program, a customized version of a Hoshin Planning Process, its Competency Program and its Leadership Retreat are other examples of applied programs that utilize the Scanlon Principles.

"Before Scanlon, we all believed in involvement," said Holata. "We laid an excellent foundation for ourselves in prior years. The Scanlon Principles, however, gave us all the same direction and put us on the same page. As demonstrated through our many

Scanlon programs and initiatives, employees now take a more proactive approach to life at SGS."

5. From Parts to Pets, Scanlon Improves Service and Profitability

When Limerick Veterinary Hospital joined the Scanlon Leadership Network, it became the most unusual member. But although Limerick was far removed from the manufacturing base of the Network, its goals for the business and its employees were quite similar: engage employees in the business for self-fulfillment, and improve the care and services of the hospital for its patients and their owners. Limerick adopted its Scanlon Plan, People at Work Succeeding (PAWS), in 1998 to help achieve these goals.

As a service-oriented practice, Limerick, located in southeastern Pennsylvania, had to adapt the Scanlon Principles and Processes accordingly. Catering to a different kind of client, Limerick implemented PAWS to strengthen its position in veterinary medicine to provide compassionate care for its best friends and their owners.

In addition to veterinary medicine "We're in the service business," said Dr. Charles Koenig, President of Limerick. "Most Scanlon companies are in the business of making parts. But just like anywhere else, if you don't know what's going on, you can't help fix problems." Since the inception of PAWS Limerick employees are more informed, and are more involved in the day-to-day activities.

"I was initially attracted to Scanlon because of Dr. Frost's approach to management," said Dr. Koenig. Dr. Frost created the Scanlon Principles and Processes. "It's the idea that we're always going through change," he added. "If you can make the employees aware that your workplace is changing, that your clients are changing and that everything you do is changing, that's the way to go. It's important to be on top of new situations that arise, and through PAWS, our employees are prepared for those situations. Management is a continuous process, and Scanlon helps us manage that change."

According to Limerick, veterinary medicine is a rapidly evolving profession because the strength of the human-animal bond is making pet owners more aware of better healthcare for their best friends. Limerick's Happy Tails facility provides animal daycare, agility training, grooming and boarding. During the day pets may engage in everything from playtime to obedience training to behavioral counseling.

"Pets and their owners love animal daycare because the animals aren't left at home alone," said Dr. Koenig. "Pet owners go to work with a clear conscience and don't worry about the health and safety of their pets or wonder what kind of mischief they may be getting into," he added. Soon Limerick will offer even more services to clients, a testament to the evolving nature of the 42-year-old practice.

In January 2005 Limerick held its first offsite Scanlon rally to map out ways to put the new ideas, such as geriatric and hospice care for pets, into action. Limerick's suggestion committee is responsible for many of the new ideas implemented at the practice, such as puppy kindergarten, puppy parties and the agility program.

"The suggestion committee makes everyone part of the process, which was our original goal," explained Dr. Koenig. "It's the best thing that Scanlon offers. On the whole it's an excellent medium through which employees can both express their frustrations and contribute new ideas for improvement."

Dr. Koenig also strongly supports customer communications. Limerick keeps in touch with clients through a postcard rating system, which makes employees aware of how they're doing.

"Before we started with the Scanlon Process, employees complained that we never told them what was going on," said Dr. Koenig. Prior to Scanlon, Limerick's management regularly reviewed financial records, but often employees were not informed and did not seem concerned because business was good. Limerick has since made substantial strides in that direction by publicizing financial figures on charts around the offices, giving employees access to information to which they weren't privy before. Now employees know what they have to do to meet practice goals, and nothing is hidden. Limerick's owners also let employees take ownership of projects from start to finish, ensuring that their voices are heard.

"Scanlon stresses communication and visibility—it's a great system," said Dr. Koenig. "I believe employees are much more aware that their opinions about their jobs count, which, in the end, helps us make better decisions," he added. "All of this helps us achieve our ultimate goal, which is to become a better veterinary hospital for the community."

Afterword

THOSE WITHOUT VISION PERISH: A CALL TO ACTION

Max DePree

The Scanlon plan now has a long history. Where organizations have implemented it in a sophisticated and responsible way, it has helped people by the thousands to grow and to develop their gifts through the opportunity to participate genuinely in meaningful work.

In a Scanlon operation, the inevitable tensions produced by innovation and change are calmed by good communications and an understanding of why things are the way they are. Instead of the demotivation of tight and limiting supervision, there is the freedom of personal responsibility and joy of new horizons in the work place. With this freedom comes the enabling dignity of authenticity as a legitimate and accountable member of the team. Over many decades and in many organizations in a variety of cultural settings (often within the same group), the results have been astonishing. Change becomes normal. New ideas and innovation become the standard. Continuing education and personal growth become routine. Organizations become more competitive and more profitable and therefore more sustainable. Horizons, both personal and corporate, expand. A reservoir of accountability and good will sustain the group in difficult times. The practice of personal involvement spills over into our communities.

In light of the condition of our society and an epidemic of errant and selfish leaders, I believe that the elegant breadth of

283

the Scanlon idea deserves further thought. With a discouraging regularity—so much so that our senses almost become dulled—we learn of researchers doctoring results, of corporate leaders on trial, of sports figures cheating. Government "servants" confess to profiting from inside information. Our entertainment industry is awash in trash. People once thought to be models for the aspiring are becoming a social fifth column, tearing down confidence and hope in our values. Are these failures even news any more? Or have we, like the prisoners in the old joke, weary of repeating ourselves, just given these tragedies numbers?

The great strength of Scanlon is the potential unleashed by freeing an entire organization to do its best, to become involved. A recent story from my friend Jill reminds me of the heart and spirit and potential of the Scanlon idea and of the enormous difference many folks, not necessarily top leaders, make in our world. Jill is a nurse and an administrator in a large health care center in southern California. She called the Red Cross and offered her services to help victims of hurricane Katrina. The mother of three grown children, she was told to pack her bags and report to Tyler, Texas, a city that had agreed to care for 1500 refugees and then had to figure out what to do. Volunteers appeared. Schools and churches, unions and business people checked in. Churches became dorms, and later families moved in with families. Pharmaceutical companies shipped in supplies and medicines. Clinics were established. Within two days after arrival, children were in schools. Communications and order were established, clothes and food and toys arrived. Work responsibilities were assigned to both volunteers and refugees. Daily rituals took hold. Lives were saved; families were reconnected; trauma was treated; health care was delivered.

What an inspiring picture repeated in many places in America of good will, love, energy, skill, and effectiveness. Why do I tell this story? Because I believe it gives us a new way to think about the elegant breadth and potential of the Scanlon idea. What happened in Tyler, Texas, you see, is an exciting example of social innovation.

In the free market system, we have demonstrated great ability in materials and process innovation, and that's good. We have a remarkable track record as custodians of the nuts and bolts side of the system, but a serious imbalance exists on the social side. Implicit in the Scanlon idea is custodianship of the whole of our life together. It must become a shared devotion.

How can the idea of custodianship—a venerable and powerful concept—help us with the growing awareness that our social condition is in need of the kind of care and ingenuity we bring to product and process?

Who will be our custodians? Is it reasonable to ask those who believe in the Scanlon idea to extend their commitments and their competence to the challenge of social innovation and moral obligation? Surely the social segment of life is in great need of equity and participation, identity and competence.

For me, custodians should be the guardians of our most prized assets. We all are, for instance, the custodians of ideas. We are required to both propose and respect ideas, which often begin as something fragile, and to imagine their consequences.

We are the custodians of beauty. Three devils threaten us in the search for beauty in our society. One devil is a concern about money, which should be after all a normal and helpful constraint, and not allowed to become a debilitating preoccupation. The second devil is the shadow of utilitarianism, the idea that something only has to work. The third devil is laziness in the pursuit of becoming the best we can be. These devils often cause us to forfeit our advocacy of beauty.

As custodians we design the kind of community we intend to be. An important concept is that we share needs—the need to belong, to be valued, to be nurtured. We seek to be a learning community and a community that shares its commitments. We honor priorities, realizing that true innovation depends on trust, thrives on constraints, and is seldom initially popular. Custodians live effectively with these ambiguities.

Custodians have the courage to be human. The quality of our relationships counts. Character counts. Our language is important, Forgiveness enables. Forty years ago a friend taught me, "Love recognizes the sanctity of another life and wishes for it nothing but good."

Can those of us who are committed to the elegant breadth of the Scanlon idea begin to consider ourselves the custodians of social innovation? Why not? Who better than the companies who believe deeply in the Scanlon idea to be the launching pad for the next wave of effective activists? Who is better equipped to marshal the organizational experience, integrity, hope, and confidence needed to produce a broad renewal in our social condition.

Those without vision perish.

Acknowledgments

Paul W. Davis would like to thank his wife Bonnie who by her example has shown that servant leadership begins in the family and his sons Douglas and Matthew–his hope for the future. He would like to thank his mother and father John and Jane Davis who through 62 years of marriage were living testaments to the power of commitment. Thanks to the Scanlon Leadership Network and the Scanlon Foundation for their institutional support. A special thanks to MIT for their gracious permission to allow us to reprint the classic Scanlon chapters from Scanlon, McGregor, and Lesieur.

Thanks also to the Scanlon Stewards, Dick Ruch, Dr. Dwayne Baumgardner, Pat Thomson, D.J., Max and Hugh DePree, Buzz Kersman, Dr. Carl Frost. Dr. William Greenwood, Tim Tindall, John Chipman, and Myron Marsh for keeping the dream of the steelworker alive. Thanks to Suzanne Busley and Majel Maes; caring and dedicated employees of the Scanlon Network. Finally, thanks to my friend Larry Spears, without whose support this Scanlon EPIC story would never have been told.

Larry C. Spears would like to offer his special thanks to his family, friends and colleagues around the world who have enriched his life, and especially his wife, Beth Lafferty and their sons, James and Matthew Spears. Very special thanks also go to Paul Davis, trusted friend and esteemed colleague.

—P.D. and L.C.S.

Contributing Authors

Anthony J. Adolfi (Chapter 20) is the founder and President of Marketing Communications Inc in Washington, PA. Adolfi, has 30 years' experience in communications with three Fortune 300 firms and two international advertising and PR agencies. Adolfi gained his Corporate Communications experience at Eli Lilly Pharmaceuticals, at Pfizer as Director of Public Relations and at Ciba (now Novartis) as Director of Communications. Adolfi also served as Senior Vice President at a Young & Rubicam Advertising agency directing major accounts for SmithKline, Ciba, Mobil Oil, Pfizer and others.

Dwane Baumgardner (Chapter 16) served as Chairman and CEO of Magna-Donnelly for over 20 years. During his tenure Donnelly doubled in size every five years and was ranked among the top ten in the 1994 book, *The 100 Best Companies to Work for in America*. Dr. Baumgardner is currently a Director of Wescast Industries, Inc., a global automotive supplier, and of Landscape Forms, Inc., a designer and manufacturer of outdoor commercial furnishings. He also serves as the President of the Scanlon Foundation. He is a Scanlon Stewardship Award recipient. He has coauthored with Russ Scaffede, *The Leadership Roadmap: What Every Leader Needs to Build a Winning Organization*.

Warren Bennis (Foreword) is one of the foremost authorities on organizational development, leadership and change. He is currently Distinguished Professor of Business Administration at the University of Southern California where he created the Leadership Institute. Dr. Bennis has advised four Presidents and has written over 27 books on leadership. His book *Leaders* was named one of the "top 50 business books of all time" by *The Financial Times*.

289

Philip G. Benson (Chapter 13) is on the faculty of New Mexico State University, where he teaches primarily in the areas of human resources management. In 1982, he was awarded the PhD in Industrial/Organizational Psychology from Colorado State University. His research focus has included compensation, staffing, and international HRM. He has taught at Al Akhawayn University in Ifrane, Morocco as a Visiting Fulbright Scholar, and he has also been a visiting professor at the Estonian Business School in Tallinn, Estonia

James Bishop (Chapter 13) is an associate professor of human resource management and organizational behavior at New Mexico State University. His teaching, research and consulting focus on work teams and employee commitment. He also specializes in statistical data analysis and organizational research. Dr. Bishop's work has appeared in over 35 journals, books and conference proceedings. He has received national research awards from the Academy of Management and the Society of Human Resource Management.

Charles Davis (Chapter 14) is a social science researcher in the field of business innovation. He currently teaches at Ryerson University in Toronto, Canada, where he holds the Edward S. Rogers Sr. Research Chair in Media Management and Entrepreneurship in the Faculty of Communication and Design. Dr. Davis is the author or co-author of more than one hundred scientific publications and reports, and has received numerous research grants from scholarly granting agencies, international agencies, and private firms.

Max DePree (Afterword) helped to grow his small family-owned business into the second largest furniture maker in the world. Under De Pree's leadership, Herman Miller had the distinction of being named to three Fortune Top Ten lists—most admired companies, most innovative companies, and best managed. DePree created a Scanlon culture that produced stellar financial results—increasing revenues from $230 million to $743 million. DePree is a member of *Fortune* magazine's National Business Hall of Fame, and a recipient of the Business Enterprise Trust's Lifetime Achievement Award. He is author of *Leadership Is an Art, Leadership Jazz* and *Leading Without Power*.

Jane Floyd (Chapter 13) had broad change management experience at Sears and IBM. She directed the Scanlon process (Goalsharing) at Sears. She is a former Board member of the Scanlon Leadership Network. Ms. Floyd has presented speeches at many U.S. locations and internationally in Montreal Canada and the University of St. Gallen in Switzerland.

Carl Frost (Chapter 5) is professor emeritus at Michigan State University. He was an instructor in the Industrial Relations Research Section at MIT from 1946–1949 where he worked with Joe Scanlon and Douglas McGregor. Dr. Frost continued the work begun by Joe Scanlon, developing the four EPIC Principles and the Scanlon Implementation Roadmap. Dr. Frost's clients included Herman Miller, Donnelly, Motorola, Wolverine Worldwide, Beth Israel Hospital, Firestone and Harley Davidson. He is author of *Changing Forever: the Well-Kept Secret of America's Leading Companies* and *The Scanlon Plan: Identity, Participation, and Equity*.

Richard Frost (Chapter 7) is Vice President for Student Development and Dean of Students at Hope College. Student development services at Hope include housing and residential life, student activities, multi-cultural life, disabled student services, special programs, career services, counseling and health services, and student judicial affairs. Prior to working at Hope, Dr. Frost was associate director of housing and residential services at the University of California-Santa Barbara.

Praveen Gupta (Chapter 17) is President of Accelper, which consults with businesses in achieving sustained profitable growth utilizing employees' intellectual participation. Prior to founding his consulting business, Dr. Gupta worked at Motorola, Inc., and AT&T Bell Telephone Laboratories. He has authored numerous books including *Six Sigma Business Scorecard, The Six Sigma Performance Handbook* and *Business Innovation in the 21st Century*.

Federick Lesieur (Chapter 4) was an apprentice machinist at the La Pointe Machine Tool Company in Hudson, Mass., when he heard about a new industrial labor-management system pioneered by Joseph N. Scanlon—the Scanlon Plan, as it later became known—that promoted labor-management cooperation on production problems. Mr. Lesieur was instrumental in introducing the Scanlon Plan to La Pointe and became union president there. When Mr. Scanlon died in 1956, Mr. Lesieur succeeded him and carried the Scanlon Plan further, in part through bi-annual conferences staged with help from the Industrial Relations Section of MIT. He edited *The Scanlon Plan: A Frontier in Labor Management Cooperation* (MIT Press, 1958). Mr. Lesieur died in 1988.

Majel Maes, (Chapter 15) Director of Programs and Administration for Scanlon Leadership Network, has been with the association since 1999. She holds a Bachelor of Science in Merchandising/Management from Michigan State University. Majel is an accredited Certified Association Executive from the American Society of Association Executives.

Douglas McGregor (Chapters 2 & 3) was a Management professor at the MIT Sloan School of Management. He recruited Joe Scanlon and Dr. Carl Frost to be part of an interdisciplinary social science research department at MIT. His 1960 book *The Human Side of Enterprise* had a profound influence on management practices. In the book he identified an approach for creating an environment where employees are motivated via integration and self-control, which he called theory Y. Dr. McGregor died in 1964.

Randy Pennington (Chapter 10) is a consultant and business author who helps leaders build cultures committed to results, relationships, and accountability. He is author of two books: On *My Honor, I Will: Leading with Integrity in Changing Times* and *Results Rule! Build a Culture that Blows the Competition Away*.

Dick Ruch (Chapter 9) served Herman Miller, Inc. for 45 years in 14 different jobs including vice-president of manufacturing, CFO, CEO and Chairman of the Board. He is author of *Leaders & Followers: Lessons from 45 Years at Herman Miller, Inc*. Known as "Mr. Scanlon" during his years at Herman Miller, Mr. Ruch was recognized with the Scanlon Stewardship Award by the Scanlon Leadership Network.

Russ Scaffede (Chapter 16) began his career with General Motors (GM) in 1971. During his years at GM, he gained

experience in engine plant assembly and machining processes. In 1986 as the Flint Engine Plant's production manager, he introduced the staff to Toyota/NUMMI lean concepts.
Later, he spent five years with Toyota in a series of increasingly responsible management positions culminating with vice
president and general manager of Toyota Power Train. Russ
joined Donnelly Corporation in 1995 as vice president of North
American Operations. Dr. Scaffede was also the vice president of manufacturing for Tiara Yachts in Holland, Michigan.
He has coauthored with Dwane Baumgarder, *The Leadership
Roadmap: What Every Leader Needs to Build a Winning
Organization.*

Joseph N. Scanlon (Chapter 12) was a prize-fighter, cost
accountant, Director of the Steelworkers' Research Department and a lecturer at the Massachusetts Institute of Technology (MIT). He was actively associated with the labor
movement for over twenty years. During World War II he
served on several labor advisory committees of the War Production Board and was a technical advisor to the Anglo American Council on Productivity of the Mutual Security Agency.
He is best known as the creator of the Scanlon Plan of union-
management cooperation. Mr. Scanlon died in 1956.

Peter Scontrino (Chapter 18) holds the Ph.D. degree in
industrial-organizational psychology. He is a licensed psychologist in the State of Washington. Born and raised in the State
of Washington, he served on the faculties of the University of
Washington and Seattle University prior to forming his own
management consulting organization in 1975. Dr. Scontrino is
a widely recognized expert in the design and implementation of
Scanlon Plans and Gainsharing Plans.

Dow Scott (Chapter 13) is a Professor of Human Resources
in the School of Business Administration at Loyola University
Chicago. His practical approaches to teaching, research, and
consulting focus on helping business leaders create more productive and satisfying work environments. He has published in
more than 100 journal articles, books, and conference proceedings; and received national recognition for high performance organization and teams, productivity improvement,

attendance control, pay-for-performance, talent acquisition and human resources development. Dr. Scott often is called upon by organizations to evaluate compensation and other human resources policies and programs.

John Schuster (Chapter 11) has built and sold two service firms in his business career. His companies were known for connecting soft people skills with hard business results. He has a passion: helping CEO's and executive teams build the necessary leadership and social capital within their enterprises so they can execute on behalf of customers and shareholders. Mr. Schuster and his team built a business simulation tool that has been used by hundreds of thousands of people in high-growth businesses, MBA programs, GE, Harley Davidson, EDS and Sprint, to name a few clients He has also authored four books, *The Power of Open-Book Management*, John Wiley & Sons, 1996, *The Open-Book Management Field Book*, John Wiley & Sons, 1998 (translated into four languages), *Hum-Drum to Hot-Diggity on Leadership*, 2006, Steadfast Publishers, *Answering Your Call: A Guide to Living Your Deepest Purpose*, Berrett-Koehler, 2003 (translated into two languages).

Terry VandeWater (Chapter 6) is author of *Principle-Based Participative Management, Making Your Principles Work for You* (available from the Scanlon Leadership Network). A writer or teacher of writing all of his work life, Terry spent 25 years working for Herman Miller. Terry graduated from Hope College and earned a Master of Arts in English Language and Literature from the University of Michigan.

Daniel Wren (Chapter 1) received his Ph.D. from the University of Illinois and is David Ross Boyd Professor Emeritus and Curator, Harry W. Bass Business History Collection at the University of Oklahoma. Dr. Wren is a Fellow of the Academy of Management and a Founding Fellow of the Southern Management Association. His latest publication is the *History of Management Thought*, published by John Wiley & Sons.

About the Editors

Paul Davis has been President of the Scanlon Leadership Network since 1993.

A frequent speaker on Leadership, Paul has been an invitational speaker for the European Foundation, the Academy of Management, the Conference Board, The Japanese External Trade Organization, the American Society for Training and Development, The Ecology of Work Conferences, The Greenleaf Center Conference and Dyad Development of South Africa.

He has worked with Scanlon Network members throughout North America, consulting/training/and developing Scanlon programs and services. He created the Scanlon 101 and Scanlon Leadership Programs. He created the E.P.I.C. Culture Inventory™ and the Scanlon Roadmap learning map. He assisted in the development of the Network's Listening Program, the Lean Sim Machine™, and Hoshin Quick Start™. He helped in the development of Scanlon Plans at Watermark Credit Union and United Building Centers.

His article "Leadership from Theory to Action" appeared in *Leading-Edge Magazine*. His article "The ABC's of Gainsharing" appeared in *Physician Compensation* and *The Employee Ownership Law Review*. His article "Hoshin Planning" appeared in the *Lansing Business Journal*. He coauthored with Dow Scott and Chuck Cockburn "Scanlon Principles and Processes: Building Excellence at Watermark Credit Union" which appeared in the *World of Work Journal* and *Incentive Compensation*. Mr. Davis received the Scanlon Stewardship Award in 2007.

Larry C. Spears is President & CEO of the Larry C. Spears Center for Servant-Leadership, Inc., established in 2008. From 1990–2007 he served as President & CEO of the Robert K. Greenleaf Center for Servant-Leadership. Spears had previously been Managing Director of the Greater Philadelphia Philosophy Consortium, a cooperative association of 12 colleges and universities in the Philadelphia area. He also served as a staff member with the Great Lakes Colleges Association's Philadelphia Center and with the Quaker magazine, *Friends Journal*, in Philadelphia, PA.

Spears is also a writer and editor and has published hundreds of articles, essays, newsletters, books and other publications on servant-leadership. Dozens of newspapers and journals have interviewed him, including *Fortune, the Indianapolis Business Journal, the Philadelphia Inquirer, the Washington Post,* and *Advancing Philanthropy*. A 2004 television broadcast interview of Spears by Stone Philips on NBC's *Dateline* was seen by ten million viewers.

Mr. Spears is the creator and editor of eleven books on servant-leadership—

- *Servant Leadership: Heart, Mind, Spirit* (with Shann Ferch, forthcoming)
- *Scanlon EPIC Leadership* (with Paul Davis, 2008)
- *Practicing Servant-Leadership: Succeeding Through Trust, Bravery and Forgiveness* (with Michele Lawrence, 2004, Jossey-Bass)
- *The Servant-Leader Within* (with Hamilton Beazley & Julie Beggs, 2003, Paulist Press)
- *Servant Leadership* (2002 Silver Anniversary edition, Paulist Press)
- *Focus on Leadership: Servant-Leadership in the 21st Century* (with Michele Lawrence, 2002, John Wiley & Sons)
- *The Power of Servant Leadership* (1998, Berrett-Koehler)
- *Insights on Leadership: Service, Stewardship, Spirit and Servant-Leadership* (1998, John Wiley & Sons)
- *Seeker and Servant* (with Anne Fraker, 1996, Jossey-Bass)
- *On Becoming a Servant Leader* (with Don Frick, 1996, Jossey-Bass)

- *Reflections on Leadership: How Robert K. Greenleaf's Theory of Servant-Leadership Influenced Today's Top Management Thinkers* (1995, John Wiley & Sons)

He is also a contributing author to the above books and others, including—

- *Robert K. Greenleaf: A Life of Servant Leadership* (2004, Berrett-Koehler)
- *Cutting Edge: Leadership 2000* (2000, University of Maryland)
- *Stone Soup for the World* (1998, Conari Press)
- *Leadership in a New Era* (1994, New Leaders Press)

Mr. Spears is Series Editor of the forthcoming *Servant-Leadership Essay Series*, and he serves as the Senior Advisory Editor for *The International Journal of Servant Leadership* (2005–Present).

Spears is also a frequent speaker on servant-leadership. The titles of some of his addresses include "Servant-Leadership and the Honoring of Excellence," "Servant-Leadership and Business," and "Robert K. Greenleaf's Influence on Trusteeship." Among his recent keynote presentations are addresses to the Servant-Leadership Research Roundtable, the Louisiana Office of Mental Health, Gonzaga University, the Greenleaf Center, and Indiana Campus Compact. Since 1990, Mr. Spears has given two hundred keynote addresses on servant-leadership on four continents, a dozen countries, and forty states. He has been called today's foremost authority on servant-leadership. He knew Robert Greenleaf and first encountered Greenleaf's writings in the early 1980s while working at *Friends Journal*. Following Greenleaf's death in 1990, he examined Greenleaf's personal papers and discovered dozens of unpublished essays, written over a fifty-year period. Many of these essays were later collected and published in 1996 in two volumes (*On Becoming a Servant-Leader*, and *Seeker and Servant*).

Among several honors, Spears was the recipient of the 2004 *Dare-to-Lead Award* given by the International Leadership Network. Mr. Spears has thirty years of experience in organizational leadership, entrepreneurial development, non-profit management, and grant writing, having envisioned and authored 30 successful grant projects totaling several million dollars. The newly established Spears Center is committed to enhancing the global understanding and practices of servant-leadership. Mr. Spears is a longtime member of the Association of Fundraising Professionals, and a Fellow of the World Business Academy. He and his wife, Beth Lafferty, have two wonderful sons: James and Matthew.

For more information, please contact:

Larry C. Spears, President & CEO
The Larry C. Spears Center for Servant-Leadership, Inc.
329 Garden Grace Drive
Indianapolis, IN 46239
317.416.8218 (Work)
www.spearscenter.org
lspears@spearscenter.org

About the Scanlon Leadership Network/Foundation/ Consultancy

The Scanlon Leadership Network is "where the best ideas come together" to create worthwhile employment, worthwhile goods and services, and worthwhile investments.

The nonprofit Network is composed on three interrelated organizations; the Scanlon Leadership Network, the Scanlon Foundation, and the Scanlon Consultancy.

The parent organization is the Scanlon Leadership Network. Founded in 1964 by Herman Miller and the Donnelly Corporation members range from small family businesses to large multinational corporations. Called "the best kept secret in Business" by business writers the Network has helped five organizations become among the top 50 best places to work in America.

The Network provides integrated products and services designed to help create cultures of excellence. Network members share Scanlon related best practices, and training programs. The Network's unique focus on all levels of an organization supports top leaders and front-line employees through training programs, assessments and surveys, conferences, tours, workshops and retreats. The Network maintains the world's largest knowledge base of Scanlon Plans, and Scanlon related training programs. The Network seeks progressive organizations interested in joining the Network. The Network web site is www.scanlonleader.org.

The Scanlon Foundation was created in 2002 to support the public mission of the Scanlon Leadership Network. The Foundation sponsors conferences and workshops for those interested in exploring Scanlon EPIC Leadership. The Foundation also conducts Scanlon related research, and develops Scanlon related books and instructional programs. The Foundation offers individual membership for those interested in EPIC Leadership, but who may not belong to a Scanlon organization. Tax-deductible donations to carry on EPIC Leadership can be made to the Foundation. The Scanlon Foundation web site is www.ScanlonFoundation.org.

The Scanlon Consultancy provides consultants and coaches who work with leaders and organizations interested in practicing the Scanlon EPIC Principles. Scanlon Consultants/Coaches are screened and approved by the Network. They are experts in Scanlon, EPIC Leadership, Group Compensation Systems, Culture Change, Labor Management Cooperation, Employee Involvement, Team Building, Open-Book Management, Lean Systems, Strategic Planning/Hoshin/Policy Deployment, Suggestion Systems, and Assessment. Scanlon Consultants can be reached at (517) 332-8927 or at www.ScanlonLeader.com.

Permissions & Copyrights

Chapter 8, "Servant Leadership and Scanlon Ideas" is an original essay created by Larry Spears for this collection. Used with permission of the author.

Chapter 9, "The Role of the Followers" is an original essay created by Dick Ruch for this collection. Printed with permission of the author.

Chapter 10, "Integrity-the Critical Factor" is an original essay created by Randy Pennington for this collection. Used with permission of the author.

Chapter 11, "Jefferson, Scanlon and Open-Book Management" is an original essay created by John Schuster for this collection. Printed with permission of the author.

Chapter 12, "Profit Sharing Under Collective Bargaining" originally appeared in the October 1948 issue of *Industrial and Labor Relations Review* and *The Scanlon Plan: A Frontier in Labor Management Cooperation* (MIT Press, 1958). Printed with permission of MIT Press.

Chapter 13, "The Impact of the Scanlon Plan on Retail Store Performance" originally appeared in the *World of Work Journal*, third quarter 2002. Printed with permission of the authors.

Chapter 14, "Organizational Culture in Scanlon Firms" is an original essay created by Charles Davis for this collection. Used with permission of the author.

Chapter 15, "The ABC's of Gainsharing: Lessons from the Scanlon Plan", is adapted from a chapter that originally appeared in the *Journal of Employee Ownership Law and Finance*, Volume 9, No 1, Winter 1997 published by the National Center for Employee Ownership 1997 and *Physician Compensation: Models for Aligning Financial Goals and Incentives*, published by McGraw-Hill. Copyright 2000. Printed with permission of the authors.

Chapter 16, "Scanlon and the Lean Enterprise" is an original essay created by Dwane Baumgardner and Russ Scaffede for this collection. Used with permission of the authors.

Chapter 17, "Scanlon, Six-Sigma, and Innovation" is an original essay created by Praveen Gupta for this collection. Used with permission of the author.

Chapter 18, "Employee Involvement and Scanlon" is an original essay created by Peter Scontrino for this collection. Printed with permission of the author.

Chapter 19, "Do Scanlon Plans Fail or Do Managers Plan to Fail?" is an original essay created for this collection by Paul Davis. Printed with permission of the author.

Chapter 20, "Scanlon Success Stories" was taken from Volume 9, Number 1, May 2005 of the *Scanlon News*. Used with permission of the author and the Scanlon Leadership Network.

The Afterword is an original essay created for this collection by Max DePree. Used with permission of the author.

Recommended Reading

Case, John. *Open-Book Management: The Coming Business Revolution*, New York: Harper Business, 1995.

Collins, Denis. *Gainsharing and Power: Lessons from Six Scanlon Plans*, Ithaca: Cornell University Press, 1998.

Dennison, Daniel. *Corporate Culture and Organizational Effectiveness*, New York: John Wiley & Sons, 1990.

DePree, Hugh. *Business as Unusual*, Zeeland: Herman Miller, 1986.

DePree, Max. *Leadership is an Art*, New York: A Currency Book, 1989.

DePree, Max. *Leadership Jazz*, New York: A Currency Book, 1992.

Doyle, Robert J., and Paul I. Doyle. *Gain Management*, New York: AMACOM, 1992

Ewing, David, *Justice on the Job: Resolving Grievances in the NonUnion Workplace*, Boston: Harvard Business School Press, 1989.

Flannery, Thomas P., David A. Hofrichter and Paul E. Platten. *People, Performance and Pay. Dynamic Compensation for Changing Organizations*. New York: The Free Press, 1996.

Frost, C.F. *Changing Forever: The Well-Kept Secret of America's Leading Companies*, East Lansing, MI: Michigan State University Press, 1996.

Frost, C.F., J.H. Wakeley and R.A. Ruh. *The Scanlon Plan for Organization Development: Identity, Participation and Equity*, East Lansing, MI: Michigan State University Press, 1974.

Golembiewski, Robert. *Men, Management, and Morality: Toward a New Organizational Ethic*. Piscataway: Transaction Pub, 1988.

Graham-Moore, Brian and Timothy L. Ross. *Gainsharing and Employee Involvement*, Washington D.C.: The Bureau of National Affairs, Inc., 1990.

Graham-Moore, Brian and Timothy L. Ross, *The Scanlon Way to Improved Productivity*, New York: John Wiley & Sons, Inc, 1978.

Greenleaf, R.K. *Servant Leadership* (25th Anniversary ed.) Mahwah, NJ.: Paulist Press, 2002.

Gupta, Praveen. *Six Sigma Business Scorecard*, New York: McGraw Hill, 2003.

Gupta, Praveen. *The Six Sigma Performance Handbook*, New York: McGraw Hill, NY 2004.

Gupta, Praveen, "Six Sigma Sense, Monthly Column", www.qualitydigest.com, 2004–05.

Heil, Gary, Warren Bennis and Deborahn Stephens. *Douglas McGregor, Revisited: Managing the Human Side of the Enterprise*, New York: John Wiley & Sons, Inc., 2000.

Huszczo, Gregory E. *Tools for Team Excellence*, Palo Alto: Davies-Black Publishing, 1996.

Katz D. & Kahn R L. *The Social Psychology of Organizations*. New York: Wiley, 1966.

Lee, William G. *Mavericks in the Workplace: Harnessing the Genius of American Workers*, New York: Oxford University Press, 1998.

Lesieur, Frederick Editor. *The Scanlon Plan: A Frontier in Labor-Management Cooperation*, Cambridge: Massachusetts Institute of Technology Press, 1984.

Liker, Jeffery, Editor. *Becoming Lean: Inside Stories of U. S. Manufacturers*, Portland: Productivity Press, 1998.

Liker, Jeffery. *The Toyota Way: 14 Management Principles From The World's Greatest Manufacturer*, New York: McGraw-Hill, 2004.

Likert, Rensis. *The Human Organization: Its Management and Value*, New York: McGraw-Hill, 1967.

Markham, S.E., Scott, K.D., and Little, B.L. (1992) National gainsharing study: The importance of industry differences. *Compensation and Benefits Review.* 24 (1).

McAdams, Jerry. *The Reward Plan Advantage: A Manager's Guide to Improving Business Performance Through People*, San Francisco: Jossey-Bass, 1996.

McGregor, Douglas. *The Human Side of Enterprise*, New York: McGraw-Hill, 1985.

O'Bannon, D.P. and Pearce, L., (1999) An exploratory examination of Gainsharing in service organizations: Implications of organization citizenship behavior and pay satisfaction. *Journal of Managerial Issues*. 11 (3), 363–372.

O'Dell, C. and J. McAdams. *People, Performance, and Pay*. Houston, TX: American Productivity and Quality Center, 1987.

O'Toole, James. *Leading Change: The Argument for Values-Based Leadership*, New York: Jossey-Bass, Inc., 1995.

Pennington, Randy. *Results Rule: Build a Culture That Blows the Competition Away*, New York: John Wiley & Sons, Inc., 2006.

Rigsbee, Richard. *The Art of Partnering*, Dubuque: Kendell/Hunt Publishing Co., 1994.

Rosen, Robert H. *Leading People: Transforming Business from the Inside Out*, New York: Viking Press, 1996.

Ruch, Richard. *Leaders & Followers: Lessons from 45 Years at Herman Miller, Inc.*, Holland: Star Publishers, 2002.

Schuster, John, Jill Carpenter, and Patricia Kane. *The Power of Open-Book Management*, New York: John Wiley and Sons, Inc, 1996.

Schuster, John, Jill Carpenter, and Patricia Kane. *The Open-Book Management Field Book*, New York: John Wiley and Sons, Inc, 1998.

Shields, Joyce L. (1999). "Transforming Organizations: Methods for Accelerating Culture Change Processes," *Information Knowledge Systems Management* 1(2): 105–115.

Spear, Steven and Kent Bowen. "Decoding the DNA of the Toyota Production System," *Harvard Business Review*, Reprint 99509.

Spears, L.C. (ed.) *Insights on Leadership: Service, Stewardship, Spirit, and Servant-Leadership*. New York: John Wiley and Sons, Inc., 1998.